AF504110

K.N. Panikkar

The Theatre of Rasa

NATARANG PRATISHTHAN SERIES ON MODERN INDIAN THEATRE

K.N. Panikkar

The Theatre of Rasa

Edited by

Udayan Vajpeyi

for
Natarang Pratishthan

NIYOGI
BOOKS

NATARANG PRATISHTHAN SERIES ON MODERN INDIAN THEATRE

© Natarang Pratishthan
B-31, Ist Floor, Swasthya Vihar
Vikas Marg, New Delhi-110 092
Tel: 91-11-22519710, 22543450
email: natarangpratishthan@yahoo.co.in
website: www.natarang.org

Published by
NIYOGI BOOKS
D-78, Okhla Industrial Area, Phase-I
New Delhi-110 020, INDIA
Tel: 91-11-26816301, 49327000
Fax: 91-11-26810483, 26813830
email: niyogibooks@gmail.com
website: www.niyogibooks.com

Edited by Udayan Vajpeyi
Design: Shashi Bhushan Prasad/Niyogi Books
Cover photos from Natarang Pratishthan Archives

ISBN: 978-93-81523-30-8

Publication: 2012

Printed at: Niyogi Offset Pvt. Ltd., New Delhi, India.

CONTENTS

PART TWO: VOICES

FOREWORD

Natarang Pratishthan was set up as a contemporary theatre archive and resource centre by the eminent writer and theatre critic, the late Shri Nemichandra Jain with his personal collection of material on theatre and literature. Now in its twenty-third year of existence, the Pratishthan has a rich and well documented collection of books, journals, photographs, posters, brochures, play scripts, clippings and audio-video recordings relating to the practice of theatre in India, particularly North India. It is attempting to preserve for posterity this information on productions, actors, directors, writers and organisations, which presents an amazing plurality of visions. The Hindi theatre journal *Natarang,* continuously appearing since 1965, is published by the Pratishthan. It also organises public events including theatre festivals, seminars, exhibitions, lectures, dialogues, etc. Through these multifaceted activities, the Pratishthan attempts to initiate new areas of interdisciplinary debate and focus critical attention to the interface between the theory and practice of modern Indian theatre.

Natarang Pratishthan started a project of documenting important theatre directors of our time, covering their visions and style, working methods and productions. The focus during this project was on the work processes of directors in order to get an insight into the creative impetus of these practitioners. The directors shortlisted for this project were a mix of the pioneers of modern Indian theatre and a few promising new ones who are still evolving their methodology and styles, so as to get a sense of continuity of the creative expression in post-independence theatre. The materials so collected are vast and complex.

To make this material accessible to a larger body of scholars and practitioners, Natarang Pratishthan is publishing a series of books, each devoted to a single director, which would use the archival material and documentation from the Pratishthan and from other diverse sources to give a comprehensive picture of the methods, development and contribution of the director in question. To begin with we have chosen Satyadev Dubey, Kavalam Narayana Panikkar and Badal Sircar. Much of the material used in these books has never been looked at before. The editors, Shanta Gokhale, Udayan Vajpeyi and Kirti Jain, have also commissioned new material on areas not covered by the archival collections. In some cases, fresh interviews have been included to get a picture of the present vision of the director. These are likely to be the most comprehensive books brought out on these directors.

What makes this series special is that the editors of these books are eminent creative people in their own right, and senior scholars who have had firsthand experience of the work of the directors they are working on and are therefore in a position to contextualize the contribution of the directors apart from analysing the collated material. The first book was on Satyadev Dubey, a stalwart of Indian theatre at a time when modern urban theatre was in the process of establishing itself.

The second book in this series is on Kavalam Narayan Panikkar, a major figure in modern Indian theatre who being deeply rooted in the soil of Kerala has not only inherited the classical concepts and practices of Indian theatre but has also reinvented and revitalised them: Panikkar's theatre is simultaneously classical and contemporary. It is a theatre which celebrates and interrogates. Folk traditions and classical conventions merge in his work in a unique and intense manner making the categories of classical, folk and contemporary seem inadequate in describing his work. It is not entirely coincidental that the contemporary theatre criticism in India has, more or less, been wanting in developing concepts and strategies to analyse, understand and evaluate Panikkar's theatre. This book, in this context, is the first serious attempt to look at this complex and significant body of theatre of our times from many different points of view and to provide critical insights into the structures, theatrical devices, vision and struggles of Panikkar's unique theatre.

Udayan Vajpeyi has edited the book for Natarang Pratisthan. He is a Hindi poet, fiction writer and critic who has been engaged for long with cinema, theatre and other performing arts. He has spent considerable time with Panikkar watching him work and talked to him at length. The material collected in the book carries many traces of a multilayered dialogue between a master and a younger inquisitive and sensitive mind.

We are happy that he agreed to undertake this project and has added a new dimension to the series.

While the documentation of Panikkar's work was being carried out by the Pratishthan, we requested filmmaker Gurvinder Singh, a student of Mani Kaul, to make a film on Panikkar. It is a matter of great satisfaction that he agreed, and has produced a film *KAVALAM* (76 minutes) that captures Panikkar's work process and the milieu in which his theatre is embedded. We are grateful to Gurvinder Singh for making the film.

We express our gratitude to Kavalam Narayan Panikkar and Sopanam for their constant help and cooperation in providing some rare material on him and thank all the contributors for their articles.

Natarang Pratishthan is thankful to the JRD Tata Trust for supporting this project and publication. Thanks are also due to the Pratishthan staff whose hard work under the guidance of its director Rashmi Vajpeyi and archive chief S.N. Khanna made the documentation work possible.

We would also like to thank Niyogi Books for publishing the first three books in this series and their editor Nandita Jaishankar for her valuable inputs.

We hope that the books would be useful for discerning scholars and help them understand better the contribution of some of the directors whose struggles and anxieties, creativity and courage have made modern Indian theatre such a rich site of imagination and human exploration.

Ashok Vajpeyi
Series Editor

Acknowledgements

I am grateful to Kavalam Narayana Panikkar ji for the love that he gave me while I was working on this book. I am equally grateful to Amma (Mrs Sharadamani Panikkar) for treating me like one of her family during the days when I was staying in Kavalam and Thiruvananthapuram. I am also grateful to all the actors of Sopanam—I remember Kalyani and her mother Maya with a lot of love.

I am grateful to all the writers whose articles are included in this book, namely Phillip B. Zarrilli, Brian Singleton, Gary Wynn, Sandra Kovacs, Sangeeta Gundecha and K.S. Rajendran. I also feel indebted to all those who participated in the discussion on Panikkar's play, *Ottayan*. I would like to thank Niraj Kunder for the photographs that he very kindly gave for this book.

Without the support of Natarang Pratishthan and its director, Rashmi Vajpeyi, this book would have been not possible. I express my gratitude to her. I also express my gratitude to the great Hindi poet Kamlesh who got all the tapes of my conversation with Panikkar transcribed. I am extremely grateful to the young filmmaker Gurvinder Singh who very passionately got involved in making the film based on the rehearsals of *Uttaramacharitam* in Thiruvananthpuram. I will remain grateful to Nandita Jaishankar for her editing.

During my stay in Thiruvananthapuram, Panikkarji's son Harikrishnan's constant support inspite of his busy schedule was truly beyond words. His sad demise leaves a void in my happiness at the publication of this book.

—Udayan Vajpeyi

PREFACE
The Creative Journey of Kavalam Narayana Pannikar

Kavalam Narayana Panikkar was born on 28 April, 1928 in the picturesque village of Kavalam, part of Kuttanad, once famed as the granary of Kerala. The rustic lifestyle of the agricultural community, in the heart of Mother Nature and the scenic beauty of the area—where the sacred River Pampa ends its journey by merging into Vembanad Lake—all provided an ideal background for the young Panikkar to develop his innate artistic talents and vision. He himself believes that the ambience of the area played a decisive role in grooming his personality in the early stages of his life.

Panikkar was born into a matrilineal joint family where the maternal uncle was the head of the family. This system gave him the first lessons of discipline in life. However, it was his father, the late Godavarma, who introduced him to the world of literature. In fact, Panikkar remembers that he was initiated to the fascinating world of the great epics like *Ramayana* and *Mahabharata* by his father. Moreover, a system of intense and regular reading of the epics existed in the house where his mother, grandmother and women from the neighbourhood participated. This tradition inspired him to organise poetry reading sessions later in life, at a time when it was argued that poetry was for private reading and enjoyment.

Panikkar, after his initial education in local schools in Kavalam and in the nearby village of Pulinkunnu, joined the famous CMS College in Kottayam, that has produced prominent personalities like K.P.S. Menon and Sardar K.M. Panikkar, the latter being Kavalam Panikkar's own uncle.

Taking inspiration from his surroundings and upbringing, Panikkar started writing poetry from his schooldays. The poems, rich with rural idioms, were the reflections of a young poet's mind on the archetypal imageries, myths and parables that had a profound influence on him.

He took his degree in Economics from SD College, Alappuzha and later Bachelor of Law degree from Madras Law College. After obtaining his Law degree, he started his career as a lawyer in Alappuzha Bar and practised for six years starting from 1955. However, he continued to pursue his artistic interests and a breakthrough came when he was nominated as Secretary of Kerala Sangeetha Nataka Akademi in 1961. He consequently shifted his base to Thrissur, the cultural capital of Kerala.

The new responsibility gave him a chance to interact with artists from all over the state. He was also introduced to different art forms, both classical and folk. He remembers how the tenure helped him to expand his relations and facilitated the growth of the artist in him.

Panikkar's tenure in the Akademi also saw the institution getting more systematic in its functioning. During this period, the Akademi organised many festivals, which gave Panikkar a deeper insight into the rich cultural heritage of the state and its deep rooted and indigenous folk traditions. He started his research in the folk and classical arts of Kerala, which ultimately led him to theatre.

Panikkar admits that his first few attempts at writing plays in tune with the established and popular realistic theatre traditions were not successful. But the journey in search of his real identity continued.

A turning point in his theatre experiments, especially as a playwright, came with the production of *Daivathar*. Panikkar did not direct the drama, but tried to actively collaborate with directors like Kumara Varma, interpreting his textual inputs to the director.

In 1974, Kavalam shifted his residence to the state capital Thiruvananthapuram. A highlight of the period was the staging of his play *Avanavan Kadamba*, directed by the established film director G. Aravindan.

In contrast to Aravindan's known style of functioning while donning the mantle of a film director, he interacted a lot with the playwright as well as the actors in the production of *Avanavan Kadamba*. This resulted in what is termed as ensemble acting.

The structure of this play and its presentation were truly path-breaking. The theme demanded an open auditorium with trees in the background with hanging lamps. The concept of proscenium and picture-frame stage with a rolled curtain divide was broken. The acting area started growing beyond its prescribed limits, creating a sense of involvement and participation among the audience.

A major breakthrough in Panikkar's career as a director came when he was offered a chance to produce and present a Sanskrit drama at the prestigious Kalidasa Samaroh in Ujjain. He selected Bhasa's *Madhyama Vyayogam*, which was his first directorial attempt.

On 2 November 1978, *Madhyama Vyayogam* was presented in Ujjain and was received with a standing ovation. The culturally sound audience could feel the strength of the Sanskrit presentation, the usage of body dynamics by the actors and their ability to combine the *sattvika* and *vachika* acting and above all, the directorial contribution of Panikkar.

Since the first production of *Madhyama Vyayogam*, Panikkar has enjoyed a special bond with Ujjain in Madhya Pradesh, which has virtually become his second home. His Sanskrit plays are performed here and almost all the debut shows of Sanskrit dramas are organised in the Samaroh at Ujjain.

The participation in the Samaroh also gave him and his team an opportunity to get exposed to a wider audience. The impression created in Ujjain had its effect in New Delhi also. Kamaladevi Chattopadhaya, the chairperson of the National Sangeet Natak Akademi, was instrumental in inviting Panikkar to New Delhi and the play presented there in February 1979, went on to have repeated shows.

Panikkar also remembers a special occasion when he was requested by Adya Rangacharaya, director of Kalidasa Akademi, to present Bhasa's Sanskrit play *Dhootavakyam* using artists from Madhya Pradesh. It was a great experience for him as well as the artists on the practical implementation of the techniques of *Natyashastra*. Later, at the National School of Drama, he produced and directed plays in Sanskrit and Hindi for the students, overcoming the language barriers through creating a 'language' of theatre. *Mathavilasom* of Mahendra Vikrama Varman translated into Hindi by N. C. Jain and a play written by Shri. B R Bhargava in Hindi adapting Bhasa's two plays, *Pratijna Yogantharayanam* and *Swapnavasavadatham*, require special mention in this context.

In 2008 he worked with the Hindi poet and writer Udayan Vajpeyi on Bhavbhooti's *Uttararamacharitam*. Udayan recreated the play in Hindi and Panikkar's direction made it possible for his Malayam-speaking actors to give a new dimension to the enunciation of Hindi in theatre.

While dabbling with Sanskrit theatre, Panikkar also wrote and directed a number of Malayalam plays. His first Malayalam play was *Sakshi*, *Kalivesham* being the latest.

Panikkar's creations, though experimental and non-conformist, often feature non-realistic tools and have themes in close proximity to real life, its anxieties, struggles and confusion. These give them a durable nature and make them suitable for *Lokdharmi-Natyadharmi* treatment. Another salient feature of his plays is the absence of the exhaustive use of language as a medium of communication. Instead, the *bhava* or expression is utilised as a powerful vehicle to provide ample space for improvisation as well as interpretation. All his plays are part of the author's experiment with structural patterns and its possibilities in the Indian context.

Kavalam Narayana Panikkar has successfully introduced the indigenous music of the region—*Sopana Sangeetham*—as an organic accompaniment to Mohiniyattam. Famous dancers like Kanak Rele from Mumbai and Bharati Shivaji from New Delhi have worked with him on this project.

Panikkar has visited many countries, including the Soviet Union. He considers his interaction with the Greek theatre in producing *Iliyayana* a memorable experience. *Iliyayana*, which he produced along with the Greek theatre group Volos, was a combination of the *Ramayana* and the Greek epic *Iliad*. In the project that saw a wonderful fusion of two great ancient cultures of the world, he was supported by Greek director Spyros Wracorites and two specialists, Dr Ayyapa Panikkar and Professor Andriades, a Greek scholar.

Panikkar prefers to call his theatre group Sopanam, consisting of twenty artists, his theatre laboratory. His wife Sharadamani has been a perennial source of strength and inspiration to him. His two sons Harikrishnan (who is no longer alive) and Sreekumar have been of great support in his creative ventures, taking time off from their official responsibilities.

Panikkar lives in Thrikkannapuram on the banks of Karamana River, away from the dust and din of the state capital, yet near to the city. He has another house in his native village on the banks of river Pampa, an abode which is a great source of nostalgic inspiration for him.

Kavalam Narayana Panikkar has carved out a niche for himself in the evolution of a regional theatre movement, which is one of the major components of national theatre in modern India. In a career spanning over four decades, Panikkar has given a new lease of life to the age-old Sanskrit drama tradition on the one hand and has, on the other hand, identified the interrelation between the evolved art forms and folk arts, successfully creating a fusion that has enthralled the contemporary audiences since then.

***

The first part of this book contains essays by poet, writer and theatre critic Sangeeta Gundecha, theatre director K.S. Rajendran, theatre person Phillip B. Zarrilli (his essay is also the introduction to the English translation of Panikkar's play, *Karimkutty*), theatre critic Brian Singleton and actors Gary Wynn and Sandra Kovacs. The second part of the book features a discussion on Panikkar's play *Ottayan* by some prominent theatre thinkers of Kerala as well as a long conversation between Kavalam Narayana Panikkar and myself.

Some of the essays in the book were published in literary or theatre journals. The Hindi original of Sangeeta Gundecha's essay was published in *Rang Prasang*, New Delhi; Brian Singleton's essay was published in *Indian Literature*, New Delhi and the Hindi original of my essay was also published in *Rang Prasang*. We are grateful to the authors and are equally grateful the journals for their permission to reproduce these essays.

Udayan Vajpeyi
Bhopal, 2012

Creating and Conversing with Panikkar

1

Kavalam Narayana Panikkar had come for three of Bhasa's plays in Bhopal. We designed the programme in such a way that after each play, there was a discussion. During these discussions, I said to him that he should also do *Uttararamacharitam*, not in Sanskrit but in Hindi. He very gently replied, 'If you work on it with me, I will do it.' I agreed. The deal was finalised. I had no idea as to where the support for such a thing would come. And, as if from nowhere, the proposal to do a book on Panikkar came from Natarang Pratishthan, New Delhi! It was like a gift from heaven. I spoke to Panikkar about the book and told him that it would contain a long conversation with him. I also spoke to him about our possible collaboration on *Uttararamacharitam*. 'Now we can also work on *Uttararamacharitam*, it will help me understand your creative process of producing a play and will also initiate me into writing plays.' He happily agreed and told me that we would do both these things in his village, Kavalam. The village was not unknown to me; I was aware of its beauty and had wanted to go there for some time. Travelling from Bhopal to Mumbai and from there to Cochin, I reached Alappuzha. I could have taken a boat to go from there to Kavalam, but Panikkar's son, Harikrishnan came to receive me. Hari bhai was a wonderful person who had worked for many years in a big company and left it to help Panikkar manage his theatre group, Sopanam. He used to avoid smoking in front of his father, and would take any and every opportunity to leave the house so he could smoke his cigarette in peace. We took the road flanked by lush green fields of paddy. The breeze rippled gently and created several shades of green across fields, serene and mysterious.

2

Panikkar has a house on the banks of beautiful Pampa River in Kavalam. The door of Panikkar's house frames the river elegantly and one can see ferries passing across it, the people sitting on them awash in golden sunlight. Kavalam is his ancestral village, where he spent his childhood. He often comes here from Thiruvananthapuram to spend time writing or thinking. He is at home there. Amma, Panikkar's wife, was also there. In fact, wherever Panikkar goes, Amma accompanies him; she is not only a great support to him but is also his memory bank; if ever he forgets something at any time, he immediately calls for her.

Without wasting even a minute, we got down to work. We decided that we would first work on *Uttararamacharitam* and then record our conversation. I had to write the performance text of *Uttararamacharitam* in Hindi. It was a great joy working on this text with him.

For the first few days in Kavalam, we continued working on the performance text (which Panikkar calls subtext). We worked all day and then, in the evening, we would go for a walk along the river. He would stop at the *paan* shop and have a *paan* and few leaves of tobacco (this was done clandestinely; because of health reasons, Amma does not allow him to have tobacco). After his *paan,* we would walk along the Pampa and he would point out places of interest in the village. Whoever saw him waved at him or greeted him with great respect. On our way back, we would sometimes buy *parotta* (paratha) for dinner, a strange mix of the Punjabi version with a distinct Kerala flair. When we reached home, Amma would immediately ask us to have our dinner. The Panikkars are vegetarian, but Amma once prepared a delicious fish dish for me, bought from the *vallam* (boat) passing on the river flowing beside their house.

Panikkar works very fast and therefore I too used to write as quickly as I could. I would try to be as brief as possible because I was aware that *vachika*, the spoken, is only one of the four elements of acting and overdoing the *vachika,* even if it is poetic, takes away the poetry in theatre. The poetry of theatre or *abhinaya* (acting) lies in the poetic coming together of the four elements of theatre namely, *vachika, angika, sattvika* and *aharya.* In fact, to write the performance text of any play is to find the essential *vachika* from the written text of the play and to discover how this *vachika* will be poetically integrated with other elements of theatre. So I would be as brief as possible but Panikkar would insist that I should give more words and images to him to work on during rehearsals. 'You are very stingy,' he would often tell me. I would then struggle to find some more lines for him. Day after day, we sat together in my room to discuss the play; we would include some scenes, exclude others, include some characters, exclude others, invent whenever we felt the need to do so. Both of us internalised Bhavbhooti's *Uttararamacharitam* and were reinventing it in a small village of Kerala.

Outside my room and in the compound of Panikkar's house there was a clothes line on which our clothes would dry in the breeze coming from the river. The sound of passing ferries would come into our rooms and float around us like a sheet of cloth filled with wind. What a time it was, imagining, writing, eating and walking beside the quietly flowing river. We once went to a nearby temple. As is custormary in the south, I removed my shirt. Initially, I felt as though I was naked. But at the same time I felt suddenly unburdened. I felt as light as a flower—was I going to offer myself there? The configuration of the spaces within the temple was so elegant that I felt as if those various spaces were lucidly opening into each other like the various scenes of a beautifully done play. The deity was not only located in the sanctum sanctorum, but could be felt in the spaces of the temple which were continuous with the infinity of the dark sky. Panikkar was known to all the priests of the temple who were walking inside and they were very respectful towards him. I could see that the temple was very significant for Panikkar; I could see him there, feeling the presence of the Divine.

3

We wanted the entry of Ram to be in the Kerala tradition. We wanted the same for Sita and Laxman. Immediately after his entry, we wanted Ram to express the three *rasas* (literally, 'juice' or essence, but widely meaning aesthetics) which were going to be the main axes of the production. Panikkar wanted me to find ways to express the sequence of the three *rasas* in the *vachika*—he was confident that his actor Girishan would do the rest through his *angika* and *sattvika abhinaya*. Months later, when I saw the production of the play in Puducherry, I was thrilled to see the richness of the acting of Girishan during the entry of Ram. One will have to see the play to believe how subtly he moves from *shringara* to *veer* to *karun rasa*s. Actually, the entire play unfolds along these axes. The play-writing continued for some days and then we decided to start recording our conversation.

It started one evening when the sun was setting. We sat in the little verandah in front of my room and began recording our conversation. I could see Panikkar going deeper into his past without leaving the present. Many characters of his past started making their presence felt but even then, he never became sentimental. We would go on recording late into the night. We started our conversation from a discussion on his relationship with Vallathol, the great Malayalam poet. I never knew that his understanding of the nature of Indian theatre had its foundation in the remarks made by Vallathol on seeing him perform a role in a realistic play. It so happened that when Panikkar was living in Alleppey, Vallathol came there. At that time, Panikkar was acting in a realistic play called *Atom Bomb*. He invited Vallathol to see it. Vallathol came for the show with his dear friend and Panikkar's uncle, Sardar Panikkar. They sat through the show for about two hours. After the show Panikkar asked them about their impression of the show. Vallathol smiled and said that what his play was trying to communicate could actually be written in half a page. Panikkar was shocked by this comment. This was the beginning of his questioning realistic theatre and its verbosity.

Sometimes his nephew Gopalkrishan would enthusiastically join us and Panikkar would speak to him in Malayalam, forgetting completely that there was someone there who could not understand his language. On seeing my blank face he would immediately go back to English. What a strange thing: English was a foreign language for both of us and yet it was our common language. Seeing this Thomas Macaulay might have been more than happy! One evening we went with Gopalkrishan to his ancestral house to drink *todi* (toddy), which had been arranged by Adawa, the caretaker in Panikkar's house. We sat under the tall trees in the courtyard of Gopalkrishan's home and drank from earthen pots. The intoxication of *todi* is unlike any other. It fills your head with a certain heaviness which you gradually realise is sleep. It is as if you are getting filled with sleep. Or perhaps the sleep that lies buried in you is brought to the fore by *todi*. We carried that folded sleep in our heads and crossed the dark streets of Kavalam to reach our place where Amma was waiting with dinner. A few days earlier, Hari bhai had left for

Thiruvananthapuram with his extremely quiet wife, Maya. For Panikkar his theatre and his family have a simultaneous existence; it is impossible to find where one ends and the other begins. He has organised his theatre around his family in such a way that the family has become a source of energy for the theatrical activities that take place not only in his theatre repertory, Sopanam, but elsewhere as well. I have seen Amma boiling water every day with a particular bark to disinfect it so that the actors can drink it. I have also seen her coming to the *kalari* (the rehearsal space located within the Panikkars house in Thiruvananthapuram) with her granddaughter Kalyani and enjoying the rehearsals.

Panikkar does not give much importance to his public image. The amount of energy that he radiates is so much that his surroundings are filled with activity. After spending a few more days in Kavalam, we went to Changanacherry, where his nephew Gopalakrishan lives, and from there we took a train to come to Thiruvananthapuram. Before boarding the train, Panikkar took me to a college. When we sat down on the stage in front of many students, I realised that in few minutes they were going to ask me to speak and even though I was totally unprepared for such a thing, I would have to talk!

4

In Thiruvananthapuram, I stayed in a house on the hill top. This was a house which Panikkar had hired for the students who come to study with him. I was told that just before me, a group of Estonian actors were living there. From beside the Pampa River we had come to the outskirts of a metropolitan city. Even then, there were lots of trees; every morning Hari bhai would come wrapped in a shawl with a thermos of hot tea. Panikkar's house in Thiruvananthapuram is full of light; there is a coconut grove and a small wavy *pagdandi* between his residential area and the *kalari,* where he works with his actors. I would go to Panikkar's place for breakfast which would invariably be wonderful. I had come to relish coconut oil with which food is made in Kerala. We would start recording our conversations in the afternoon and would continue till late at night. We would go for walks on the winding hill roads where the Panikkars live. He was extremely worried about the salary grant of his repertory which was getting delayed and was therefore causing difficulties to his actors. Sopanam has one of the most talented group of actors in our country and the reason for this is the training techniques that Panikkar has evolved during the last few decades. Panikkar treats his actors as equals and pays them well, unlike many directors of other theatre groups.

I came back to Bhopal after spending a few more days with him and his family. For the next few months he went on thinking about the play and also started rehearsing. Sometimes he would call me to say that some more lines were to be written for the play or he would ask me to compose a song for some character. One morning he called me to say that we should begin the play with a mating song of birds. I liked the idea, and wrote another song. Our writing the play in this way continued for many more days.

5

Panikkar's theatre is the theatre of imagination and *rasa*. Let me give an example. He was rehearsing the opening scene of *Uttararamacharitam*. He wanted to show the famous *kraunch-wadh* (killing of the crane) at the beginning of the play. He felt that we should show a forest scene where the killing of the bird takes place. He told me his idea; I liked it and elaborated upon it. Then he told me to write a mating song of the birds. When this song was being rehearsed he asked the actor who was doing the role of Valmiki to enter the scene along with the actor who was doing the role of the hunter. The hunter was to hunt the bird and Valmiki was to see the killing and utter his first verse (*shloka*). He imagined these two acts as done on two different axes but woven in one rhythm. The moment Valmiki utters his *shloka*, groups of actors come from all sides and join the celebration of the birth of the first human *shloka*. The result is a beautiful theatrical moment full of *rasa*.

Panikkar spent his childhood in Kavalam where he was exposed to various performing traditions of Kerala like Kathakali, Kudiyattam, Mudiyattu, etc. From a young age he started absorbing the pleasure and spirit of these arts so much so that they almost became part of his being. When later in his life he became Secretary of Kerala Sangeetha Nataka Akademi, he went to various remote places of rural Kerala to get an intimate experience of almost all the folk (*deshi*) and classical (*margi*) art forms of Kerala. He did extensive research in these art-forms and tried to understand their creative dynamics. He started writing plays much before he started directing them. His first directorial attempt was the production of Bhasa's *Madhyama Vyayogam*. It seems that while directing this play, Panikkar understood very clearly that if Sanskrit theatre is to be practised it will have to be connected to the *deshi* theatrical practices which means that during the direction of his very first play, Panikkar was able to establish a creative and imaginative link between the Sanskrit *Natyashastra* and the folk practices of theatre. One can say that his theatre is both *Natyadharmi* and *Lokdharmi*, it is neither totally classical nor is it entirely folk (it is neither totally *margi* nor is it entirely *deshi*). It is neither totally stylised nor is it entirely mimetic. He picks elements from all these traditions and creates his own unique theatre which is sensuously philosophical and the other way round. Panikkar's theatre is the most philosophical theatre of the country and yet his is a theatre of imagination, a theatre of *rasa* where all four elements of *abhinaya* (acting) are brought into play. In this regard, his is a rare theatre. There are theatre directors in the country who give more importance to the spoken word (*vachika*) in their theatrical practices and thus turn their theatre into a kind of story-telling. There are some directors who give importance to the costumes and props (*aharya*) but in my view, Kavalam Narayana Panikkar is the only Indian theatre director in whose theatrical practice all four elements of acting are poetically balanced and yet are able to maintain their independent existence as is envisaged in the traditional Asian dramaturgy.

In Panikkar's theatre many folk forms of Kerala are in fact creatively conserved and allowed to realise their potential. This becomes possible because in his theatre Panikkar is able to connect the vitality of the folk elements with the refinement of the classical ones. This connection gives Panikkar an enomous amount of freedom to create and yet remain rooted into the collective memory of the civilisation. Let it be said again and again that *deshi* or folk elements are not at all decorative for Panikkar's theatre. They are most creatively and philosophicallly used. For example, in his production of Bhasa's *Urubhangam,* Panikkar used the folk form of Theyyam to interpret the character of Duryodhana. One sees two Duryodhanas on the stage— the character Duryodhana and the other is his *theyyam* that is, his self. By bringing both of these on the stage together he could bring to the fore what was almost whispered in the written text of the play: Duryodhana too had a Self which could see through his misdeeds.

6

I went to Thiruvananthapuram two more times. Filmmaker Gurvinder Singh accompanied me on both these visits, documenting the way we worked on the text, the way rehearsals were carried out, and the various sources of the theatre practice of Panikkar. He called his film *Kavalam*.

I worked with Panikkar on *Uttararamacharitam*, enjoying the enunciation of Hindi by Malayalam tongues, fine-tuning a thing or two, here and there. But most of all, I enjoyed the way Panikkar worked with his imaginative actors. They not only gave substance to his imagination, but also elaborated it whenever it was possible.

Panikkar's theatre decolonises the theatrical practices of India. It opens various ways of relating to the *margi* and *deshi* traditions of India, not only for itself, but also for other directors. Our tradition believes and practices the continuity between *nritta* (pure dance based solely on rhythm and pace), *nritya* (dance with acting) and *natya* (theatre). Perhaps Panikkar's theatre is the only contemporary urban theatre where such continuity is most beautifully realised. And this makes it possible for him to create many textures of time for his viewers to take immense pleasure in.

Part One
WRITINGS

The Panikkar Phenomenon in
Modern Indian Theatre
K.S. Rajendran

Kavalam Narayana Panikkar's seminal contribution to contemporary Indian theatre practice is that he evolved a distinct performance idiom integrating several traditional/folk/popular, classical and dance-music forms of Kerala, the southern state of peninsular India. Kerala, known for its varied performance traditions ranging from ritualistic practices to highly evolved codified systems of acting inspired Panikkar, an undisputed pioneer, to initiate and practice a system of acting and play productions strikingly different from the earlier theatre practices that were developed under the influences of colonial modernity. Before coming to the world of theatre, he had the advantage of being a very popular Malyalam film lyricist. His association with music dates back to his younger days when he evinced keen interest in learning Sopanam music. His interest in Mohiniyattam, a classical dance form of Kerala for which he wrote songs, gave him an opportunity to closely interact with the eminent practitioners of Mohiniyattam like Bharati Shivaji. His brief stint in Kerala Sangeetha Nataka Akademi as its secretary perhaps also enabled him to watch and learn from a whole variety of performance and theatre traditions existing and practised in Kerala. With his understanding and acquaintance of these indigenous forms, Panikkar entered the national theatre vista in the late 1970s with his production of Bhasa's *Madhyama Vyayogam*.

To put his work in proper perspective within the frames of 'modern Indian' theatre, we must have a brief understanding of the Malayalam theatre that prevailed prior to his arrival on the Indian theatre stage. Professors G. Shankara Pillai, S. Ramanujam and Kumara Varma were actively involved in the *nataka kalari* movement in the twentieth century. They conducted a series of theatre workshops all over Kerala and paved the way for a meaningful modern Malayalam theatre to emerge. Professor Pillai also established a theatre training school at Thrissur for Calicut University. Professor Ramanujam and Professor Varma, after graduating from the National School of Drama (NSD), were actively involved in the promotion of modern Malayalam theatre. This was the time when the so called 'theatre of roots' was generously patronised and supported by the cultural establishments of the state which never had any understanding of the term nor of the future of 'modern' Indian theatre. Theatre practitioners who conformed to this postcolonial project of reviving Indian theatre exploited traditional theatre and performance forms by failing to understand the generic characteristics of these forms. They produced theatre along a distinct style for quick fortune and fame by producing a spectacle of 'Indianness' which was distant from the authentic practice and appropriation of traditional Indian theatre. The urban consumer (audience) with nostalgia and limited knowledge of traditional theatre, enjoyed a 'pure Indian' flavour on the theatre-stage; alongside the practitioners of 'pure, unadulterated' Indian theatre who promoted and produced such theatre.

At this time when both traditional and modern Indian theatre were struggling to find a niche for their own rhetoric, Panikkar entered the scene with his innovative skill and capability to stage Sanskrit plays. This immediately brought him into the national limelight and he held the position of sole authority on contemporary productions of Sanskrit plays for decades. Besides staging Sanskrit plays he also wrote and produced plays in Malayalam. His plays were significantly different from the well-known Malayalam plays in theme and structure. They were based on myths and legends whereas most of the popular Malayalam plays were highly political and represented the contemporary issues directly in a well-knit dramatic structure, which was closer to modern European plays. He created a more flexible performance structure that takes us back into the past centuries in practice and performance while simultaneously critiquing the *contemporaneity*. The basic rhythm (*tala* pattern) that guides the flow of such performances was the strength of his performance-idiom. Every small detail of stage setting was meticulously governed by this *tala* pattern, discernible only to the informed audiences who were well-versed with the basic knowledge and understanding of the styles, text, content and theatre. The movement pattern in Panikkar's productions did not follow any single style of Kerala's performing art traditions. He was able to extract the best styles from the traditional theatre forms of Kerala and mix them artistically to evolve a coherent performance style that was unique and distinctive in functioning and performing. His grasp on the varied modes of performance forms and the ability to permute and combine several performance forms like Theyyam, Ottan thullal, *Chakyar* koothu, Nangiar koothu, Padayani, Chavittunatakam, Tholpavakoothu besides the well known forms of Kerala namely Kathakali, Kudiyattam and Mohiniyattam was simply outstanding. A condensed version evolved by exploiting certain features of all the above mentioned traditional forms in order to create an alloy of original is not any small achievement of Panikkar's.

His first production of Bhasa's *Madhyama Vyayogam* was something contemporary Indian theatre had never witnessed. This production was first noticed by the critics and scholars at Kalidasa Academy, Ujjain. Later Panikkar brought it to the national theatre workshop organised by Sangeet Natak Akademi (SNA) in 1981 at New Delhi where he spoke in great detail about his production process and his actors demonstrated scenes from the play. Music, stylised acting, stylised speech, recitation, song and dance/movement were all at the centre of his work. However some argue that it was not at all a theatrical production. But the impact of this production on modern Indian theatre was so great that no criticism was heard. He emerged as an indisputable contemporary theatre director with all the means and methods that he extracted from Kerala's performance traditions. He successfully brought alive the almost forgotten perfunctory text of performance in Bhasa's plays that were discovered in the beginning of the twentieth century by Ganapati Shastri.

Indeed, Panikkar deserves a special position in modern Indian theatre for his theatrical rendition of Sanskrit plays, but the absence of criticism of his works needs to be discussed. If the so called learned Sanskrit scholars and critics of Indian theatre failed to posit any question on the relevance, evaluation and appropriation of his works with regard to the evolution of modern Indian theatre then we have failed to understand the necessity and significance of Panikkar's works. His involvement and practice in theatre has set a new trend in modern Indian theatre which will go unnoticed if we do not critically engage in re-viewing and re-analysing the process and performances of Panikkar. As a practitioner and researcher of Sanskrit plays for several years, I have realised the significance as well as the limitations of Panikkar's works especially regarding the Sanskrit plays. It is time we critically analyse the birth, evolution, success and limitations of the Panikkar phenomenon in modern Indian theatre.

Resensualising the Theatrical Experience[1]
Udayan Vajpeyi

1

I recently read somewhere that before starting his journey into theatre, Kavalam Narayana Panikkar received a degree in Law and in fact practised law for some time. Practising law, what does that mean? I think it means to interpret the written law to suit the contemporary situation of the case one is handling. Someone who practises law has to relentlessly interpret the written law, interpret to contemporise it. To give it a new temporality that it may lack otherwise, which, in other words, means not to accept the law as given but to reinterpret it, reconfigurate it, to redesign it. Or to recreate it.

2

Two words that perhaps Kavalam uses most in his conversations are *Natyadharmi* and *Lokdharmi*. With due respect and understanding of these terms and their connotations, I prefer using *margi* and *deshi* in their place. I will let you know the reason for that a little later. I am aware that these terms were and are primarily used with reference to music and dance. But then I am also aware that Bharat Muni says that music (*gaan*) is the bed of theatre, *gaan* is the *natyashayya*; therefore, by using these terms to describe theatre, I am not too much off the mark. *Margi* and *deshi* are used loosely for the classical (which is, of course, a misnomer in the Indian context) and folk forms (another misnomer) but in fact, these words have much wider and deeper connotations than these blatant meanings.

Margi has come from *mrigaya* that is, hunting. *Marg, mriga* and *mrigaya* are all connected words. *Marg* is the way that one takes for *mrigaya* or hunting. It is the way that one takes to search for the *mriga*, the animal to be hunted, to do *mrigaya*. One has to invent a new way every time one hunts. That's

---

1 This essay was written on the occasion of Panikkar's 80th birthday in 2008. It included the subtitle Or Shall We Call Him Margi Kavalam Narayana Panikkar?

what *marg* is—a new way. From this perspective *margi* art forms can be seen as those where the artist incessantly tries to find new ways of creating. He or she has to be on the look out for a possible new way to create his or her art-form. *Deshi* art forms are something different but not lesser in any way. They are, ontologically speaking, repetitive in nature. Here the artist tries to repeat the ways of creating and rightly so because *deshi* art forms are not only a repertoire of the ways of creation and therefore, primarily memory based, but they perform a very significant function of invoking collective memory of the community in which they are practised.

In *deshi* forms the stress is not on inventing new ways of creating but on repeating ways of creating. *Margi* art forms are different; their axes lie in inventing and searching new ways of creating. I think the *margi* form does not primarily evoke collective memory and thereby a sense of community but stimulates the imagination of its audience to think differently, to think new and thereby to help them to be self-reflexive.

The mode of being *margi,* as we have seen, is such that it takes much more time and effort for it to be accepted.

3

Panikkar's theatre, as I know it, is primarily *margi* theatre. It has taken many elements from the *deshi* theatre of Kerala, but he has invested them all into creating a scintillating *margi* theatre. In other words, this is a theatre grounded in *deshi* but incessantly searching for new ways of being. Seen from this angle his is a unique theatre: the theatre which attempts to find new openings within the *deshi* to create a sensuous *margi* theatre thereby establishing continuity between the two or creating a scale of which *margi* and *deshi* become parts of.

One can appreciate presence of such a scale not only here but in almost every element of Panikkar's theatre, in the *angika, vachika, sattvika,* or even *aharya abhinaya* of his theatre. It is as if all the *deshi* components of his theatre gradually undergo a radical transformation, a kind of *bhavantaran* and instead of carrying the burden of repetition, they become vehicles of search—search of the new ways of creating theatre. They, then, do not remain *deshi* but acquire a new life as details of a *margi* theatrical experience.

4

I will take two of Kalidasa's plays that Panikkar has performed. Kavalam's *Malavikagnimitram* and *Vikramorvashiyam* are unique productions. Kavalam has dug out a different Kalidasa from these plays, a Kalidasa, of course, more suited to our times but also a Kalidasa who would have remained embedded in these plays if Kavalam had not dug him out. It is as if this new Kalidasa was waiting for centuries for Kavalam to bring him out into the lights of the contemporary stage. He is the same Kalidasa we have known for ages and yet is completely different.

Through his *margi* theatrical practice, Kavalam is able to restate the essential feature of great writing: it is never self-same. It has many possible ways of coming into being which lie dormant in it. Whenever it is approached with an open creative mind, it reveals its less known way of being. Kavalam has done precisely this. He approached Kalidasa with his *margi* intentions and has brought out a new Kalidasa for us. What are those *margi* ways of Kavalam? They are innumerable and are there to be seen in his theatre instead of being talked about and yet we can talk about a few. One which is most noticeable is his interpretation of Malavika and Agnimitra and Urvashi and Pururava. In Panikkar's theatre they are the embodiment of *prakriti* and *purush*. Malavika and Urvashi are the embodiment of *prakriti* and Agnimitra and Pururava are *purush* embodied. But even here Panikkar does not accept the established Sankhya notion of *prakriti-purush*. He reinterprets them and brings them close to what a poet like Bulle Shah envisaged:

> *Ajja ajo ki preet na jani*
> *Laggi rose azal di aahi*

> Love of her and me is not of this day, it is
> there since the day of creation of the Universe.

In the Sankhya tradition, *prakriti* is *jad* or inert whereas *purush* is consciousness. It is through *prakriti* that *purush* is able to experience itself. Kavalam reinterpretes this notion of *purush-prakriti*. For Kavalam in the light of love, *purush* and *prakriti* become lover and the beloved and then he adds another dimension to *prakriti*; in his theatre it becomes not only the loved one but also the embodiment of nature. In this way, a completely novel Malavika and Urvashi come into being. It is not something which Panikkar has added or grafted on the plays of Kalidasa; this interpretation was lying in wait in those plays. With his imaginative perception, Panikkar allowed it to unfold and take the centre stage in his presentation of these plays. He then went one step further and redefined the most mysterious of all emotions: love. Love, as the *mangalacharan* of Kavalam's *Vikramorvashiyam* seems to suggest, is to invoking the *prakriti* in all its meanings within oneself. Therefore love of Pururava for Urvashi is an attempt of his to find the external nature (*prakriti*) and internal nature (*swabhav*) within himself. Strangely enough as a result of the *margi* imagination of Kavalam the Ashok tree comes into the centre of the *Malavikagnimitram* and in *Vikramorvashiyam* Urvashi becomes one with the forest where she disappears. She makes her individual appearance again only when Pururava is able to internalise the forest and is able to see the forest as the description of Urvashi, not as *aharya* of Urvashi but as her *angika*.

5

The flow in Panikkar's theatre comes not only from the flow of the narrative of the play but more so through the use of scales. I think this is extremely significant for any theatrical practice—the imaginative use of scales. There are and can be various scales in theatre. The scale of *vachika* or speech pattern potentially ranges from simple straightforward speech to song. (It is interesting to note that most of the Sanskrit plays do not only have more than one language but have multiple language-gestures ranging from plain speech to *shloka*s). The scale of *angika* or various styles of movements of actors ranges from a simple walk to what is almost dance. The scale of syntax of the placement of actors ranges from the so called realistic way to highly imaginative ways like one finds in Kudiyattam. Panikkar's theatre moves in multiple axes along all these scales producing something like microtones (*shruti*) in these domains of performance. The movement along all these scales leads in his theatre to the unleashing of various forms of energies which prepares and makes his audience experience the cascades of *rasa* of the play with much greater depth and intensity. But at the same time it also allows one to experience what Henri Bergson called duration because the movement along these scales leads to subtle disjunctions in temporalities causing various *chhanda*s to be born, thus allowing the audience to experience not only the movements but the material of the movements—Time.

6

The entry of Semitic religion traditions[2] caused at least one big problem in the way Sanskrit and other traditional Indian texts were read. It went through the process of desensualisation—desensualisation and de-eroticisation. The thing that has to be restated is that in almost all pagan traditions, like India, the continuity of man and nature is established and practised through erotic or *shringara rasa*[3]. It is one of the ways through which homocentricity is avoided but then semitisation of the reading of Sanskrit and other traditional texts also had its impact on the way theatre, especially Sanskrit theatre, was performed. It may seem strange but most Sanskrit theatre which developed in the last century is highly de-eroticised theatre. It is not a coincidence that in most of the performances of *Malavikagnimitram*, Agnimitra is shown as some kind of lumpen and not a lover without which, in any case, the true erotic *rasa* can not emerge.

I have a feeling that Kavalam Narayana Panikkar is one of those very few theatre directors who resensualised not only Sanskrit theatre but modern theatre practice in India. He took his theatrical elements from all possible sources—from *deshi* theatre of *theyyam* to much more refined *margi* Kudiyattam dance-drama traditions—and used them all to create theatrical experiences which are truly pagan in nature. In this way he showed not only the way theatre can be done but also gave a glimpse of the ways theatre might have been done in civilisations similar to India.

---

2 By Semitic traditions, I mean those world views which believe that the moral or otherwise ordering of the things and human beings leads inevitably to divine 'grace' as against the wisdom of the 'pagans' like Bulle Shah who said, *ain wain chah dikhaya*, 'grace was given without any rhyme or reason'.
3 Rati, the *sthai bhava* of erotic or *shringara rasa*, unlike *sthai bhava* of any other *rasa*, is present in all living beings.

7

Kavalam has relentlessly tried in his theatre to find what I would call pagan ways to describe pagan world views. Instead of appropriating the various manifestations of pagan consciousness into Semitic paradigms, he has tried to invent and discover unique ways of describing traditional insights of India, those we so much need in this overtly semitised world of ours.

The lawyer in Kavalam Narayana Panikkar whom we met in the first section of this essay may have stopped interpreting the law, but he is working day and night with his theatre director persona to reinterpret and recast the plays of Sanskrit playwrights like Kalidasa and Bhasa and many of his own into remarkably innovative and sensuous yet spiritual that is, *rasayukta* gestures of theatre to pave the possibility and realisation of a truly rooted and therefore truly universal artistic experiences in our times.

I wish him a long life. I wish, of course, for his sake but also for mine so that I may get many more beautiful artistic experiences born in my life.

Actors Speak[1]
Gary Wynn and *Sandra Kovacs*

Having been trained as a Shakespearean actor at the London Academy of Music and Dramatic Arts with no prior knowledge of Bhasa, much less Sanskrit, I approached the role of Baledeva with mixed feelings of enthusiasm and trepidation. At the moment of casting I knew that my task was enormous and that this role would be one of the most challenging and frustrating assignments of my acting career. Our situation was thus: we would perform a play based on foreign mythology in an ancient language which was completely alien to our western ears, tongue and culture. We would have to undergo intensive physical training in both Kalari (the indigenous martial art of Kerala) and Bharatnatyam (classical dance of India). Fortunately some of the cast had previous experience in Kalari. This training was meant to enrich our bodies with Indian aesthetics. We had to study or familiarise ourselves with specific *talas* for characterisation. We attempted to become intimate with the great Indian epics; and last, but certainly not least, we rehearsed.

The performance would be a culmination of nearly a year's worth of blood, sweat and many tears. Some thought the project both absurd and improbable. I did the best I could in all our studies and trusted that our labours would bear fruit. We proceeded to vigorously stamp our untrained feet onto the floor; our eyes went through the daily routine of circular motions and diagonals to increase our expressiveness and our fingers were stretched out through the *mudras* of Bharatnatyam. Each day a Sanskrit scholar would patiently go through our text with us for pronunciation and meaning. I desperately tried to create mental images through the language as a means of memorising. It is impossible to memorise abstract sounds, images are needed. Our intensive weapons-work in Kalari took place each and every day since our production would begin with a combat prologue, which Bhasa conceptualised as verbal imagery through the soldiers. Professor Zarrilli, a master at Kalari,

---

1 This text was written in 1987 when Gary Wynn and Sandra Kovacs were Fellows of the American Institute of Indian Studies.

wisely chose to stage these images. After six months of this rigorous routine we had developed a collage of Bharatnatyam characters, realistic delivery of dialogue, actual combat intermingled with abstract classically danced combat and the use of some Kathakali techniques. As actors we trusted the direction we were receiving from our present director and choreographer and thus continued in the mixed style of production. However the style that was emerging instinctually seemed wrong to me. The abstract and stylised characterisation did not seem to merge with our realistic vocal patterns. I felt that all the characters had a flatness, a uni-dimensional quality that was far from theatrical. My fear was that we would have an esoteric production on our hands which would not communicate to our audience even if they were Sanskrit scholars. Yet I continued in this direction.

The use of classical dance in a theatrical production frustrated my beliefs as a theatre artist. I thoroughly enjoy the grace and beauty of Bharatnatyam, but not in the theatre genre. The form is much too stifling and restrictive for true characterisation. And my own insecurities in the form affected my work as an actor. I found it quite presumptuous on our part to attempt the innovative use of a highly developed form without mastering the form itself. However, whenever I attempted to break the mould, either by heightening the vocal delivery or modifying the dance form I was quickly put into my place as an actor. The work continued.

Urubhangam was to be presented for the Festival of India in Chicago in one month. Our unique style was taking shape and I discovered a way to make it somewhat work for me. Yet my frustrations continued. At this point we received good news; our guest director's visa was cleared and he was scheduled to arrive in a few days. The cast figured there was not much he could do at this stage of the process. Maybe he would polish some of our rough edges and crystallise the style a bit. We anxiously awaited his arrival.

We met Kavalam Narayana Panikkar for the first time at a run-through rehearsal. He watched, made mental notes and we did the best that we could. That day will certainly remain in my repertoire of theatre stories to tell my grandchildren. My Bharatnatyam form was in pretty good shape: shoulders back and down, elbows up; my *mudras* were fairly precise and my legs turned out. The flatness of my feet resounded the floor with Baledeva's occasional stamping. And my vocal style remained realistic and low key as directed. 'He must be impressed,' thought this naive American actor. After the run-through the cast was asked to leave as all three of our directors conferred. The cast eagerly awaited approval, as all actors tend to, and expected that Mr Panikkar would be able to relax for the next month.

Baledeva and Duryodhana, I and my wife Sandra Kovacs, were asked to enter the space. This was when our rehearsal truly began. This was also when *Urubhangam* was lifted from the depths of a Bharatnatyam bore and began to take shape, finally reaching the heights of a dynamic theatrical experience. Panikkarji began work with me. He demonstrated the vocal and physical style of Baledeva's first entrance. I was awestruck by the powerful use of the vocal mechanism and expressiveness of the body language. I attempted to copy. Again he demonstrated and again I attempted to copy. This process of copy-cat continued for some time until I was able to internalise this new and highly theatrical form and make it my own. I was released from the harness of a pure form and discovered the freedom of a dramatic form. It was truly amazing how our American production of *Urubhangam* took shape within that last month of rehearsal. Originally Duryodhana was shown as crawling on the ground since his thighs were shattered. Panikkar did not agree with this interpretation. He lifted Sandra off the ground and allowed her to enact the textual images visually. This alone helped the production tremendously since she is a wonderful dancer and was finally free to enact this fabulous role of Duryodhana. Panikkarji stated that if Duryodhana's thighs were truly broken then we must send him to the hospital immediately! Mr Panikkar taped all of our *shoka*s utilising his powerful mode of vocalisation which we went home and copied. This was truly the moment when the form gives one the freedom to perform. The new style gave us the freedom to expand our acting choices and test the limits of our performance.

With one month remaining, K.N. Panikkar entered the scene in our rehearsal process, a journey which began eight months prior. This eccentric-looking fellow, as I had thought at our time of meeting, commenced to revamp our production totally. It seemed as if all of our previous labours were for naught and a new style would emerge—thank goodness! This sudden metamorphosis was not universally accepted by the cast. In fact, most of the cast refused to make these enormous changes; therefore, Mr Pannikar concentrated on Baledeva and Duryodhana. The method of watch and copy is certainly not new for the Asian performer; this is the traditional form of study. Of course, this is not true in the West. We must 'feel' our role and characters, a very self-indulgent means of expression. Whereas through copying Panikkar's voice and body movements, my own instrument was fine-tuned thereby giving me more freedom in my final choices in creating Baledev. I was released from the confines of classical dance and a rich character emerged. Miraculously, our production became exciting. No longer an esoteric theatre piece for stuffy intellectuals, it became theatre for all to watch and enjoy, despite the language and culture differences. Even if the audience did not fully understand the production, due to the language, they certainly were entertained. Theatre should be intellectually stimulating, socially meaningful, aesthetically pleasing and above all entertaining. Our work finally bore fruit which was very pleasing to the senses.

Urubhangam was more than an exciting experience for me. It gave my wife and I a strong direction to head in for the next few years. My training in Kalari continued under the very able guidance of Professor Zarrilli and the Asian forms that we encountered inspired my wife and myself to create our own performance pieces based on international mythology. The spark of travelling to India for the purpose of receiving first hand training in traditional performance forms was ignited through our work with Mr Panikkar. This led to an American Institute of Indian Studies fellowship of intensive study with master gurus in indigenous environments. For this we gratefully thank Mr Panikkar for the inspiration and knowledge he has shared with us. I can't help but feel that only after our studies here in India should we have attempted the monumental task of performing a Bhasa play in his own language of expression, Sanskrit. We hope to use the work, training and inspiration we are receiving in Kerala to present an original movement theatre piece for a village audience based on a Native American parable. We wish to share cross-cultural ideas and hopefully give back a bit of ourselves to India, thus fostering cultural exchange through performance techniques.

(From the Nemichandra Jain Collection)

Recitation and Performance
Sangeeta Gundecha

The dramatic reading of any play is like pulling apart balls of cotton for Kavalam Narayana Panikkar. He listens to each layer of cotton carefully and makes threads for himself out of these. Then he weaves them together and expands them to create the play like a fine shawl.

On 5 May 2007 Kavalam Narayana Panikkar phoned me to tell me that he is thinking of preparing *Avimarakam* in memory of late Ayyapa Panikkar[1]. He asked me to reach there early because he wanted to start the play soon. On another occasion, during a conversation he had told me that till now he has already staged *Madhyama Vyayogam, Karnabharam, Dootavakyam, Urubhahgam, Pratimanatakam, Swapnavasavadattam* and *Pratijnayaugandharayanam*—a total of seven plays from *Bhasanatakacakram*. But Ayyapa had wanted him to stage *Avimarakam* as well. I had then requested Mr Panikkar to inform me whenever he wished to start the preparations for the play.

It was the month of May; days and nights were very hot and one could find coolness only in the water of the wells. No seats were available on trains going from Bhopal to Thiruvanathapuram for the next two months. Then Brajesh Dixit, a friend of the Hindi author Udayan Vajpeyi helped me and I reached Thiruvanthapuram after a forty-hour train journey on 9 May.

While doing my research on the great poet Bhasa, I had already had long conversations with some of his important contemporary practitioners such as Habib Tanvir, Ratan Thiyam and Kavalam Narayana Panikkar. In fact, I had stayed with Panikkarji at Sopanam for some time in this context. Then I had travelled with him in the train to Thiruvananthapuram after presenting my paper on Dhrupad at the Swathi Thirunal Samaroha organised by him at Kochi. In the train, I observed that many people were expressing their appreciation for his contribution. On seeing him a woman had exclaimed, 'Kavalam!' Conversing with him in Malayalam, she told him that she too

---

1 Ayyapa Panikkar was an eminent Malyalam poet and a close friend of Kavalam Narayana Panikkar.

was from the village Kavalam and that her daughter's school textbook had a beautiful poem authored by him.

It is a specialty of some non-Hindi speaking provinces such as Kerala, Bengal and Maharashtra, where an intimacy is easily established between people and their writers and artists. The reason for this is certainly their rich cultural ambience, but language emerges as one of the major constituent elements. While sharing this, the boundaries of identity between the people and the artist-writers quickly become fuzzy.

When I reached Sopanam,[2] situated amidst dense trees, far away from

Thiruvananthapuram city on Tagur (the Malayalam version of Tagore) Road, I could hear the *Mangalacarana* (invocation) of *Avimarakam* before I could reach the Kalari (theatre), after passing through Panikkar's house.

Utksiptam sanukampam

salilanidhijaladekdanstragrarudhamakrantamjimadhye

nihataditisutamekapadavadhutam.

Sambhuktam preetipurvam swabhujavsagatamekcakrabhiguptam

srimannarayanaste

pradisatu vasudhamuchchhritaikatpatram.

The *Mangalacarana* composed in the *Sragdhara chhanda* (metre)[3] by Bhasa invokes the various incarnations of Visnu such as the Matsya and Varaha avatars (the Fish and Boar incarnations) who rescued the earth from within the sea, *Nrisimhavatara* (the Man-Lion incarnation) who slew the demons for her protection, *Vamanavatara* (the Dwarf incarnation) who took a single step to measure the earth, *Ramavatara* who nurtured her with love and *Krisnavatara* who protected her with his *cakra* (disc), etc. In Panikkar's presentation, it is the Varaha or the Boar incarnation which is at the centre. He was giving instructions to actor Sathish Kumar who was playing Varaha regarding how to portray the boar rescuing the drowning earth and putting her on the tip of his tusks. But first the sea had to be created. Following Panikkar's directions the singer Anil Kumar Payaveedu and Sathish Kumar were repeating a phrase of the *Mangalacarana, Salilanidhi* four times on the note *Sadja* of the *madhya saptaka* (middle octave). Six actors were standing

---

2 Repertory directed by Kavalam Narayana Panikkar

3 The *Sragdhara* metre has four phases (*charanas*) and twenty-one beats (*matra*)

in a row, each holding two strips of different coloured cloth. They were waving them with their hands. Because of their waving action the effect of the sea was being created on the stage. The drummers (players of *tala-vadya*) were playing the adakya and the mizhau following the beat of the singing of *Salilanidhi*.

Tattatakit   tattatakit   tattatakit   tattatakit

The actors were waving their coloured cloth strips without lifting their feet off the ground, to the same beat.

Now Anil and Sathish were singing on the fifth note of the *madhya saptaka*—

Salilanidhi   Salilanidhi   Salilanidhi   Salilanidhi

Six actors were continuously creating the wave of the sea on the stage. Then the singers shifted to the high sixth (*Tara Shadja*) note of the *Madhya Saptaka*—

Sassss   Sassss   Sassss   Sassss
Salilanidhi   Salilanidhi   Salilanidhi   Salilanidhi.
Tattatakit   Tattatakit   Tattatakit   Tattatakit

A huge sea had now been created on the stage. The actress Saritā could now be seen bobbing up and down in this sea. The waves of the sea threw her upwards sometimes, and at other times tried to take her into its arms. She was about to drown now. In order to show the earth drowning, Saritā, who was portraying the earth, had the coloured strips on her head, so that the audience could experience the surface of the water and the drowning earth within it. As soon as she began to drown the Boar entered, picked her up and placed her on the tip of his tusks. The actor takes his hands close to his teeth and with two fingers indicates his tusks. He pretends to take these tusks close to the surface of the sea and then lift them upwards. This is where the singing of the lines of the *Mangalacarana* begins.

One of the singers sings a line and the second one repeats it—

First singer—*Utksiptam*
Second singer—*Utksiptam*

First singer—*Utksiptam*
Second singer—*Utksiptam*

First singer—vasudham utksiptam
Second singer—vasudham utksiptam

First singer—vasudham utksiptam
Second singer—vasudham utksiptam

First singer—Utksiptam
Second singer—Utksiptam

First singer—Utksiptam
Second singer—Utksiptam

First singer—vasudham utksiptam
Second singer—vasudham utksiptam

First singer—vasudham utksiptam
Second singer—vasudham utksiptam

First singer—sanukampam utksiptam agraruham utksiptam
Second singer—sanukampam utksiptam agraruham utksiptam

First singer—utkśiptām vasudhām utkśiptām
Second singer—utkśiptām vasudhām utkśiptām

First singer—utksiptam vasudham utksiptam
Second singer—utksiptam vasudham utksiptam

First singer—akrantamajimadhye
Second singer—akrantamajimadhye

First singer—nihataditisutam
Second singer—nihataditisutam
Ni ha ta {Here each syllable of the phrase *Nihata* is recited with a pause in between and then only the beats of the drum (tala-vadya) are played}.

First singer—ekpadavadhutam

Second singer—ekpadavadhutam

First singer—sambhuktam preetipurvam

Second singer—sambhuktam preetipurvam

First singer—swabhujavasagatam

Second singer—swabhujavasagatam

First singer—ekcakrabhiguptam

Second singer—ekcakrabhiguptam

First singer—srimannarayanaste

Second singer—srimannarayanaste

First singer—pradisatu vasudham

Second singer—pradisatu vasudham

First singer—uchchhritaikatpatram

Second singer—uchchhritaikatpatram

When the phrase *Ekapadavadhutam* (measured with one foot) is sung the *Vamanavatara* (the Dwarf incarnation) of Visnu is enacted. When Visnu enters the stage, all the actors present on the stage reduce their height and stretch their necks upwards and look at him with large eyes. This is how his vastness is indicated. Then the actors, who were sitting, gradually stand up and the actor playing Visnu bends to his right and proportionately reduces his height to the same beat. Thus, it is indicated that Visnu has entered his *Vamanavatara*. This dwarf incarnation of Visnu takes a leap and measures the earth. First he takes three small steps and then he suddenly stands up and measures it with a single step. The coloured strips which were the sea previously, now become Visnu's umbrella, under which the earth is shown receiving blessings from Visnu. This is where the *Mangalacarana* comes to an end.

Kavalam Narayana Panikkar believes that the playwright leaves clues in several places within the texture of the play which indicate how the play is to be performed. The director's job is to find these clues submerged within the play and bring them out in practice. He unravels the playwright's intentions at several levels. Whatever he achieves in this unravelling process becomes his performance. He did the same with the *Mangalacarana* of *Avimaraka*. He determined the beat and rhythm of the drums *Adakya* and *Mizhau* from the embedded metre of the *Mangalacarana*. The rhythm and beats played on the drums determine the pattern of movement and rhythm of the actors and also the rhythm of the dialogues spoken by them (i.e. the speed of delivery and the pauses). And along with this the subtle actions (*sattvik*) too continue to be determined. In this way, the interdependence between different forms of action and their mutual co-ordination enables the audience to fully enjoy their experience. A noticeable feature of the performance of the *Mangalacarana* by Panikkar is that although he keeps the rhythm of the metre of the *Mangalacarana* intact in the singing, he breaks up the phrases according to his own interpretation of the play and the requirements of the performance. This kind of division can be seen in the *astavrikriti* (eight forms of recitation) of the Vedas. For example the fourth *Vak* of the *Rudraprasna* occurring in the *Vaiswadevakaandam* of the *Taittiriya Samhita* of the *Krisna Yajurveda* may be considered:

Samhita patha (Textual recitation): This is the basic recital:

siva saravya ya tav tayano rudra mridaya

Pada patha (Word recital): In this form of recital, the sentence is divided into individual words of padas. The padas are written with *yati* (musical pauses)

1	2	3	4	5	6	7	8
Siva	saravya	ya	tav	taya	no	rudra	mridaya

Kram patha (Sequential recital): Two words are paired at a time for recital:

1+2	2+3	3+4	4+5	5+6	6+7	7+8
Siva saravya	saravya ya	ya tav	tav taya	taya no	no rudra	rudra mridaya

Jata patha (Braided recital: the words are braided together and recited back and forth):

1+2	2+1	1+2
2+3	3+2	2+3

3+4	4+3	3+4
4+5	5+4	4+5
5+6	6+5	5+6
6+7	7+6	6+7
7+8	8+7	7+8

Siva saravya	saravya siva	Siva saravya
saravya ya	ya saravya	Saravya ya
ya tav	tav ya	ya tav
Tav taya	tav taya	tav taya
Taya no	no taya	taya no
No rudra	rudra no	no rudra
Rudra mridaya	mridaya rudra	rudra mridaya

Ghana patha (Bell recital): the words are repeated back and forth in a bell shape):

1+2	2+1	1+2+3	3+2+1	1+2+3
2+3	3+2	2+3+4	4+3+2	2+3+4
3+4	3+4	3+4+5	5+4+3	3+4+5
4+5	5+4	4+5+6	6+5+4	4+5+6
5+6	6+5	5+6+7	7+6+5	5+6+7
6+7	7+6	6+7+8	8+7+6	6+7+8
7+8	8+7	7+8+9	9+8+7	7+8+9
Siva saravya	saravya siva	siva saravya ya	ya saravyasiva	siva saravya ya
saravya ya	ya saravya	saravya ya tav	tav ya saravya	saravya ya tav
tav ya	ya tav	ya tav taya	taya tav ya	ya tav taya
Tava taya	taya tav	Tav taya no	no taya tav	tav taya no
Taya no	no taya	taya no rudra	rudra no taya	taya no rudra
No rudra	rudra no	no rudra mridaya	mridaya rudra no	no rudra mridaya
Rudra mridaya	mridaya rudra	rudra mridayeti mridaya		

(Since it does not have more than eight phrases, this sequence ends here.)

We can see this form of recitation embedded in the structure of Sanskrit poetry. This can be understood from the following example of a famous Sanskrit poem:

Saile saile na manikyam, mauktikam na gaje gaje

sadhavo na hi sarvatra, candanam na vane vane[4]

If we change the pattern of the third phrase of the loka, it will be something like the following:

Sadhavo na sarvatra

sarvatra nahi sadhavo

Na hi sarvatra sadhavo

Sarvatra sadhavo na hi

The pattern of other phrases can also be similarly altered. Here, the change in the sequence of the phrases does not fundamentally alter their meaning. The difference is merely in the pattern. The possibility of altering the pattern unravels the various new layers of meaning within it. This is why the poet keeps the intended pattern embedded in the structure of the poem. We can also see that, in Hindustani classical music (and in Classical Carnatic music too) the *Bol-baant* (division of musical phrases) which is done constitutes a continuum with Vedic recitation. The musical composition based on a work by the famous Bhakti poet Raskhan, *Manus hon to wahin raskhan*[5] was presented by the well-known exponents of Dhrupad, Naseer Aminuddin Dagar and Naseer Moinuddin Dagar in raga Kambouji with the following *Bol-baant*:

Manus hon to wahin raskhan

Ma manu manus wahin ras

Manus hon to wahin ras ras ras hon to wahin

Hon to ras manus hon to wahin raskhan basaon

Brij gokul basoon basoon braj gokul basaon

Manus hon to basoon manus hon to bosaon

Manus manus hon to basoon braj gokul ke gwalan hon to wahin

Manus hon to wahin raskhan

Gaon ke gwalan gwalan gwalan gwalan hon to wahin

4 Not every mountain contains diamond, not every elephant has a pearl. Not everywhere one finds gentle soul, not every forest has the sandalwood tree.

5 If I am born as man Raskhan, I would be settled as a milk man in Gokul village of Brij.

If I am born as animal, I can't help it, I would like to be a cow, grazing every day amongst many cows of Nand.

If I become a stone, I would like to belong to that mountain which was lifted by Krisna like an umbrella.

If I be a bird, I would like to live on the branches of the Kadamba tree which stands on the banks of dark Yamuna River.

Manus hon to wahin raskhan
Manus manus hon to wahin
Manus hon to wahin raskhan

Gaon ke gwalan gwalan gwalan gwalan hon to wahin
Manus hon to wahin raskhan
Manus manus hon to wahin
Hon to wahin raskhan gokul gwalan gwalan ke gokul

Gaanv ke gwalan gwalan gaanv ke
Hon to wahin
Manus manus raskhan
Manus hon to wahin raskhan
Manus hon to wahin
Goan ke gwalan
Goan goan ke gwa gwalan
Hon to wahin raskhan

Raag Kambouji has always been a favourite of the Dagar brothers. It is thought to have come from Kambouja (Cambodia). Perhaps we should reconsider the study of ancient Geography from the viewpoint of the expansion of ancient India. The India which is designated *Jambudwipa* (the island on which Jambur is found) in the *Natyashastra*, what was its extent, where the Meru and Sumeru mountains were situated in it and what were the conceptions based on them— these questions should form important themes of our study and discourses.

The special feature of this composition by Raskhan is that it contains poetic beauty as well as musicality (that is, it can be easily put to music or sung). Surely Raskhan did not compose it to be sung in the Dhrupad style.

In India, the source of every art form is the *Natyashastra* and the source of *Natyashastra* is in the Vedas. This is why every art and craft form is related in some manner to the Vedas. But every art form must have evolved through a different path and in each there comes a juncture where its form altered independent of its association with Natya. The same has happened with Dhrupad.

The point is that the division of phrases in the recitation of Vedas and in the practice of Dhrupad music is somewhat similar to the way Kavalam

Narayana Panikkar divides the phrases in his presentation of the *Mangalacarana* of *Avimaraka*. It is difficult to find a sequence of division of phrases in the recitation patterns of the Vedas similar to his divisions, but the nature and style of presentation is approximately the same. We have to identify the Vedic recitations as the source of his inspiration. It is an appropriate thought, because he is a connoisseur and scholar of the Kudiyattam form of Kerala and closely follows its conventions in his theatrical works with great subtlety. It is said that the verbal actions (*Vacik abhinaya*) of Kudiyattam have evolved from Vedic recitations. There is a saying in Kerala that when Vedic recitations became distorted, the *vacik* of Kudiyattam was born.[6]

Until now it was our understanding that the inspirations of the four forms of action (*angik, vacik, aharya* and *sattvik*) depicted in the *Natyashastra* are different in theatre. But after understanding the dramatic process of Kavalam Narayana Panikkar's theatre, we find that in his case (even if we leave aside the *aharya*) music is the basis and inspiration of all forms of action. And music is rooted in Vedic recitation. Vedic recitation has certain special characteristics. Here, the high (*Udatta*), the low (*Anudatta*) and the middle (*Swarit*) notes are recited in a variety of rhythms and these have specific rules. These various rhythms evolve through Kuttiyattam and become the root sources of the various elements and interweave in Panikkar's theatre. In his performances, the subtle non-verbal actions (*sattvik*) based on the physical movements (*angik*), which in turn are based on the patterns of rhythm and beats, are inspired by music. The sage Bharata says that music is the bedrock of theatre: *Saiyyam hi natyasys vadanti geeta*[7]

If we consider the context of the performance of the plays of Panikkar, we can say that Vedic recitation is the bedrock of his theatre. It may have been invisible to the audience, but its echoes can always be heard by cultured audience and connoisseurs.

Translated from Hindi & Sanskrit by Pragati Mohapatra
Rang Prasang-36, Oct.-Dec. 2009

---

6 The exact saying in Malayalam language: *Kutta pidachcha otta kuttai.*

7 *Natyashastra-* 32/436.

References:

Avimarakam: Bhasanatakacakram, Chowkhamba
                                    Surbharti Prakasan, Varanasi, 1986.

Babulal Sukia Sastri: Natyasastram (Hindi), Chowkhamba
                                    Surbharti Prakasan, Varanasi, 1996.

Chhandomanjiri: Chowkhamba   Surbharti   Prakasan,
                                    Varanasi, 1990.

Acarya Brihaspati: Dhrupad, Sangeet Karyalaya, Hathrase (U.P.)

Rigved: Ramgovind Trivedi (Hindi Translation)
                                    Chowkhamba, Vidya Bhavan, Varanasi,
                                    2001

Sahasarasa: Edited by Dr Premlata Sharma, Sangeet
                                    Natak Akademi, New Delhi, 1972

Ustad Naseer
Moinuddin Dagar: Raga Kambouji (Audio Recording) The
                                    Royal Collection of Mewar, Virgin.

Malvikagnimitram by Kavalam
Narayana Panikkar
Udayan Vajpeyi

1

Whatever is going to be written here about the production of *Malvikagnimitram* by Kavalam Narayana Panikkar is not a criticism of the performance but a salute to it. I had watched the performance with Pakistani storywriter Intazar Hussain in rapt attention. We both were astonished to see the performance—can a theatrical performance be so bewitching? So full of *rasa*?

2

Whenever I go to watch any performance of *Malvikagnimitram,* a fear lurks somewhere in my mind lest I should come across the same clichéd interpretation of the play; lest the performance should again be woven around the general (Christian) moralist rendition that tends to characterise Agnimitra as a lustful king. Such interpretation not only showcases a belittled Agnimitra, but also narrows down many more characters of our fictional literature, such as Vatsaraj Udayan of *Kathasaritsagar.* Therefore whenever I go to watch *Malvikagnimitram* I become nervous. When I got to know that in the Kalidasa festival in Ujjain, my favourite stage director Kavalam Narayana Panikkar was coming with *Malvikagnimitram* I was very excited, though I was apprehensive as well. I had seen Panikkar's *Vikramorvashiyam* and it was an unforgettable experience. The interpretation that Kavalam had given to the love between Pururava and Urvashi was too incredible for words to express. Oh! It was truly wonderful. Will he be able to repeat his feat in *Malvikagnimitram* too?

3

Notwithstanding that a dance-drama genre in Sanskrit like Kudiyattam has survived for more than a thousand years, Sanskrit theatre has deteriorated in our country over the years. Post-Independence we did not put the required effort to reopen the obliterated sources of our tradition. It is no secret that the British had wilfully undermined the Sanskrit education system, as they knew that in this language and in its inherent insight lay our inherited intellect, our world view, etc. These world views also pulsated in the folk life here. By undermining Sanskrit, the British ensured that out of our many sources of folk life an important one was dried up. As we kept on eschewing Sanskrit gradually, Sanskrit theatre too shrivelled. There had been many fresh attempts to revitalise it though (and it is a matter of great satisfaction) but since we put in no genuine effort to bring Sanskrit close to our lives, all these attempts, in place of better Sanskrit drama, mostly resulted only in speaking Sanskrit in costume on the stage. For most of our people associated with Sanskrit theatre, it is nothing more than a formality. It is formality because they take it as the limit of their creative responsibility to present it in its dried form without using their imagination and creative discretion. It is clearly reflected in their performance that Sanskrit drama signifies to them what the portraits of Mahatma Gandhi do in thousands of government offices. Instead of identifying vividly with the ethos of the Sanskrit plays, they end up exhausting their energy only in expressing them in the so-called 'classical' manner. Therefore the revelation of the disposition of theatre directors or actors is nowhere visible in them. You feel as if you are seeing some old photograph (in which a wooden actor keeps his hand on the right side of his mouth and utters: *Mareesh*!).

In this scenario Kavalam Narayana Panikkar is an exception. His practice of Sanskrit theatre is perhaps the most unique.

4

Panikkar treats Sanskrit as a contemporary language. It is a living language for him and not a fossil. Sanskrit plays are not plays of some bygone era to him; they belong to such a time which is still active in us. He does not look at them in retrospect; he finds them standing side by side to him. He has a natural rapport with these plays and thus carves out a way to sneak himself into them. These plays do not belong to some remote era and setting, but are contemporary to him and his surroundings. In other words Kalidasa's plays for him do not transcend time for the sake of saying; they transcend their own time in the real sense. Kalidasa has really bridged the gap between his times and ours. That is why when Panikkar approaches his plays, he can see all that which remains invisible to other directors: he manages to see their essence or more aptly, with Kavalam Narayana Panikkar's insight a new meaning is revealed in the plays of Kalidasa and then he gives theatrical expansion to that meaning by his gift of imagination. It results in a theatrical experience that bewitches you for long, that gives you an opportunity to see your own life in a new light, that makes you experience many levels of acting and enunciation so that you are able to hear the possibility of singing in every enunciation and feel the pulsations of simple dialogues in every song.

5

In Panikkar's *Malvikagnimitram* the Ashoka tree is in the centre of the play. Malvika is not just a princess of the neighbouring state, but is *prakriti* or true feminine nature herself. Agnimitra is not just a king and lover, but also a *purush* who has the prowess to understand *prakriti*. The space between the *prakriti* Malvika and *Purush* Agnimitra is occupied by Agnimitra's wife, Queen Dharini and another woman Iravati and the *vidushaka* who, as his name suggests, is engaged in undoing this space. In Panikkar's *Malvikagnimitram* the well-being of the people of Agnimitra's kingdom and the splendour of nature are interlaced, as if they are two parts of the same phenomenon. When people are deprived of their happiness, nature also starts withering away and when the people of the kingdom are restored their happiness and well-being, *prakriti* also blooms up. Panikkar has suggested this change through the blossoming and withering of the Ashoka tree. Malvika seems to be *prakriti*'s soul for whom Agnimitra has spontaneous attraction and love. If the *purush* will not fall in love with *prakriti* how will his selfhood of being a *purush* be characterised? Therefore in Panikkar's *Malvikagnimitram,* Agnimitra's attraction for Malvika is not mere superficial fondness of a lustful king—as it had appeared to many of the moralist directors—because in that situation there would have been only a semblance of *shringara rasa* that is *rasabhaas* and no real *shringara rasa* in this play of Kalidasa. In that way the play would not have qualified as a piece of of art nor would it have been so popular in the public. The presence of *rasa* in art is not only a pre-requisite of its greatness, but also a quintessential condition of its being an art object. And if this work has been traditionally accepted as a work of art, the relationship between Agnimitra and Malvika must have been seen as love. We must scrutinise the cause of the difference that has been crept into our eyes whereby Agnimitra has started looking lustful to us. It's true that Kalidasa could not present Agnimitra's love with that finesse with which he had portrayed Dushyant's love. But it may be pertinent to know here that *Malvika* is an earlier work of Kalidasa.

Panikkar's Agnimitra is not only a true lover, in a way he is also a natural companion to *prakriti* (Malvika) on account of being the *purush* of the *purush-prakriti* couple. As if there were an eternal familiarity between them, and Malvika's coming before Agnimitra as a maid to Dharini were just a renewing, a recognition of that primeval familiarity. A creation becomes possible in such an eternally renewing familiarity and this is what causes the blossoming of the Ashoka tree.

<h1 style="text-align:center">6</h1>

In Kavalam's *Malvikagnimitram,* and as has also been shown by Kalidasa, love flourishes during the interval of two wars. Here love sprouts and grows in the dusk of victory and defeat. The *vidushaka* speaks the modern vernacular of northern India, Hindi. This experiment is exceedingly meaningful. It implies the understanding that the use of vernacular languages in Sanskrit plays in fact was a mechanism to incorporate other languages in those plays and not a device to belittle or glorify characters; an attempt to charge the space of the plays by different languages. It is not a mere coincidence that when Vidyapati wrote Sanskrit plays, he invariably wrote all lyrics in his dialact, Maithili. When Panikkar's Malayali *vidushak* speaks Hindi, he not only reminds us of the meanings of the vernacular but also brings out the beauty of the Malayali enunciation of Hindi. And his acting? It is only by seeing one can say how precise it was. Just as many levels of enunciation from the common utterances to singing become lively in Panikkar's performances, similarly, acting ranging from *Lokdharmi* to *Natyadharmi* is also realised there. The same 'range of levels' are seen in the movements of actors (and actresses) too: Their movements range from straight walk to the highly stylised one. And so they manage to lend many rhythms to their theatrical space. What

I am trying to say is that in the theatre of Panikkar there are simultaneous practices at many layers in enunciation. It can also be said in a different way that Panikkar's theatre moves on these different levels of *vachika* and *aangika* acting like a musician moves on the musical scale. Here the theatrical sense is continually enriched by multi-layered significations. And during the course of the play, the flow of *rasa* remains uninterrupted. It is almost impossible to express the beauty of Panikkar's theatre in any other way. And it has been said that the experience of *rasa* of theatre is *aprameya* that is something which cannot be measured.

7

Ajj ajau ki preet na jaani
Laggi roje azal di aahi.

The love between him and me is not a love starting from today. It has been coming down since the day of creation itself.

—*Bulle Shah*

Panikkar's unique interpretation of Kalidasa's plays interconnects all three of them. As we already saw in Panikkar's interpretation of the Malvika-Agnimitra relationship, they have eternally been familiar to each other because they are embodiments of *prakriti-purush*. Their love for each other is in fact just a renewal of their eternal togetherness. Panikkar has also shown something similar to this in his production of *Vikramorvashiyam*. The very title of the third play of Kalidasa's contains the word *abhijnan*, renewal of an old acquaintance. Thus on the basis of Panikkar's theatrical interpretation we can say that all the plays of Kalidasa are *abhijnan* annals of *prakriti-purush*. They separate and they come together. The heroes and heroines of Kalidasa's plays are living embodiment of *prakriti-purush* whose alienation and reunion, separation and proximity weave the narratives of his plays and in the meanwhile all the nuances of *shringara rasa* are evoked in an exceptional manner.

Translated from Hindi by Dr Ghanshyam Sharma
From Rang Prasang—25, Jan-March, 2007

Karimkutty by Kavalam Narayana Panikkar
Phillip B. Zarrilli

In a country like India with its many regional languages, its regional versions of both traditional and modern theatrical forms and styles and variety of socio-economic structures, attempting to work as a modern creative artist is often a thankless, much less an economically viable, occupation. That someone like Kavalam Narayana Panikkar, so far removed physically as he is from the major urban centres of contemporary Indian theatre, has begun to emerge from within modern theatrical circles as an innovative director and playwright at a pan-Indian level is something verging on the miraculous. Panikkar is best described as a true and vibrant man of the theatre, in love with the rich possibility that the Indian theatre today can serve as a bridge between traditional and modern life. Kavalam Panikkar lives with a foot firmly placed in both worlds—and it is his peculiar talent to be able to draw them together in a manner which respects the traditional, yet recognises both the limitations and the changed circumstances in which any particular tradition exists today in India.

Panikkar grew up in Alleppey district, Kerala, in southwestern coastal India's agricultural area with a wealth of folk traditions. His first involvement with theatre came through writing poetry rich in rural idioms and images. During the early 1960s he began his first practical production work in theatre, drawing together a group of performers trained in a variety of disciplines. In 1974 he moved (along with several of the original performers with whom he worked) to Trivandrum, the capital city of Kerala, and there he established his theatre company, Sopanam. Five of the original members are still with the company today, after eleven years.

Panikkar's love for the rich, indigenous performing arts of Kerala has led him time and again out into the villages, where he has gathered, documented, learned from, appreciated and championed Kerala's classical and folk traditions. For years he has been intimately involved in an attempt to rediscover and reconstruct some of the sources and performance styles of

Kerala's Mohiniyattam, a solo female dance and Kerala's counterpart to the much better known Bharatanatyam.

In his practical production work, what makes Kavalam Panikkar so unique is his ability to serve as a non-exploitative bridge between the past and the present, between the rich indigenous traditions and the modern urban world of the creative arts. What makes Panikkar and the members of his theatre company somewhat unique in India is the level of practical hands-on knowledge they possess of traditional performing arts. Panikkar himself has had training in many forms of instrumental and vocal music. And perhaps even more importantly, Panikkar insists on having the members of his company receive substantive, long-term training in at least the basics of the traditional arts, so that they are able to possess a substantial vocabulary of movement and vocal skills, which they may put to creative use in producing particular plays. Panikkar is not interested in having his performers reproduce precisely any specific traditional performance techniques but in having them use the basics of such techniques as a springboard for creative expression by transforming them into something new.

Panikkar's search for the roots and expressive possibilities of Indian theatrical traditions has taken him to the earliest sources: the Sanskrit dramas themselves. Kavalam Panikkar, if nothing else, has been a major factor in the revival of a pan-Indian interest in and understanding of the great theatrical potential of the Sanskrit classics by producing them in Sanskrit—but not as tired spoken dramas which make use of outmoded and totally unsympathetic colonial/British Shakespearean-based modes of production. Rather, he has revived the Sanskrit dramas in modern productions by drawing on the extant regional performance traditions he knows so well: in particular, Kerala's Kudiyattam, Kathakali, Mohiniyattam, and many lesser known pretheatrical forms such as Theyyam (ritual performance), Padayani (folk dance) and Kalarippayattu (martial art).

His creative work, though, is not exhausted by his Sanskrit drama productions. He is equally well known for the productions of his own plays in Malayalam, Kerala's regional language. His productions of Malayalam dramas, like the productions of Sanskrit dramas, interweave dance, music, stylised movement, vibrant vocalisation and acting into a unique whole.

Panikkar's vast knowledge and practical experience as a musician and composer are manifest in the aural surrounding he creates in his productions by weaving a tapestry of instrumental sound and by the energised treatment of the *vacikam* utterance aspect of the actor's performance. I say utterance because Panikkar's actors are called upon to make each utterance a 'vocal act' in the most fundamental sense—sound uttered is filled with the vibrancy of meaning and *bhava*—the feeling tone of that dramatic moment. But most importantly, the substance and content of his Malayalam dramas is based on revitalisation and a simultaneous transformation of traditional legends, stories, and social roles into viable vehicles for a modern means of discovering through the past a new vision of one's present.

The Parable Plays

In one of Panikkar's earlier Malayalam plays, *The Lone Tusker* (*Ottayan*), the major role goes to a Kudiyattam Sanskrit drama *Chakyar* (a caste of temple servants whose specific temple function was to perform in a Kudiyattam-style production) as a means to explore the dynamic tension between theatre and caste life. *The Lone Tusker*, like *Karimkutty*, should be considered a modern parable. Each takes traditional social roles and through delightfully theatrical means, Panikkar makes these roles vehicles for subtle commentary on the explosive transition from the traditional to the modern world. Panikkar's plays, however, are far from being simple moral quips about 'isn't it awful what is happening to our traditions and traditional social roles?' He provides virtually no answers. Rather, he introduces a vibrant theatrical world in which these roles are re-presented in a different milieu, in the course of which he raises questions, but ultimately provides no moralistic answers.

Karimkutty was first produced in Trivandrum, Kerala, in 1983, by the Spanam (theatre troupe) company, directed and with musical settings by Kavalam Narayana Panikkar. Costumes were designed by G. Aravindan. In brief outline, the events of the play *Karimkutty* are as follows. Kondadimadan, a sorcerer, is the master of a vast array of spirits (*chaattan*), including Karimkutty, the invisible chief of the spirits. Kundunni, Kondadimadan's trusted family servant, is terrified of Karimkutty even though he is invisible. Sundaran, a handsome young *chaattan*, exchanges words of devotion with

Kondadimadan's daughter, Pumala. When the father realises that the lovers have met during the annual day in which the *chaattan* have free rein of the village, he chastises the young spirit and banishes his daughter. Mantravanan, a former disciple of Kondadimadan, has learned enough of the sorcerer's magic to enable him to garner considerable wealth and to put his former master in his debt. When Mantravanan offers to take one *chaattan*—a power he has long desired to possess—in payment of the debt, the *chaattan* become so incensed that they drive him from the scene. At the conclusion of the play, Kondadimadan agrees not only give Mantravanan control of a *chaattan*, but that it will be Karimkutty himself. The whole host of *chaattan* rises up against Kondadimadan in outrage, leading to the fall of the traditional master.

A play like *Karimkutty* is so rich in its suggestive multivocal imagery and theatricality that it leaves an audience with many suggestive resonances of possible meaning long after the night of seeing the production.

Let me merely suggest several of the many possible resonances of *Karimkutty*. Kondadimadan is and represents the traditional family and caste-specific role of master of a certain order of magical practice. His confrontation with the limits of his own power over the spirits supposedly under his control is an existential dilemma that the traditional artist himself must confront today. Even more poignantly presented, and more forceful as well, is the dilemma of the traditional artist faced with an eager, power-hungry, wealthy outsider. Mantravanan is not a traditional practitioner. He is there at the periphery of the tradition, ready and willing literally to 'buy' *chaattan*, as if such traditional spiritual knowledge could ever be bought or sold.

Here the poignant resonance of but one suggestive dimension of the play begins to be felt. Kondadimadan's fading power over his traditional practice places him, as a representative of all such masters in today's world, in the existential dilemma of questioning his own powers. His anger is the anger of the confused, self-doubting artist or ritual specialist in a world no longer under his control. Ready, willing, and able to buy up what he can no longer utilise and control are those pretenders who hang about at the periphery of such traditional arts—the Mantravanan of modern India. Indeed, such traditions and practices, in today's harsh marketplace economy, are being bought and sold. To what end? Pai does not tell us. There is no 'resolution' to this resonating aspect of the story. It resonates because it must be left open-ended—it is open-ended. What becomes (is becoming) of Kon the traditional artist? Will the spirits of a traditional art turn on the master/practitioner who 'sells,' as they turn on Kondadimadan? And what of Mantravanan the pretender to knowledge, the buyer of power? This is a question to be asked by all who might buy their way into such arts, even the researcher, scholar, or artist.

Another resonating set of relationships in *Karimkutty* is the parallel between the *chaattan* and the working class. The powerful masters hold them under their sway, and possess the power to buy and sell them. Although based on the social system of the hierarchical feudal order that was supposedly swept away with land reform in Kerala, the play keeps in the foreground the interplay between today's exploiters and exploited, even though presented in parable form. Indeed, the parable form of Panikkar's dramas allows for a freer play of such resonances between the traditional and the modern, the old and the new.

Asian Theatre Journal, 1985, Vol. 2, No. 2

Kavalam Narayana Panikkar's *Theyyatheyyam*: Resisting Interculturalism Through Ritual Practice
Brian Singleton

Indian theatre practice under British colonial rule was marked by differing strategies of resistance agitprop drama to promote social and political reform; the preservation of classical dance as cultural heritage; and the continuing practice of folk rituals in rural areas outwit the immediate control of the colonial authorities. Post-Independence India, however, has witnessed those deviant practices of resistance become the dominant ideological performance practices of modem India. Much actor training continued to be modelled on British drama schools such as RADA (Royal Academy of Dramatic Art), classical dances have survived to incorporate certain aspects of western ballet (for example, group sequences in Kathak) and the folk rituals have come increasingly under the microscope of western cultural tourists. Indian theatre practice, therefore, succumbs to the power of the dollar as western academies and practitioners, with their financial and technological power, act as legitimising agents for the global recognition of Asian culture. We are at a time when great currency is being attached to the notion of intercultural rejuvenation of home cultures by acts of productive reception of foreign cultures (a more positive definition of the practice by Erika Fischer-Lichte in direct response to Edward Said's charge of cultural colonialism which he terms Orientalism). It is worthwhile taking note of how certain forms of modern Indian theatre are resisting intercultural practices, not by refusal or direct opposition but by theatrical acts of intracultural rejuvenation, without the injection or the foreign culture as a serum.

One of the main accusations of intercultural approaches to theatre is of the political incorrectness of plundering stable source cultures (more often than not the theatre of traditional societies in Asia) to meet the increasing demand of the postmodern, floating, unstable cultures of the western world. A look at the relatively stable performance culture of Kerala reveals a 'plundering' of quite a different nature. Instead of the assimilation of western culture, it is the ancient folk traditions of rural Kerala which are being established as 'the other' in a modern India in the sense that they are the source which the modern (and essentially urban) theatre is tapping. This type of theatre practice is intraculturalist, a genre which depoliticises the nation of regeneration by dispelling any sense of exploitation, as one culture is simply tapping its source.

One of the chief characteristics of the postcolonial world in Asia has been the economic desire for productivity which fosters a belief in a rational view of the world, as A.J. Gunawardana asserts: 'Rationality presents an attitude critical of the past and suggests the direction for change.' The rational view of the world urged upon Asians is a fundamental criticism of indigenous culture. It claims that many of the received ways of thinking and behaving depend on non-rational (magical, superstitious, religious) beliefs, which are obstacles to economic and social progress. How then do ritual practices survive in an urbanised world in which the populace is being urged to reject inherited culture and to think and behave in ways which promote material success? Intracultural theatre practice, therefore, takes on an added political significance in that it is giving currency to inherited culture, and both an allegorical and vital place in the post-colonial world.

Arguably Kerala's (and India's) leading exponent of this type of practice which weaves together a modem urban theatre with the popular, rural folk traditions of his native state, is Kavalam Narayana Panikkar, writer and director of the Sopanam Institute of performing Arts in Trivandrum. His recent play *Theyyatheyyam* takes the North Keralan folk tradition of Theyyam and by learning it and practising it in a new, modern context, turns it into an allegory of modem life. Sopanam is an institute for performing arts and research established in Kerala in 1964. It was formed with the declared aim of contributing to the evolution of a new Indian theatre based on the long theatrical tradition of the country through the productions of Sanskrit and Malayalam plays with an emphasis on contemporaneity. Their research has led to a rediscovery of traditional theatre practices and the evolution of a system of training actors in the traditional disciplines. In the last thirty years the company has presented twelve Malayalam and five Sanskrit plays.

The emphasis in training is to help the actor discover this inner spirit and to project his body and mind as tools of expression. As the basis for all physical work, the performers (like their traditional counterparts) practice Kalari, the martial art of Kerala, and traditional folk rituals such as Padayani, Theyyam and Mudiyettu. The rendering of the Vedas and the various practising traditions of the local systems of music place maximum emphasis on rhythm which links movement, vocalisation and *bhava* (expression). Much of their work and study has been in the North Keralan district of Cannanore where the Dravidian ritual Theyyam is practised, the aim being ultimately to combine the elements of ritual with the dramatic. The Sopanam Company goes back to its traditional roots in search for a way forward for the modem Indian theatre which, since Independence, has separated itself from its origins in performance terms. In his introduction to Panikkar's play, *Karimkutty*, Philip Zarrilli sees the work of Sopanam operating as a non-exploitative bridge between the past and the present, between the rich indigenous traditions and the modem urban world of the creative arts. Far from any sterile replication of tradition, Panikkar's actors exploit their form and practice for new creative expression.

Lying at the root of all the folk traditions of performance in Kerala is a great significance ascribed to the notion of the transformation of villager to character. On a primary level there is the transformation first of villager to performer and then of performer to character. The identification of villager with the role is at first physical; he learns the codes of gesture, mime, facial and body language—the language of theatre; second, the performer identifies with the role in a metaphorical sense, that he, the villager, is being transformed into the role he is representing. On a secondary level this process of transformation takes place in the mind of the other villagers/ spectators. The spectator sees at once the villager/actor and actor/character and, since surface realism is impossible to achieve in a village context the spectator is being asked to make an even greater suspension of disbelief. It could be said, in fact, that the actor only plays a minor role in the process of transformation, in that his primary function is to act as facilitator of the spectator's mental transformation.

In most traditional performances in Kerala (including Theyyam), performed in the courtyards of Hindu temples, the demarcations between life and performance are not fixed. Times are announced for the beginning of the performance but these are never adhered to, as the enactment of the ritual is driven by social factors, and is not considered an exhibition of fabricated aesthetics. The action emerges from the villagers' preparations without any significant ritual marker. In the Padayani ritual of central Kerala (another Dravidian ritual of dancers costumed in elaborately painted masks of areca nut palm's spathes) the village men don the masks of the gods as much out of necessity to perform the ritual as by rehearsed design. One villager can substitute for another and the masks once painted are taken out of the temple courtyard simply in order to process them back in again. This procession is accompanied by flaming torches, the singing of Padayani songs and then a few men leap into the centre, swinging pieces of cloth, ostensibly to clear the performance space. The succession of dances then proceeds, often punctuated by gaps during which performers may or may not be cajoled into performing, and unruly spectators ejected. The performance emerges from a shared knowledge of the ritual between a group of core performers. The emphasis is on the accomplishment of the ritual, rather than the completion of a performance. With such life and performance markers being so fluid, it is up to the spectator to transform the performer (who minutes earlier may have been acting as bouncer) into a trance-possessed masked spirit. It is also the spectator who transforms the hyperventilating, writhing performer into the living embodiment of the god represented.

In Theyyam there are two types of transformation. First, every human being is transformed into a Theyyam after death (Theyyam means the deification of the spiritual and the word 'theyyam' derives from *deivam* or God). This type of transformation is a metaphysical one: from death to deification, from human to the divine. The social rationale behind the transformation after death is that persons who suffered untimely deaths or who suffered injustice in an unequal society (as well as those whose earthly life needs to be rewarded) also achieve deification. M.L. Varadpande notes the origins of the cult: any object inspiring reverence, awe and fear was made into Theyyam by the folk and tribal communities and worshipped with appropriate rituals which included dance, drama, music and poetry. The Theyyam deities were propitiated for the welfare of the community, village or individual and they in turn appeared before the devotees through the medium who may be a priest or chosen person and granted their wishes. The Theyyam, then can also be a functional tool for a society to assuage its guilt and the dancing, an act of contrition as well as an attempt at appeasement.

The second type of Theyyam is of gods whose different reincarnations are enacted as Theyyams. These gods are Dravidian, the protectors of humanity from natural disasters. They do not sit in judgement over humanity in a shroud of morality, but actively participate in the day-to-day life of humankind. Demon gods such as Ravana (Rama's arch enemy in the Ramayana), are included in this list. The rationale is that there is no distinction between hero and demon gods. On the human side, too, it is not just the heroes and protagonists who are made Theyyams, it is also the antiheroes and antagonists. The result is a flattening out of a hierarchical value system in the human and godhead, which leads to the humanisation of gods and the deification of humans.

Such a value system is evident in everyday life, is what Kavalam Narayana Panikkar discovered, and his particular version of the Theyyam ritual is based on a real-life incident. While travelling in Payannur, North Malabar, the author called on a Theyyam dancer. The dancer's mother was unsure as to her son's precise whereabouts and gradually it became clear that the dancer had been accused of murder and had gone into hiding. Here was a case of a traditional performer also being involved in a real-life drama similar to the drama he was preparing to enact and the duality of the situation was the inspiration for a play based on an ancient myth, and set in a modern context.

This duality leads inevitably to two parallel plots which eventually merge. In the first (Story A) it is harvest time and Ramunni, an agricultural worker and Theyyam dancer, hears of the attempted seduction and rape of his girlfriend, Kannipoo, by the local landlord, Mekkantala in an effort to exert his non-existent *droit decuissage,* Ramunni, after killing Mekkantala, elopes with Kannipoo. Kannipoo's father, Satgunni, is outraged by the incident and immediately wants retaliation for the unlawful abduction of his daughter. It is the abduction, and not the murder of the landlord, which must be avenged. Ramunni's mother appears and affirms that her son is undergoing a period of forty-one days' penance in preparation for the Theyyam for which he will, she assures, return to the village to dance. The village policeman prepares his handcuffs to make the arrest, but Satgunni and the other villagers prepare to teach Ramunni a lesson, which ultimately leads to his death.

Running parallel to this is the villagers' version of the Ramayana (Story B) in which the villain Ravana arrives on shore to continue his plundering of wealth because he believes all things good on earth should belong to him. One thing he plunders is Sita (the hero Rama's wife). In the villagers' version Sita becomes Poonkanni (played by the same performer as Kannipoo in Story A). Poonkanni (which translates as 'virgin of the soil') is abducted by Paranki (the villagers' name for Ravana) and taken to his ship. Beppooran (the monkey-god Hanuman, and friend of Rama in the Ramayana) sets off in search of Poonkanni and attempts to rescue her. He steals Paranki's belt which he has discovered is the source of his strength and is thus able to beat Paranki to death. Subsequently Paranki is deified by the very same society that he had ill-treated when he was alive, in keeping with the Theyyam tradition that deification is not based on moral judgements. As this character, Paranki—played by the agricultural worker—Ramunni returns to the play, the two story lines merge. The villagers armed with sticks approach Ramunni playing Paranki and the personalities of both characters are confused. It is not just the character from Story B (Paranki) who is beaten to death; it is the character from Story A (Ramunni) as well. Consequently there is the Theyyam of a Theyyam: hence the title *Theyyatheyyam*.

The irony, of course, is not lost that the character Paranki is deified after having committed an unjust act. He had stolen another man's wife, and therefore his killing could be seen as just. But on the village level of the story, Ramunni is killed for avenging an act of injustice, an attempted rape and he thus appears to be an innocent victim. Given the nature of the value system however, it must be remembered that Ramunni abducted, rather than eloped with, another man's daughter. Both Ramunni and Paranki are deified and it is at the point of *Theyyatheyyam* that the audience is confronted with the irony that surrounds the act of deification. This cultural processing of a noble religious ideal is based on shaky social and moral foundations, even—the spirits are attributed with godliness.

This irony is dramatised by the transforming ability of performer to the role and this forms the very crux of the play. The villager first transforms by acts of penance into performer, and then from performer, by learning the dance tradition, transforms into character A-Ramunni. The performer next transforms into character B Parankichamundi (the deified Paranki) and still further into character A (the deification of Ramunni). And so the author, Panikkar, takes the mirroring of the two roles and reflects them into infinity. The essence of this mode of theatre is the dramatization of the impossibility of totally separating performer from the role.

This is also taken one step further by highlighting the lack of boundaries between spectator and performer. Although spectators are not invited to perform, the performance of *Theyyatheyyam* can take place even if the divisions between spectators and performers are at their loosest: in an open space with the performers on the same level as the audience. The actors can emerge from anywhere to perform. As well as breaking down barriers it does much to suggest that theatre takes place in life: the stage has an important role to play in the act of transformation. This vital act of transformation in the modern theatre is an allegory of the regional and religious value system. The religious belief represented through theatrical allegory not only resists urbanising and westernising rationality, but also any metatheatrical self-consciousness on the part of the spectator. Resistance, therefore, becomes theatrical as well as social, religious and non-rational.

The drama does not unfold chronologically. The villagers' story and the *Ramayana* story are woven together textually, achieved in performance through the use of chorus. No character exists discretely. Both antagonists and protagonists emerge from and return to the chorus. Simple acts such as putting on a headdress, an item of costume, picking up a sickle, or staring in a hand mirror, all achieve the transformation from the choral text to character. Character identities are transient and fleeting, for as the narrative moves on, the performers must move from one plot to the next and also take part in the chorus. Costumes are minimal, parts represent the whole, and the result is that we are always aware of the duality of the performer's function. The chorus not only narrates but chants and sings and is accompanied by percussion instruments in measured rhythm. The members of the chorus also punctuate the action in their pseudo-Brechtian self—introductions directly to the audience. The inference is of the multiple identities we all assume in everyday life.

Everyday life and the tools associated with it take on added significance in this production. The sickles used by the villagers at harvest time are threatening instruments of death. When Paranki puts on his belt, he is possessed by superhuman strength. Performers become characters by looking into mirrors and seeing themselves reflected back as characters, not as performers. The performer playing Bepporan (the monkey-god Hanuman) builds up an increasingly large vocabulary of monkey-like gestures, in south Keralan Ottanthulal style, in order to become the character. There is no pretence at realism. All action is stylised and the dualities between the two story-lines are maintained only by minimum use of gesture and costume. The spectators are always made to feel that the difference between past and present and between the two fictional realities of the drama, is minimal. The stage is a constant among these acts of transformation and the chorus represents society as 'a perennial narrator of the stories, as a witness to the drama of events'. The dramaturgical and theatrical continuum is an index to a belief system based on deification.

Although performed in the urban cultural centres of Mumbai and Chennai, Panikkar's play has not divorced itself from its original rural blueprint. The plot involves all the vestiges of the rites, passions and concerns of an agricultural community and the transformability of the actor/ villager as sign, is as intact as in the original Theyyam dance. So if this type of performance is a modernisation of a rural folk ritual for an increasingly urbanising society, what then is Panikkar resisting? Is he resisting the influx and influence of the cultural tourists who have left a bad mark on the Keralan consciousness?

Peter Brook is not only criticised by directors/scholars such as Rustom Bharucha in India for his appropriation of a religious text and performance traditions, but also more significantly at the basic ground level. In Kerala many of the actors I encountered had been made bitter by his broken promises of employment. Is Panikkar's aim to achieve a stability and a sense of ownership of Keralan culture in the face of cultural tourists such as Brook? Is he resisting the rationality of post-colonial modernisation by practising, and thereby reaffirming, aspects of either forgotten or marginalised ritual practices?

Panikkar's theatre practice is not out of step with other post-Independence practices. Without reconfiguration from two-dimensional iconic forms and also sculptures after Independence, dances such as Odissi and Bharatnatyam would probably be extinct by now. Without returning to the cultural roots of rural ritual practice, as advocated by Panikkar, modern Indian theatre would still be prey to the emulation of the colonisers' performance forms. In an interview with me in January 1992, Panikkar expressed the idea that we must first discover who we are and what made us, before we begin to assimilate other cultural traditions. He said: 'We felt it necessary to dig deep into our own tradition, not cut across the surface to purloin the tradition of another culture.'

For many years he has been berating post-colonial theatre practices in his own country—with the exception of very few art forms like Theyyam of North Kerala, in which rituals provide the inner force, our folk drama has generally been corrupted by the pervasive influence of western civilisation. The *Natyadharmi* concept laid down by Bharta in *Natyashastra* lost its meaning when our theatre started imitating the naturalistic and realistic techniques of the western stage. Yet, Panikkar's strategy of resistance is not targeted solely at the superficiality of interculturalism. His interculturalist approach to modern theatre is a defiant attempt to legitimise his performance heritage by resisting the dominant ideology through ritual practice.

Indian Literature, 205, Sept.- Oct. 2001

Actors: K.N. Panikkar and others; Play: *Panchayath*, (Malayalam); Source: K.N. Panikkar, Thiruvananthapuram; Note: This is the only photo available of earlier plays with K.N. Panikkar acting in the play.

Actors: Sreekumar, Vasantha Gopalakrishnan; Play: *Avanavan Katamba* (Malayalam); Playwright: K.N. Panikkar; Director: G. Arvindan/K.N. Panikkar; Group: Sopanam, Thiruvananthapuram 1985; Source: Nemichandra Jain Collection, Natarang Pratishthan, Delhi.

Actors: Saji S.L.; Play: *Avanavan Katamba* (Malayalam); Playwright: K.N. Panikkar; Director: G. Aravindan/K.N. Panikkar; Group: Sopanam Thiruvananthapuram; Performed in: Thiruvananthapuram, 2010; Source: K.N. Panikkar, Thiruvananthapuram.

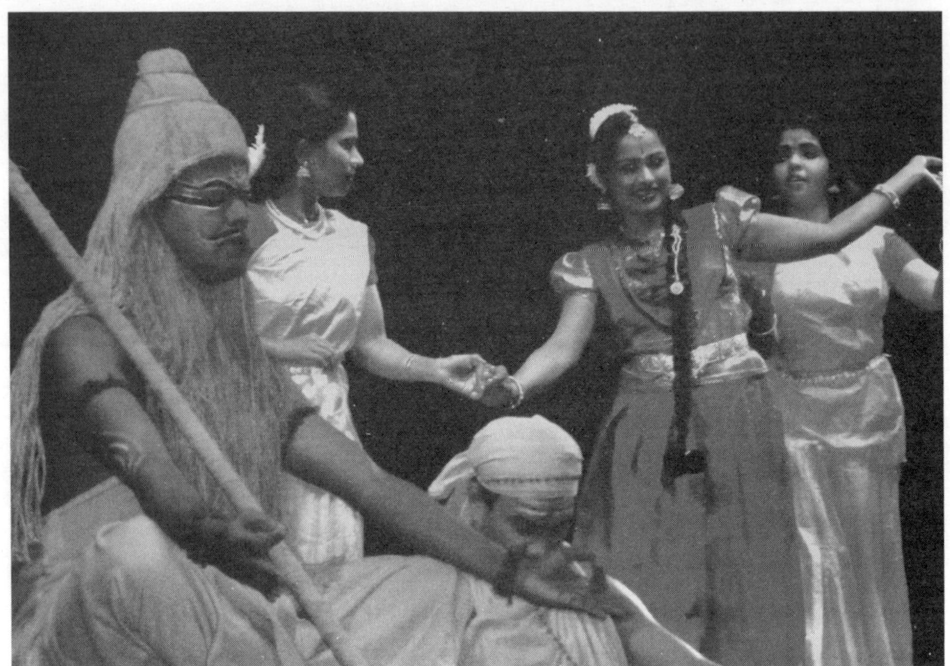

Actors: Gireesh, Saji S.L., Saritha, Sreerekha and Karthika; Play: *Bhagavadajjukam* (Malayalam); Playwright: Bodhayana; Translation: K.N. Panikkar; Director: K.N. Panikkar; Group: Sopanam, Thiruvananthapuram; Performed in: Manav Sangrahalaya, Bhopal 2010; Source: Neeraj Kunder, Sidhi.

Actors: Raj Anand, Vasantha Gopalakrishnan, Sree Rekha; Play: *Bhagavadajjukam* (Malayalam); Playwright: Bodhayana; Translation: K.N. Panikkar; Director: K.N. Panikkar; Group: Sopanam, Thiruvananthapuram; Performed in: Manav Sangrahalaya, Bhopal 2010; Source: Neeraj Kunder, Sidhi.

Actors: Jagannathan, Krishnankutty Nair, Rugmini, Jayarj, Subramaniyan Pillai; Play: *Madhyama Vyayoga* (Sanskrit); Playwright: Bhasa; Director: K.N. Panikkar, G. Arvindam; Group: Sopanam, Thiruvananthapuram; Performed in: SNA Theatre Festival Delhi 1980; Source: Nemichandra Jain Collection, Natarang Pratishthan, Delhi; © Sangeet Natak Akademi, Delhi.

Actors: Dhirendra Kumar, Virendra Singh; Play: *Dootvakyam* (Sanskrit); Playwright: Bhasa; Director: K.N. Panikkar; Group: Kalidasa Akademi, Ujjain; Performed in: Kalidasa Samaroh, Ujjain, 1980; Source: Nemichandra Jain Collection, Natarang Pratishthan, Delhi.

Actors: Jayraj, Mohini; Play: *Shakuntalam* (Sanskrit); Playwright: Kalidasa; Director: K.N. Panikkar; Group: Sopanam Thiruvananthapuram; Performed in: Kalidasa Samaroh, Ujjain, 1982; Source: Nemichandra Jain Collection, Natarang Pratishthan, Delhi.

Actors: Jayraj, Mohini and others; Play: *Shakuntalam* (Sanskrit); Playwright: Kalidasa; Director: K.N. Panikkar; Group: Sopanam, Thiruvananthapuram; Performed in: Kalidasa Samaroh, Ujjain, 1982; Source: Nemichandra Jain Collection, Natarang Pratishthan, Delhi.

Actors: S.R. Gopalakrishnan, Vasantha, Lolamani, Lekshmi; Play: *Vikramorvasiyam* (4th Act) (Sanskrit); Playwright: Kalidasa; Director: K.N. Panikkar; Group: Sopanam, Thiruvananthapuram; Performed in: Kalidasa Seminar, Ujjain 1982; Source: Nemichandra Jain Collection, Natarang Pratishthan, Delhi.

Actor: S.R. Gopalakrishnan; Play: *Vikramorvasiyam* (4th Act), (Sanskrit); Playwright: Kalidasa; Director: K.N. Panikkar; Group: Sopanam, Thiruvananthapuram; Performed in: Kalidasa Seminar, Ujjain 1982; Source: Nemichandra Jain Collection, Natarang Pratishthan, Delhi.

Actors: Vasudevan Namboothiri, Kaladharan, S. Gopalakrishnan, Prathapan; Play: *Karimkutty*, (Malayalam); Playwright: K.N. Panikkar; Director: K.N. Panikkar, Group: Sopanam Thiruvananthapuram; Performed in: Trade Fair, Manzar Theatre, Delhi 1985 Source: Nemichandra Jain Collection, Natarang Pratishthan, Delhi.

Actors: Balakrishnan, Vasantha Gopalakrishnan etc; Play: *Karimkutty* (Malayalam); Playwright: K.N. Panikkar; Director: K.N Panikkar; Group: Sopanam, Thiruvananthapuram; Performed in: Trade Fair, Manzar Theatre, Delhi 1985; Source: Nemichandra Jain Collection, Natarang Pratishthan, Delhi.

Actors: Yuvraj Sharma, Uttara Baokar, Govind Namdev and others; Play: *Mattavilasam*, (Hindi); Playwright: Mahendra Vikrama Varman; Translation: N.C Jain, Urmi Bhushan Gupta; Director: K.N Panikkar; Group: N.S.D Repertory, Delhi; Performed in: Delhi, 1984; Source: Nemichandra Jain Collection; Natarang Pratishthan, Delhi.

Actors: Govind Namdev, Lalit Mohan Tewari, Hema Singh; Play: *Mattavilasam* (Hindi); Playwright: Mahendra Vikrama Varman; Translation: N.C. Jain, Urmi Bhushan Gupta; Director: K.N. Panikkar; Group: N.S.D. Repertory, Delhi; Performed in: Delhi,1984; Source: Nemichandra Jain Collection, Natarang Pratishthan, Delhi.

Actors: Sreekumar, Babu, Prathapan; Play: *Karnabharam* (Sanskrit); Playwright: Bhasa; Director: K.N. Panikkar; Performed in: Trade Fair, Manjar Theatre, Delhi 1985; Group: Sopanam, Thiruvananthapuram; Source: Nemichandra Jain Collection, Natarang Pratishthan, Delhi.

Actors: Mohanlal, Gopinath; Play: *Karnabharam* (Sanskrit), Playwright: Bhasa, Director: K.N. Panikkar; Performed in: Bharat Rang Mahotsava 1999, National School of Drama, Delhi; Group: Sopanam Thiruvananthapuram; Source: National School of Drama, Delhi.

Actors: Mohnlal, Gopinath and group; Play: *Karnabharam* (Sanskrit); Playwright: Bhasa; Director: K.N. Panikkar; Group: Sopanam Thiruvananthapuram; Performed in: Bharat Rang Mahotsav, 1999, National School of Drama, Delhi; Source: K.N. Panikkar, Thiruvananthapuram.

Actors: Gireesh and Komalan; Play: *Urubhangam* (Malayalam); Playwright: Bhasa; Translation: K.N. Panikkar; Director: K.N. Panikkar; Group: Sopanam, Thiruvananthapuram; Performed in: Bhopal 2010; Source: Neeraj Kunder, Sidhi.

Actors: Kenneth Desai, Rohit Gaur, Suwarn Rawat, Sitaram Panchal, Pawan, Vani Singh; Play: *Raja* (Hindi); Playwright: Rabindranath Thakur; Translation: Ageya; Director: K.N. Panikkar; Group: 3rd Year Students National School of Drama, Delhi; Performed in: Delhi 1989-90; Source: Nemichandra Jain Collection, Natarang Pratishthan, Delhi.

Actors: Sitaram Panchal, Navneet Kaur Virk, Suwarn Rawat, Rohitashwa, Pawan, Sanjay Mishra; Play: *Raja* (Hindi); Playwright: Rabindranath Thakur; Translation: Ageya; Director: K.N. Panikkar; Group: 3rd Year Student National School of Drama, Delhi; Performed in: Delhi 1989-90; Source: Nemichandra Jain Collection, Natarang Pratishthan, Delhi.

Actors: Mohini, Biju, Saji, Murali, Promod; Play: *Raja* (Malayalam); Playwright: Rabindranath Thakur; Translation: P. Narayana Kurup; Director: K.N. Panikkar; Group: Sopanam Thiruvananthapuram; Performed in: Kolkata, 2006; Source: K.N. Panikkar, Thiruvananthapuram.

Actors: Biju Kumar and group; Play: *Raja* (Malayalam); Playwright: Rabindranath Thakur; Translation: P. Narayana Kurup; Director: K.N. Panikkar; Group: Sopanam Thiruvananthapuram; Performed in: Kolkata, 2006; Source: K.N. Panikkar, Thiruvananthapuram.

Actors: Kaladharan, P.A.M Rashid, P.J. Radhakrishnan and others; Play: *Kaikuttappadu* (Malayalam); Playwright: K.N. Panikkar; Director: K. Kaladharan; Group: Rasika Art and Cultural Society, Thiruvananthapuram; Performed in: Delhi 1990; Source: Nemichandra Jain Collection, Natarang Pratishthan, Delhi; © Sangeet Natak Akedmi, Delhi.

Actors: Sivan, Manikantan and others; Play: *Kalanetheeni* (Malayalam); Playwright: K.N. Panikkar; Director: K. Kaladharan; Group: Rasika Art and Cultural Society, Thiruvananthapuram; Performed in: Chennai 1987; Source: Nemichandra Jain Collection, Natarang Pratishthan, Delhi.

Stage Set of *Theyya Theyyam*; Play: *Theyya Theyyam* (Malayalam); Playwright: K.N. Panikkar; Director: K.N. Panikkar; Group: Sopanam, Thiruvananthapuram; Performed in: Bharat Bhavan, Bhopal, 2010; Source: Neeraj Kunder, Sidhi.

Actors: Gireesh, Satheesh, Saji. S.L, Suresh, Raj, Komalan, Manikantan, Reghu, Gagan, Sreerekha, Saritha, Anil Kumar, Venugopu, Krishna Kumar, Maneksha; Play: *Theyya Theyyam* (Malayalam); Playwright: K.N. Panikkar; Director: K.N. Panikkar; Group: Sopanam, Thiruvananthapuram; Performed in: Bharat Bhavan, Bhopal, 2010; Source: Neeraj Kunder, Sidhi.

Actors: Komalan, Satheesh, Saji. S.L, Krishna Kumar, Maneksha, Anil Kumar, Venugopu, Sivan; Play: *Theyya Theyyam* (Malayalam); Playwright: K.N. Panikkar; Director: K.N. Panikkar; Group: Sopanam, Thiruvananthapuram; Performed in: Bharat Bhavan, Bhopal, 2010; Source: Neeraj Kunder Sidhi.

Actors: Raj, Sreerekha, Manikantan, Satheesh, Saji. S.L, Komalan; Play: *Theyya Theyyam* (Malayalam); Playwright: K.N. Panikkar; Director: K.N. Panikkar; Group: Sopanam, Thiruvananthapuram; Performed in: Bharat Bhavan, Bhopal, 2010; Source: Neeraj Kunder Sidhi.

Actors: Sonamoni Banerjee, Kashish Agnihotri, Gita Guha, Seema Yadav, Samresh Routray, Nirmal Kant Chaudhary, Jayant Gadekar, Teekam Johsi; Play: *Swapna Katha* (Hindi); Playwright: Bhasa; Hindi Adaptation: Bharat Ratna Bhargava; Director: K.N. Panikkar; Group: 2nd Year Students National School of Drama, Delhi; Performed in: Delhi 1999; Source: National School of Drama, Delhi.

Actors: Sivan, Shaji etc.; Play: *Pratima*, (Sanskrit); Playwright: Bhasa; Director: K.N. Panikkar; Group: Sopanam, Thiruvananthapuram; Performed in: Delhi 2002; Source: Natarang Pratishthan, Delhi.

Actors: Sivan, Shaji etc; Play: *Pratima* (Sanskrit); Playwright: Bhasa; Director: K.N. Panikkar; Group: Sopanam, Thiruvananthapuram; Performed in: Delhi 2002; Source: Natarang Pratishthan, Delhi.

Actors: Shaji, Saritha; Play: *Malavikagnimitram* (Sanskrit); Playwright: Kadidasa; Director: K.N Panikkar;
Group: Sopanam Thiruvananthapuram; Performed in: 2006; Source: K.N. Panikkar, Thiruvananthapuram.

Actors: Sivan, Ayyappan, Shaji; Play: *Tempest* (Malayalam); Playwright: Shakespeare; Translation: K.N.
Panikkar; Director: K.N. Panikkar; Group: Sopanam, Thiruvananthapuram; Performed in: Bharat Rang
Mahotsava Delhi, 2001; Source: National School of Drama, Delhi.

Actors: Sujith Sankar, Sivan, Saji, Shaji; Play: *Tempest* (Malayalam); Playwright: Shakespeare; Translation: K.N. Panikkar; Director: K.N. Panikkar; Group: Sopanam, Thiruvananthapuram; Performed in: Bharat Rang Mahotsava, Delhi, 2001; Source: National School of Drama, Delhi.

Actors: Manikantan, Krishnakumar, Shaji, Saji S.L, Sujith Sankar etc.; Play: *Kallurutty* (Malayalam); Playwright: K.N Panikkar; Director: K.N Panikkar; Group: Sopanam, Thiruvananthapuram; Performed in: Thiruvananthapuram, 2002; Source: Natarang Pratishthan, Delhi.

Actor: Bijukumar M, Sarita JL; Play: *Kalivesham* (Malayalam); Playwright: K.N. Panikkar; Director: K.N. Panikkar; Group: Sopanam, Thiruvananthapuram; Performed in: Bharat Rang Mahotsava, Delhi, 2004; Source: National School of Drama, Delhi.

Actors: Murali, Manikantan; Play: *Charudattam* (Sanskrit); Playwright: Bhasa; Director: K.N Panikkar; Group: Sopanam Thiruvananthapuram; Performed in: Thiruvananthapuram 2005; Source: K.N. Panikkar, Thiruvananthapuram.

Actors: Gireesh V. and others; Play: *Uttara Ramacharitam* (Hindi); Playwright: Bhavabhooti; Recreation: Udayan Vajpeyi; Director: K.N. Panikkar; Group: Sopanam, Thiruvananthapuram; Performed in: Bharat Rang Mahotsava, Delhi 2010; Source: National School of Drama, Delhi.

Actors: Saritha (Seetha) and Gireesh (Rama); Play: *Uttara Ramacharitam* (Hindi); Playwright: Bhavabhooti; Recreation: Udayan Vajpeyi; Director: K.N. Panikkar; Group: Sopanam, Thiruvananthapuram; Performed in: Manava Sangrahalaya, Bhopal 2010; Source: Neeraj Kunder, Sidhi.

Actors: Saritha, Reghu, Raj Anand; Play: *Uttara Ramacharitam* (Hindi); Playwright: Bhavabhooti; Recreation: Udayan Vajpeyi; Director: K.N. Panikkar; Group: Sopanam, Thiruvananthapuram; Performed in: Manavasangrahalaya, Bhopal 2010; Source: Neeraj Kunder, Sidhi.

K.N. Panikkar with his wife, Shardamani and sons, Harikrishnan and Kavalam Srikumar. Source: K.N. Panikkar, Thiruvananthapuram.

K.N. Panikkar was Secretary of the State Sangeet Natak Akademi between 1961-71. From left to right: the late Shri V.S. Nampoothripad, a musicologist; K.N. Panikkar and the late Shri Premnath, a research scholar in Kerala folk arts. Source: K.N. Panikkar, Thiruvananthapuram.

K.N. Panikkar receiving the Sangeet Natak Akademi Samman from Shri APJ Abdul Kalam, President of India in 2002. Source: K.N. Panikkar, Thiruvananthapuram.

Udayan Vajpeyi, K.N. Panikkar and Sree Rekha going for rehearsal at Bharat Bhavan, Bhopal, 2010. Source: K.N. Panikkar, Thiruvananthapuram.

Mukund Lath, K.N. Panikkar, Ashok Vajpeyi during Nemichandra Jain Smriti Samaroh 2005, organized by Nemi Nidhi and Natarang Pratishthan, Delhi, 2005; Source: Natarang Pratishthan, Delhi.

Part Two
VOICES

A Discussion on Kavalam Narayana Panikkar's Play *Ottayan*

Participants:

Kainikkara Kumara Pillai: late playwright, actor and professor

Dr Ayyapa Paniker: poet, professor and scholar

K.S. Narayana Pillai: literary critic

D. Appukuttan Nair: late Kudiyattam scholar, critic and engineer

P.K. Balakrishnan: late novelist and literary critic

Professor Narendra Prasad: late film actor, literary critic, playwright, director and actor

S. Natarajan: late actor and secretary in Sopanam

Nedumudi Venu: film actor, original member of Sopanam

Kavalam Narayana Panikkar: poet, playwright and theatre director

Circus and Art

Kainikkara Kumara Pillai: Before we start the discussion on this play, *Ottayan*, there are a few basic things we should discuss. When we see a good circus show, we enjoy it. There are movements which affect our emotions. Can we say that this enjoyment is 'art'?

Dr Ayyapa Paniker: Do you mean we don't get a deep insight about life in a circus? We can't enter into the reality of a circus? Or do you mean to say it is not a spiritual experience?

Kainikkara Kumara Pillai: The circus exhibits something special. The members show their expertise. Because of that we accept their show. The basic *rasa* in the circus is that of wonder. We get a feeling of amazement, mostly where there is no emotional involvement.

Dr Ayyapa Paniker: We cannot say that amazement is not emotional. However, in the case of the circus, the spectator is not getting amazement in the form of *rasa*.

Kainikkara Kumara Pillai: If it is real art, it has to touch your heart.

Dr Ayyapa Paniker: No matter what the *rasa*, it will affect our emotions.

Kainikkara Kumara Pillai: All of Kavalam Narayana Panikkar's dramas create a feeling of amazement rather than emotion. Amazement is a very superficial feeling. Does it create anything more than that amazement? So, do you mean to say that the circus is also an art?

Dr Ayyapa Paniker: A circus is a performance.

Kainikkara Kumara Pillai: My question is, how does something that does not affect your emotions become art?

Dr Ayyapa Paniker: Art should not only affect the emotions, but emotions should be sublimated in the audience to become *rasa*. Let us say that this is the difference between a circus and art.

Kainikkara Kumara Pillai: Only art that touches your heart can communicate *rasa* and ultimately bliss.

Kavalam Narayana Panikkar: Emotion, when couched in rhythm, can communicate this bliss, can't it?

Dr Ayyapa Paniker: Let us examine each factor and not talk about which factor gives us happiness. This depends on each person's individual experience. Can we say a production has made an impact on you by making you want to see it again? How can I convince another person that the piece has made an impact of sublime feeling on me? When we talk about *rasa*s, I feel that in our classical and folk art forms, the *hasya rasa* (comic/laughter) is applied just as much as the *karuna rasa* (pathos/compassion).

Kainikkara Kumara Pillai: I agree.

The Subtle Feel of *Rasa*

Dr Ayyapa Paniker: I feel that in *Ottayan*, the most pivotal aspect is not the *Chakyar*'s efficiency in acting or the building of the house for the woodsman or the *Chakyar*'s transformation into an elephant or his escape from the woodsman. It lies in the quarrel with his wife and later the realisation of his attachment to her through the symbol of cymbals, which help him escape from a dangerous situation. These are salient aspects. Based on this point, can we say that there is *karuna,* pathos? If you see this play only once, you will probably only get the *atbhuta* (wonder) *rasa*. I have seen this play three times. I feel that the way the *kuzhitalam* is taken from his knapsack is reminiscent of *hasya* (humour) in Kudiyattam. I make this the central point that connects the whole drama. If you take any drama, you can see the underlying *rasa* only in the pivotal point. For example, *Hamlet*—I take this as an example because it is completely different from Ottayan ….

Kainikkara Kumara Pillai: From the beginning of the play to the end, *Hamlet* affects our emotions deeply.

Dr Ayyapa Paniker: Many scholars have said that *Hamlet* is an artistic failure. It is a great play to read, but the criticism is that there is a distraction from the underlying *rasa*.

K. S. Narayana Pillai: In one way or another, aren't all art forms stylised? It differs only in proportions. Is it possible to present any play as the event happened? Only through selected techniques can we present the drama.

Kainikkara Kumara Pillai: In the case of *Hamlet*, the actual Hamlet does not play the role of Hamlet. Whoever plays the role of Hamlet presents his or her own version of the character. They have the possibility of presenting different views. They had interpreted the character in different ways.

Dr Ayyapa Paniker: Take the case of the ghost in *Hamlet*. We are made to believe something that is not real in life.

Kainikkara Kumara Pillai: Please don't say that. A ghost is not unreal. We are made to feel that it is a reality. In that sense, the ghost is real. The fact is that it makes us believe it is real. I don't see anything that affects my heart in Panikkar's plays.

Dr Ayyapa Paniker: When you encounter *karuna* on the stage, do we react as we see it in real life?

Kainikkara Kumara Pillai: We have to find an answer for that question ourselves. Yes *karuna* creates a sense of pain. But after that, the reaction changes and we enjoy the experience. This process of change is involved in all art. To me, *Ottayan* has not created any such feeling. That feeling should create an experience of real life. Maybe for a shorter period of time, but that should be created. We have to cry. After that we have to laugh. If at least that is not there, I will not agree that the *rasa* was created.

Kavalam Narayana Panikkar: Not only in our theatre, but also in the theatre the world over. There are people like Bertolt Brecht who would argue against empathy in theatre.

Kainikkara Kumara Pillai: I beg to differ from the so-called 'modern'.

Dr Ayyapa Paniker: Do you think we could include Kudiyattam in this so-called 'modern'?

Kainikkara Kumara Pillai: When we see a play, do we feel pathos?

Dr Ayyapa Paniker: Yes, if it is pathetic in the theatre connotation. Even that is only a feeling. If it is genuine sorrow, then we would not go to see a show.

Kainikkara Kumara Pillai: We like that sorrow.

Dr Ayyapa Paniker: Why?

Kainikkara Kumara Pillai: Does anyone worry about that? There is no need for such inquiry.

Dr Ayyapa Paniker: It is not the sorrow of real life and that is just the reason why we like it.

Kainikkara Kuniara Pillai: You can give any reason; we don't have to inquire about that.

Dr Ayyapa Paniker: Of course we should inquire about it! Otherwise, there is no meaning to any further probe!

Kavalam Narayana Panikar: Can he be a discerning spectator who cries the most?

Dr Ayyapa Paniker: Not that, we like this sorrow. This is a very old issue.

Is The Text Flawed?

K. S. Narayana Pillai: In this play, we don't find such sorrow. Is it because of a flaw in the text, or is it due to bad performance?

Kainikkara Kumara Pillai: It is definitely because of the text.

Dr Ayyapa Paniker: Let us assume that it is the fault of the text. Just recall the dialogue when the *Chakyar* enters. He introduces himself and mentions that he is going to enact a drama. The commencement of the talk is before the actor assumes his role. The actor begins in a *Natyadharmi* way, which is not real, but artificial, and does not exist in the context of real life. Do we, therefore, get a feeling that it is not real life?

K.S. Narayana Pillai: He enacts that he reaches a forest in a stylised way. Is this the reason why we do not feel convinced?

Kainikkara Kumara Pillai: There is artificiality in all these stylised forms. Even when we are artificial, we have to find something meaningful. You find the extensive use of *Natyadharmi* in Kathakali.

Dr Ayyapa Paniker: So the problem is not because of how *Natyadharmi* is used? The uniqueness of the content of the play is the problem. The content of the play involves the *Chakyar* coming to the forest, meeting two woodsmen and making an escape after placing them in a trance. On the other hand, aspects like the human struggle, family disintegration and the deterioration of a matrimonial relationship are not developed. Is it because of the simplicity of the storyline that we cannot bring out emotions?

K.S. Narayana Pillai: Are emotions not aroused when the *Chakyar* wanders helplessly in the forest and remembers his wife when he sees the *kuzhitalam*? If not, why?

Kainikkara Kumara Pillai: No impressions are created.

K. S. Narayana Pillai: I feel that it is artistically created.

Kainikkara Kumara Pillai: It is possible. It depends on the mental condition of the audience.

Dr Ayyapa Paniker: We have this experience when a character like Duryodhana enacts on the stage. When that character assumes the outfits, like headgear, makeup, etc., even when that character appears artificially, we don't find any hindrance to our artistic experience. Why is this? Because such outfits justify that particular experience. There is a lot of difference between experience in real life and experience in art.

Dr Ayyapa Paniker: We are not getting this experience because of the simplicity of the storyline or because of the method of presentation.

Training and Aesthetic Experience

K.S. Narayana Pillai: In Kathakali, uncommon techniques are used. The same techniques are used in the presentation of this drama.

Kainikkara Kumara Pillai: Once I had the chance to go to the house of a very famous Kathakali actor, Thottam Nambudiri. I'll describe the experience I had. He presented a very famous situation in acting, namely *Ekalochanam*[1]. Behind that effort, there is strenuous training.

K.S. Narayana Pillai: In this drama, is it the fault of the actor that such an experience is not possible?

---

1 A technical demonstration exhibiting the efficacy of the artist by creating anguish in one eye and anger in the other eye.

Kainikkara Kumara Pillai: The Kathakali actor to whom I referred earlier performed with only a loincloth. The performance is a good example of the extent to which the actor can make the performance powerful. The enactment of this piece, *Ekalochanam*, could not be acted by anyone perfectly like this actor in theatre. We should try for that. Nothing else is important.

K.S. Narayana Pillai: Will it become genuine only if you present actual life in the drama?

Kainikkara Kumara Pillai: Whatever it is, the play should be convincing for us. At least while watching it.

Dr Ayyapa Paniker: Is it not by artificiality that Thottam Nambudiri could do that in his *Ekalochanam*?

Kainikkara Kumara Pillai: No, there was nothing artificial in it. It was an exhibition of his talent.

Dr Ayyapa Paniker: Yes, it is training.

Kainikkara Kumara Pillai: Yes, but it is due to that training. I don't mean to say that training is not required in such performances. The most important thing is the result that such training creates. We have to see whether it creates an aesthetic experience in us.

Dr Ayyapa Paniker: That means to create emotion, realism is not very essential. Is it the fault of the techniques of Kathakali that such emotions are not created?

Kainikkara Kumara Pillai: No.

Art should be Emotive

K.S. Narayana Pillai: The audience need not cry in reaction to the *karuna rasa* shown by Thottam Nambudiri.

Kainikkara Kumara Pillai: They should be taken up to the level of crying. Will anyone go to see an art form if it is only to weep? The spectators should feel it intensely when the actor enacts *shloka*.

K.S. Narayana Pillai: As in the case of Kathakali, drama also can create an emotional experience with the help of technique and practice.

Kainikkara Kumara Pillai: It is definitely possible, but it is difficult to make it possible, especially in the play *Ottayan* because it involves so many complex aspects. Kathakali has deeply affected me in certain situations, especially in the situation when Krishna meets Kuchela when it is properly presented.

Kavalam Narayana Panikkar: Even if it is not enacted well, it will affect certain people. The involvement and contribution of the audience are very important in this.

Kainikkara Kumara Pillai: Yes the part of the audience is very important.

Laughter and Poignancy

K.S. Narayana Pillai: In *Ottayan*, the *Chakyar* transforms into an elephant, tames the woodsmen and builds a house for them. Do you mean to say that these events are not convincing?

Kainikkara Kumara Pillai: We can believe all those things. What I mention is the totality of the play. The actor is imitating the elephant to transform into an elephant, but that does not deeply affect emotions.

K.S. Narayana Pillai: Even in a play like this, I believe it is possible.

Kainikkara Kumara Pillai: That is only conjecture.

Dr Ayyapa Paniker: Can we say that the text of the play has failed?

Kainikkara Kumara Pillai: We can say that. The possibility is not in the story. We have talked about Kathakali. These types of stories happen in the Thullal art form also. In Thullal, is it possible for the actor to create such an emotion?

Dr Ayyapa Paniker: In Thullal, we mainly see the *hasya rasa*. Can we say that this *rasa* does not affect our emotions?

Kainikkara Kumara Pillai: It can never affect us on a deep level.

Dr Ayyapa Paniker: All *rasas* will affect the emotions. Can we say that *karuna* is the only *rasa* and there should only be *karuna* in all dramas?

Kainikkara Kumara Pillai: I don't mean that.

Dr Ayyapa Paniker: If so, it is also not correct to say that *hasya* does not give any emotions.

Kainikkara Kumara Pillai: Only certain emotions can give both pervading and deep feelings.

Dr Ayyapa Paniker: Should we have such a distinction among the nine *rasas*? Is it like that?

Kainikkara Kumara Pillai: It is not like that. Out of nine *rasas*, we should see which *rasa* creates the most powerful and deep impact.

Dr Ayyapa Paniker: In the case of *hasya*, Kuncham Nambiar also does the same thing. Can we say that one *rasa* creates more impact than another *rasa*?

K. S. Narayana Pillai: In Thullal, don't you think that life has been depicted on a deep level? Take the example of Bhima and Hanuman in the story 'Kaliyana Saugandhikam'. We see in Thullal that both these characters penetrate people's hearts.

Kainikkara Kumara Pillai: Is this *hasya*?

K. S. Narayana Pillai: Is there not *hasya* in it? *Hasya* is prominent in that. Other *rasas* are also there to complement *hasya*.

Kainikkara Kumara Pillai: It is not *hasya* that touches us. *Hasya* is only in the beginning stages. What do we finally get from *hasya*?

K.S. Narayana Pillai: We get the same feeling from *hasya* as we get from any other *rasa*.

Kainikkara Kumara Pillai: In the story 'Kaliyana Saugandhikam', it is not *hasya* but intense brotherly love that is depicted.

K. S. Narayana Pillai: If such a situation were presented without *hasya*, it would have become a melodrama.

Kainikkara Kumara Pillai: What I am asking is whether it is *hasya* that we ultimately receive from that situation.

K.S. Narayana Pillai: This is the result of any *hasya* when it reaches its zenith.

Dr Ayyapa Paniker: Are we getting any emotion other than *hasya* in 'Kaliyana Saugandhikam'? Do you think Thullal is incompetent to create sublime feelings?

Kainikkara Kumara Pillai: I did not say that Thullal couldn't create the feeling. There are two sides for *hasya*. One is the absurdity in *hasya*. The other is that it creates tears.

Dr Ayyapa Paniker: We get a holistic vision of life from the absurd characters of Don Quixote or Falstaff. Whatever the *rasa* is, we are not sticking to that *rasa*, but it becomes an artistic enjoyment.

Kainikkara Kumara Pillai: Only certain people can experience this.

Dr Ayyapa Paniker: Can we connect this concept with the fact that there is no tragedy in Indian drama?

Kainikkara Kumara Pillai: There is no point in saying that we don't have tragedy. We can see very powerful tragedy in our epics and folktales.

Dr Ayyapa Paniker: In Bhavabhuti's *Uttararamacharitam,* some modification was made to keep it from becoming a tragedy. We can consider *Uttararamacharitam* as a drama evolved later, only to demonstrate tragedy.

K. S. Narayana Pillai: When we see many of the realistic plays, don't we forget the fact that drama is something that should be an aesthetic representation?

Kainikkara Kumara Pillai: A drama which depicts ordinary life should necessarily be an artistic representation. Here in *Ottayan,* the actor enters and introduces himself and then transforms into another character. Is there any necessity in his doing so and how does it become artistic?

Dr Ayyapa Paniker: Do you mean to say that there is nothing like transformation in theatre?

K.S. Narayana Pillai: Can't the transformations in this play arouse the imagination? One actor is representing several emotions and when he passes from one *rasa* to another, do you feel that there is artificiality?

Dr Ayyapa Paniker: In the presentation of this play, many rhythms have been used. How is the use of *touryatrika* (song, dance and rhythm) effective in this play? How is the combination of body acting and rhythm effective? Don't you think it is against realism?

Kainikkara Kumara Pillai: But the same thing can be seen in Kathakali also. I don't find anything wrong with the use of rhythm in this play also. But it did not create any reaction in my mind.

Dr Ayyapa Paniker: There are two opinions on this. One is that the elements of dance and music were not effective as they are in art forms like Kathakali. The other view is that this is no drama at all and there is no real life seen in it.

Kainikkara Kumara Pillai: Yes, such a criticism is possible.

Lokdharmi and *Natyadharmi*

Dr Ayyapa Paniker: You have seen the presentation of *Ottayan.* Do you think the acting has done justice to the *Natyadharmi* style of acting? It is stated in the text of *Ottayan,* 'It is a purely *Lokadharmi* play; by this, I simply mean that the story really took place. I will certainly do my best to make it a *Natyadharmi* play...I shall try to add the necessary embellishments, clothe it in attractive outfits and enact it in a suitable manner, nay in the most befitting and appropriate style.' Do you think this claim has succeeded?

D. Appukuttan Nair: We can say that a definition for *Natyadharmi* is that which is not *Lokdharmi*. Take for example, the act of crying. If you cry silently with tears in your eyes, it is *Lokdharmi* and if you cry with action it will be *Natyadharmi*. If will become *Natyadharmi* if we convey through songs, but not through dialogue. Likewise, if we walk in a normal way, it will be *Lokdharmi*, but it will become *Natyadharmi* if we walk in a stylised manner. There should be the atypical in each step in Kathakali. We should not simply walk and call this artificial. It is purposeful. Consciously, the ordinary is avoided.

Dr Ayyapa Paniker: What is the purpose of this unusuality?

D. Appukuttan Nair: The characters in Kathakali are superhuman, so their behaviour should be such.

Dr Ayyapa Paniker: The *Chakyar* in *Ottayan* is not a supernatural character.

D. Appukuttan Nair: Even though the *Chakyar* is not a supernatural character, he takes us to a different world. The *Chakyar* creates that supernaturality through his rhythm. Even though the language is worldly, the style is not.

K. S. Narayana Pillai: Why then, is it necessary for the character to be supernatural? The emotion is to be transformed to a supernatural level.

D. Appukuttan Nair: Look at the naturality in Kathakali. In *Kamsvadham*, the mahout acts in a *Lokdharmi* way. In an extraordinary situation, if the actor acts in an ordinary way, he becomes a joker. In our ordinary plays, if an actor acts superhuman, we call him either a buffoon or a lunatic. In the extraordinary situation of *Kathakali*, if an ordinary person appears, he will become a buffoon. That is why we may feel that the carpenter in *Bakavadha* and the mahout in *Kansvadham* behave like buffoons. In a supernatural situation, an extraordinary character fits in with the mood. *Natyadharmi* is against the natural situation.

Dr Ayyapa Paniker: Can we say that our behaviour in everyday life is *Lokdharmi* or is behaviour on the stage made *Lokdharmi*?

D. Appukuttan Nair: The behaviour in everyday life is *loukikka*. Imitating the *loukika* is *Lokadharmi*.

Dr Ayyapa Paniker: That means *Lokdharmi* and *Natyadharmi* are two systems of stage presentation. *Lokdharmi* is not there in everyday life.

D. Appukuttan Nair: The word, 'lokdharmi', comes from our acceptance of the dharma of everyday life.

Imitation of the Imitation

Dr Ayyapa Paniker: Can we connect the presentation of *Ottayan* with *Lokdharmi* and *Natyadharmi*?

D. Appukuttan Nair: Let me be very frank in saying I did not like the presentation of *Ottayan*. The *Chakyar* enacts in *Natyadharmi* way. *Natyadharmi* itself is an imitation. It will not be correct if we imitate it again. For example, we record our dialogue. If we make a copy of what is recorded, it will not have the quality of the original. That is what happened in the presentation of *Ottayan*. The *Chakyar* in *Ottayan* tried to imitate the real *Chakyar*.

Dr Ayyapa Paniker: Do you mean to say that the actor has been ridiculing the acting method of a *chakyar*? *Natyadharmi* itself becomes a subject matter of the play. Do you think it is done as prescribed in the book, *Natankusam*[2] (*nata*, actor and *ankusam*, reign)?

D. Appukuttan Nair: The way the *Chakyar* was imitated was not aesthetically convincing. The dialogue presentation was also a poor imitation.

A Shortcoming in the Presentation

Dr Ayyapa Paniker: So you mean to say that the acting did not keep to the *Chakyar*'s style?

D. Appukuttan Nair: It never came up to that style. It was like children playfully aping the actions. It lacked expertise.

Dr Ayyapa Paniker: Can you ascribe the reason for this flaw in the text? Is it solely due to faulty acting or is it because of the play's lack of potential?

D. Appukuttan Nair: There is a possibility for acting in the play. The problem happened in its presentation. It was not only due to the actor who played the *Chakyar* but also the woodsmen who imitated the style of *Kathakali*. The elements of Kathakali and Kudiyattam were mixed. There was also lack of proper costumes.

Dr Ayyapa Paniker: Can we say that because the woodsmen have adopted *Lokadharmi* style of acting, the *Chakyar*'s acting did not prove effective?

---

2 *Natankusam* is a book by an unknown author that is a *Chakyar*'s acting method.

D. Appukuttan Nair: In our system we are justified in combining *Lokdharmi* and *Natyadharmi*. Is that the reason why the acting has become flawed here?

Kavalam Narayana Panikkar: We said the shortcoming in the presentation happened because Kudiyattam and Kathakali were imitated. Can you suggest any other method for presenting this play? Mr Krishnankutty Nair and Mr Gopalakrishnan who played the role of the woodsmen did not have Kathakali training. Mr Jagannathan, who did the *Chakyar's* role, also did not learn Kudiyattam. They did learn the basic steps required for acting and they used the rhythms required for their respective roles. Actually, nothing was imitated. The chanting method used by the *Chakyar* was developed for creating *bhava*s (expressions). The phrases in Kudiyattam have been developed from the chanting of the Vedas. Was that an imitation? Here, in this case, the most important thing was to intensify the *bhava*. Those who seriously enjoy Kudiyattam may have felt that it was an imitation because of the similarities in our art forms. *Talam* (rhythm) is not meant only for Kathakali and Kudiyattam.

D. Appukuttan Nair: Those who saw this play have felt that this is an unsuccessful imitation.

K.S. Narayana Pillai: When we present a *Chakyar* as a character, is it required that the elements of a *Chakyar's* chanting be present?

D. Appukuttan Nair: The *Chakyar* in *Ottayan* did not present it properly. When *Natyadharmi* acting is employed, technical perfection is expected.

Dr Ayyapa Paniker: Was there any problem in the acting of the elephant because of the failure of rhythm and the heightening of percussion?

D. Appukuttan Nair: Those who have gone deep in Kathakali and Kudiyattam have found the *Chakyar's* acting irritating. But those who have not seen these types of art forms will say that the acting was good.

K.S. Narayana Pillai: Did you feel that the transformation was not proper in the character, Ottayan?

D. Appukuttan Nair: Generally, the acting was not up to the mark.

Dr Ayyapa Paniker: So, you don't mean that the possibility of transformation is missing in this play; you mean that its application was not up to the mark. It may be because of the actors' lack of experience in Kudiyattam and Kathakali. What do you say about the use of percussion?

D. Appukuttan Nair: Even though a *mizhavu*[3] was not used, the use of percussion seems to be done well. The body movements and the percussion synchronised well.

Dr Ayyapa Paniker: How was the scene in which the house was built?

D. Appukuttan Nair: There also it was felt that the dance and rhythm were synchronised. With all that, since the actor has failed in his techniques, the presentation was also substandard.

The Importance of Audience Participation

P.K. Balakrishnan: Some art forms will receive the cooperation and respect of the audience. We can't say that this play has that ability. I came to see this play on the belief that this special type of work could be done only by a rare person so there is no need of appropriating appreciation or cooperation from me. Still, the audience should develop a special kind of cooperation. That is required for Kathakali also. It is also required while reading a book. If you read a book and you don't get an impression even after reading ten pages then it will be difficult to finish it.

What is special in Panikkar's plays? When you see influence of ancient art forms of Kerala in them, people who believe in tradition will feel bad. They will also feel that art forms like Kathakali and Kudiattyam are presented in a very stupid way. This type of work will not be liked by the spokesmen of the realistic European theatre either. It has to be seen in order to get convinced that this is neither traditional nor realistic, but a new creation and that those who work in this would have the ability to manifest this creation. In order to achieve this, the audience should have that mental attitude. Then they will have no problem to be convinced that an elephant is being represented on stage.

Dr Ayyapa Paniker: It is necessary for any art form to build an audience for itself. It is said that for those who enjoy Kathakali and those who enjoy western drama, it will be difficult to enjoy this style. Do you mean to say that a new type of audience should be created for this type of play? Since all art forms require the cooperation of the audience, what is special about the audience cooperation in this style of presentation?

---

3 A rhythm instrument used in Kudiyattam.

P.K. Balakrishnan: Since this is a new style of presentation, we have to create a feeling of cooperation in the audience; in these plays, the elements of folk art are used. Does that mean we are going back to the past? I feel that such a return is not possible. While going back, a person who actually knows about the past reaches a totally new form. Kavalam Narayana Panikkar, when going back to traditional theatre roots in Kerala, is investigating a new space. The cooperation in that also becomes a creative endeavour. I don't think that an audience who has that ability will have any problem for enjoying this. I could enjoy the performance of the *Chakyar* and the woodsmen who appeared in this play. I'm not a person who is closely familiar with Kudiyattam. Still, I have been able to enjoy this. I can't say whether it is due to my special liking for this style. I didn't want to say that my attitude should be applied to the average audience.

Dr Ayyapa Paniker: In this situation, rather than an affinity for Kudiyattam or western drama, what is required for the audience is an open mind. Only from such a situation can an art form create a receptive audience.

Enjoyment and Intellectuality

Narendra Prasad: The transformation in Kudiyattam need not be identification. In the case of realistic plays, the audience has developed the experience to believe the illusion; this was made possible through association. Likewise, the audience in the past has been trained to believe the illusion created in Kudiyattam. We cannot expect that the same illusion be created when a contemporary playwright uses the same technique. It is possible to witness these plays and enjoy them only with the application of intellectuality as it is found in the appreciation of the plays of Brecht. The audience will be convinced that the elephant has come and gone only by keeping the intellectual distancing.

P. K. Balakrishnan: I meant the same when I referred to audience participation, both intellectual and otherwise.

Narendra Prasad: I believe that in modern times, these plays can only get an audience which can keep intellectually at a distance. Today, the audience should be able to establish an emotional relationship with Kudiyattam as it is conceived by some in the realistic plays. People could imbibe the transformation in Kudiyattam in the past, but it need not be the case in the present.

Dr Ayyapa Paniker: What went wrong was the example of Brecht that we quoted. What Brecht meant was that when a character praises war, the person who watches the play will feel hatred towards the war and those who support it so that opinion against war could be created. What Brechtian scholars say is that his theory failed when put into practice. The audience believed that these are all good things. The intention of Brecht was not realised. In the play, *Mother Courage*, the audience believed that the actors were saying that war was good through their skillful acting.

Narendra Prasad: That is only an opinion.

Dr Ayyapa Paniker: No, that still stands as criticism.

S. Natarajan: We should realise that intellect and compassion should not come into conflict. Along with the intellect, when logic comes into play, certain members of the audience will question why a house will be built for the woodsmen when woodsmen do not live in houses. Here it is necessary that the audience should have both intellect and compassion beyond logic.

The Extent of Involvement

Narendra Prasad: Stylisation is employed in art with the intention that the audience will not become personally involved in the story. The audience should be able to keep away from the life experience.

Dr Ayyapa Paniker: Don't you think that this intellectual approach works in all arts? In the case of a novel many things may happen after the first chapter. The novelist does not mention all those things. Those things are accepted by us. Even in a realistic art form, we cannot depict everything as it is. An intelligent application is required.

Narendra Prasad: When a character speaks in lines, he tries to communicate the feelings with the same energy as the text envisages. This was the old practice. But today, it is not like this. Sometimes the audience may have to take the opposite meaning from a character's dialogue. For this, the audience requires an intellectual approach. This should be the yardstick to appreciate stylised plays. There is no need for any emotional communication. This is not expected in stylised plays.

Dr Ayyapa Paniker: Alienation and stylisation do not mean that there is no communication of emotions. Only very few people get lost in the belief that the actor is the character. Even in realistic plays, this belief does not exist. The audience feels when they see *Hamlet* that they are watching Lawrence Olivier acting the role! We have never seen the 'real' Hamlet. The audience may be thinking about the Hamlet as represented earlier by some other actor. They may think how this actor differs from the older one, how he vocalises his lines and how his face suits the role of Hamlet. When we see the play after the first time and see the play a second and third time, our mind will be thinking all these things. An audience who has seen the play many times may not experience these situations.

Narendra Prasad: Should it not be the purpose of the performance that the audience experiences such involvement?

Dr Ayyapa Paniker: That involvement does not imply full involvement. I don't believe that *Natyadharmi* and *Lokdharmi* are contradictory. There is no play that is cent per cent *Natyadharmi* or cent per cent *Lokdharmi*. In any play we see the variations of the two acting methods. Let us see how the ratio works in *Ottayan*. Was there any special use of technique in this play?

Kavalam Narayana Panikkar: The *Chakyar* starts initially in *Lokdharmi*. When he introduces himself where he comes from, etc., he proves to be an actor getting ready for a performance. A performance, however stylised (*Natyadharmi*), is essentially rooted in *Lokdharmi*. We cannot say that these two *dharmi*s contradict each other.

Dr Ayyapa Paniker: If the *Chakyar* himself had enacted the roles of the woodsmen, it would have been more stylised (*Natyadharmi*). In realistic plays, there exists the concept of *apavarya* (aside). In *Ottayan*, the *Chakyar* says, 'If only I were in my theatre, how interestingly I could have re-enacted an elephant running in rut.' He uses an aside, which is common in the realistic theatre also. The variations and the combinations of *Natyadharmi* and *Lokadharmi*, have to be noted specially.

Two Levels of Illusion

Narendra Prasad: The actor becomes the *Chakyar* and when the he speaks, we believe it. Then, there is a situation of conflict when he enacts the elephant appearing. There we tend to be aloof from what happens and we have to make ourselves convinced that this is like this. I don't mean to say that this is artificial. This is the second level of illusion. These two levels of illusion are special for this play. Why is this created? That is my complaint about this play. How is this technique beneficial to the modern audience?

P. Balakrishnan: Can't we change the term 'modern' and use contemporary instead? I think modern has a wrong connotation.

S. Natarajan: The two levels of illusion occur to us only after we see the play and analyse it. I believe that all these become convincing if it is handled by a competent actor.

Dr Ayyapa Paniker: Here we create one level of illusion and then we destroy it, to create another and thus the creative process goes on.

Alphabets of a Special Language of Theatre

P.K. Balakrishnan: Let me bring up something different from what we have been discussing. We have referred to the difficulty in communication as an impediment to the enjoyment of the audience. For a person who has not seen *Avanavan Kadamba*[4], it will be difficult to understand *Ottayan*. All of Panikkar's plays form the alphabets of a special language of theatre. I don't say that the alphabet is complete, but to those who are not familiar with his other plays, whatever the number of layers of illusion present in *Ottayan*, the expected level of audience participation will be the same. In Dostoyevsky's *The Brothers Karamazov, Possessed* and *Crime and Punishment,* we see almost similar moulds of characters. Still, each one is an extremely new creation. If you deeply examine these works, you may find many differences in techniques. If Panikkar's plays are construed as a garland of alphabets to make theatre language forms, it is certain that a person unfamiliar with the earlier alphabets will be in his proper appreciation.

Dr Ayyapa Paniker: In Sanu's[5] opinion, Panikkar's best play is *Sakshi* in which there is comparatively less *Natyadharmi*. Its subject matter is a comtemporary social situation. It is easy to understand. There is a conflict. A realistic presentation of this conflict is evident in spite of the presence of

---

4 An earlier landmark play of Panikkar's.
5 Prof. M K Sanu has referred this in his introduction to Panikkar's earlier work *Sakshi.*

dance and music. When *Daivathar* and *Avanavan Kadamba* were presented, people doubted whether they were dramas at all. It is a fact that these plays have a chronological structure and we can go into one play only after we have gone into the earlier one. But should the audience be concerned with this? Maybe it is relevant for the playwright.

P.K. Balakrishnan: Without directly being related to any specific visual art, yet imbibing elements from many available forms, these plays belong to a new category. So in order to engage with them fully, a special training is required. In order to understand the creative individuality of a person, we have to have a holistic approach to the same. I don't mean to say here that his one work is better than the earlier one or vice-versa. In each case, we may find its plus or minus points. Still, there is a totality of the whole. The audience must be aware of that. There is a comprehensive quality in *Ottayan*, *Daivathar* and *Avanavan Kadamba*. Without any earlier reference, there is individuality in the expression. It is a kind of firework. What is important is the totality of the form. We do not get the meaning of a poet's complete works by reading just one poem alone. We may feel that the poem is great, but only by reading the poet's other works do we get a sense of his total personality. The question is whether these plays could survive all the above-mentioned problems. I feel that the relationship of *Avanavan Kadamba* with *Ottayan* is organic. At the same time, they maintain vivid differences also. It should be like that. That is why I said a complete understanding of the plays is required to enjoy them.

Freedom from Technique

Narendra Prasad: I believe that after *Daivathar*, this playwright cannot create a great work. I felt *Daivathar* was a very different and serious theatre experience. There was a purpose behind its stylisation, related to its content and creativity. This is evident from the fact that the play could create the feeling of a great tragedy even in an extremely comic situation. For example, when the crowd of devotees moves with comic utterances, the situation on the whole communicates a sense of tragedy combined with sarcasm and it touches your heart. The startling reaction that its totality creates moves us at every point. The irony that is created at a single moment could help the audience to experience a comprehensive feeling. Not only that, we find that the actor, even while following the techniques, is able to feel free from such techniques and engage in his creativity. Such theatrical freedom was not seen in the subsequent two plays of this author.

Dr Ayyapa Paniker: Narendra Prasad was asking about what benefits the audience expects by crossing barriers created by the two illusions. That can be asked in the case of the first illusion also. The question of what we ultimately get from a production depends on the audience. Each one gets a different impression.

Narendra Prasad: We cannot question the first illusion like that because the spectator comes prepared to face that.

Dr Ayyapa Paniker: We see a realistic play or a circus show. We don't get the same experience of seeing a play. When we seek the second level of illusion with so much care, our experience should also justify it. We get back from *Daivathar* more than what we give by way of cooperation; whereas in *Ottayan* we don't get back anything commensurate to our involvement. We should be able to get something unique after passing through the double illusion. That may be a special experience and need not have enough strength. It will be better to evaluate *Ottayan* on the basis of the reaction of the audience at the time of presentation.

Nedumudi Venu: The *Chakyar* in *Ottayan* has more freedom when compared to the characters in other plays. In *Avanavan Kadamba*, the importance was placed on group acting. Only a few characters can stand on their own. In *Daivathar*, also, the actor had the freedom to perform individually, but the freedom that the actor gets in *Ottayan* is supreme when compared to any other play.

The Responsibility and Freedom of the Actor

Dr Ayyapa Paniker: Kalankaniyan, the main character in *Daivathar*, had the responsibility of a *sutradhara*.[6] The *Chakyar* in *Ottayan* has the same responsibility. He is an actor and a *sutradhara*. In what sense have you mentioned that the chakyar has freedom?

Nedumudi Venu: The actor enjoys more freedom to deviate from the techniques.

Dr Ayyapa Paniker: Kalankaniyan in *Daivathar* also has the same freedom.

6 Stage manager in Sanskrit plays who presents the play in the prologue.

Nedumudi Venu: The *Chakyar* is alone in stage and he gets all the focus.

Dr Ayyapa Paniker: Is that not a responsibility? Is the freedom not reduced, as a result? Are the techniques like transformation and *Natyadharmi* not creating more responsibility? And then how can such responsibility be treated as freedom? Kalankaniyan does not keep away from the focus of the audience. On the other hand, since the *Chakyar* has to convince the spectator through his techniques, his responsibility increases. It will be in correct to say that the actor gets more freedom if there is nobody else on the stage. There is no truth in saying that the actor will have freedom if he is alone and that he will have less freedom if others are with him. We say all this on the basis that the actor is well trained and the audience discernable. So there is no point in saying that the actor's freedom is restricted when there are more actors. Here, how can the responsibility become freedom?

S. Natarajan: For an actor who acts well, if alone, and has the freedom to act, it will be a hindrance if there are other actors.

Dr Ayyapa Paniker: Do you mean to say that the actor has responsibility because he has to take care of other actors?

Nedumudi Venu: If five people act jointly, it will not be effective if only one person is good. Everybody must act well.

Dr Ayyapa Paniker: In that case, one has only one-fifth of the freedom. Out of five, he has four hindrances. In *Ottayan*, just one actor can make the whole production shine. Is this freedom? In this play, the spectator has greater responsibility. Even the actor has to act in a peculiar way. In that case, will the actor have less freedom?

Nedumudi Venu: As far as our theatre is concerned, an actor who is acting in a realistic drama will find it difficult to do a role suddenly, without practice. What I mean to say is an actor who has thoroughly practised the techniques and then acts according to his creativity has a special responsibility that becomes freedom.

Narayana Prasad: Since there is a necessity of *touritrigu*[7], I can't understand the fact that freedom increases.

Kavalam Narayana Pannikar: For an actor who has conceived the technique

---

7 The amalgam of vocal music, dance and instrumentation.

properly there is no problem with this responsibility. Has Nedumudi Venu meant that to present that technique is his freedom?

S. Natarajan: The freedom becomes practical when there is co-ordination between people who handle *touritrigam* and the actor.

Nedumudi Venu: The understanding between actor and percussionist is important. If there is an understanding, the actor can create according to his will on the stage.

Dr Ayyapa Paniker: If the percussionist is controlling the actor, can we say the actor has freedom? I will give an example. In *kekiattam*[8] there is a movement choreographed by the actor. For that dance, there is the accompanying percussion that gives its effect. The actor in *kekiattam*, creates a build-up with different kinds of dance movements and while he enacts flying, he communicates joyful moments to the spectator. The actor's body movements and the accompanying rhythms coupled with the attention of the audience can create not merely the happiness of the peacock but the mental state of the actor also which transforms into the total happiness of the play which produces an aesthetic satisfaction. The freedom about which we discussed is enjoyed like this and not by the actor being alone. Whatever is possible for one actor can be made possible by two actors also.

Kavalam Narayana Panikkar: There is no point in saying that there will be less freedom if other actors are there. In the *Nalacharitam* Kathakali, where Damayanti and Hamsam jointly act, they get freedom because of their technical expertise. This freedom will be enjoyed only if the percussion also joins. With the help of technical expertise, the actors are getting freedom from the group.

Style and Improvisation

Narendra Prasad: Is it possible in such a play for the actor to situate freedom from the practised techniques?

S. Natarajan: Practice means learning the rhythm and the steps. Do you mean to say that the actor will be free if he goes wrong in techniques? With that freedom, do you think that the actor can make his acting effective?

Narendra Prasad: Can't the actor make an emotional situation by breaking

8 A sequence in Kathakali depicting the dance of the peacock.

away from the rhythm and steps? For that he may depend on another rhythm. Is that possibility seen more in *Ottayan* than in *Daivathar*?

Dr Ayyapa Paniker: If required, the actor can get that freedom in *Ottayan*. Until now, whenever the play was done without using that freedom, it was found using the same style. That freedom was never used at the cost of the style.

Narendra Prasad: I believe that following established practice and at the same time breaking it, *there* begins the real acting. This is in the case of stylised plays.

Kavalam Narayana Panikkar: To go against a practice, another practice is to be adopted. The breaking of a rhythm is to be done by switching on to another rhythm.

S. Natarajan: As far as the play is concerned, if you intend to break the practice, it should be decided at the time of the rehearsals. One practice can be broken only by meticulously changing to another practice.

Kavalam Narayana Panikkar: Even though the percussionist is aware of what the actor is going to do, he has a concept of time regarding the detailed plan of action. Even though this is within the general structure of practice, the execution of his action is not based fully on established norms. The actor should be able to control these norms according to situations. Have we to understand that when we cross the established rules, it is *manodharma* (improvisation) that takes place? When you stick to a simple rhythm, the rules can be made more flexible for the purpose of improvisation. When you change the established rules, it need not be that you should go out of rhythm. You have to stick to the rhythm dictated by heartbeats. Keeping to that, an able actor can cross the rules and create his own norm. Basic rhythm is the link in such cases, which help the percussionist to synchronise with the actor. When you give supreme importance to emotion and use the rules as a medium to communicate the same, you can afford to break the norms in consonance with such emotions. But as pointed out, some deviations should be perfected in the rehearsals, themselves.

Narendra Prasad: When a spectator who does not know anything about the style sees *Ottayan*, he will feel that the play is performed after proper practice. But creative stylisation demands that such a feeling should not be created.

Dr Ayyapa Paniker: Jagannathan in his acting might have tried to go against the established norms, but I doubt if he succeeded. Whereas in the action of Krishnankutty Nair as woodsman, we could see that he goes against the rules, maybe because of lack of following systematised rules. Jagannathan has been able to improvise many situations like seeing the tree, then rejecting to cut the tree, etc. within the given rhythm structure, but beyond that, his creativity could not develop as you find in the case of able actors in Kathakali and Kudiyattam.

Classical and Folk

Narendra Prasad: Do you think that the classical quality of the *Chakyar* and the folk character of the woodsmen could create a concord? In the costumes of the woodsmen the *Natyadharmi* characteristics of the folk arts have been adopted. Still, why did they not harmonise with the *Chakyar*?

Dr Ayyapa Paniker: In *Ottayan*, the author has attempted to combine the classical quality of *Chakyar*s and the folk elements of the woodsmen. In previous plays like *Daivathar*, where folk elements are predominantly seen, we find that there was a fusion of *Lokdharmi* and *Natyadharmi*. The *Chakyar*s also combine these two acting methods in a brilliant way in productions like *Surpanakhankam*. Their costumes and movements match very well. This is because they have a long tradition in the presentation of these styles. We don't have that. We face the problem of how to judiciously combine these elements when we do something new on stage. This forms an important problem.

Narendra Prasad: Although you can say that the woodsmen are the mental creation of the *Chakyar* on a subtle level, they visibly appear as characters. They are nothing but his tools. This art is to be viewed differently from Kudiyattam. Such a theme never appears in any Kudiyattam. This play is written to be staged for a contemporary audience. Folk elements could not be given to the woodsmen on the same way that the importance is given to the *Chakyar*'s stylised acting. This is because the Kudiyattam style was adopted. If this is so, is it desirable to have this occur in a modern play?

Dr Ayyapa Paniker: There has never been a production of this play to show that the woodsmen are the mental creation of the *Chakyar*. The interpretation so far given is that, at least for some time, the *Chakyar* is obedient to the woodsmen and he could outwit them by his efficiency in acting. There can be a further attempt to make a different interpretation.

Narendra Prasad: Is it desirable that the classical actor is given undue importance in a play where both classical and folk elements are combined?

Dr Ayyapa Paniker: I don't think there is any contradiction between classical and folk, as it is generally understood. I had once discussed with the great musician Balamuralikrishna about classical and folk music. He opined that classical is to be considered a refined product of folk. They are not contradictions although they have differences. If the acting is organised to prove this, then it will establish the variety of both.

Narendra Prasad: That is why I said there should be flexibility while adhering to the rules. If the *Chakyar* is more flexible in his acting, then the folk quality will blend with his.

Acting Itself is the Theme of the Play

Dr Ayyapa Paniker: The special feature that makes this play interesting is that it raises many problems about play-acting itself. When we deal with a theme like this, that is, when we make acting itself the theme, we will have to face such problems, as we discussed. I don't think this playwright will write on a theme like this again. In the literature on world theatre, there are only a few plays that deal with acting as a theme. This play also has that quality. That is all. We don't have to compare this with other plays of the author's. We can compare this play only with plays having the same theme. This is like music concentrated on the life of a musician. It is not the life of an artist that is the theme, but art itself is the central theme and, as such, it belongs to a special category. Only then do the dual illusios and such problems Prop up. It has many points of restriction.

This play, compared to other plays is very short. Here the *Chakyar* is not the main character; the significant one is acting itself. Then, the human element will be lacking when compared with other ordinary plays. But, there human elements are seen to some extent. One example is the reference about his beloved *Nangiyar* when the *Chakyar* happens to see the cymbals. Even the woodsmen are very near to humanness. The *Chakyar* is an actor, but he dwells in a different dimension. Did the author envisage the acting techniques in his earlier plays when he adapted a theme like this? I'm asking this only because this subject has many limitations. I'm sure the playwright will not try a similar theme to this again. I may say that in one way, this play is a rehearsal, more than the enactment of an occurrence—it is an attempt on how the art of acting can be made effective. I feel that in this context, it can be treated as an experiment. The other play of the same author cannot be viewed like this and that, itself, can be viewed as the uniqueness of this play.

Translated by Harikrishnan Kavalam

Geography and the Poetics of Continuity
and Imagination

A long conversation with Panikkar on the banks of the Pampa River

Udayan Vajpeyi: Let us start our conversation with the Malayalam poet Vallathol. You were telling me about your relationship with him. How did you meet him?

Kavalam Narayana Panikkar: Vallathol used to visit our home whenever my uncle Sardar Panikkar was in town. He would join him from Cochin. During the formative years of the Kalamandalam, when he was struggling to get proper support for the project, he made my eldest uncle Dr K.P. Panikkar the treasurer of his institution. He used to bank on Sardar Panikkar for help from North India. My uncle was keen to help him because Vallathol was like a guru to him and he respected his seniority and also his position as 'Mahakavi', a great poet. Sardar Panikkar also wrote poems.

Actually, seniority apart, Vallathol and Sardar Panikkar were very close friends, so he used to visit us more as a member of our family. My uncle used to visit us once a year and Vallathol would also come with him. Sardar Panikkar was living away from home working earlier as administrator in some native Indian states and later, on assignments like Indian Ambassador to Egypt, China and other places and lastly as Vice Chancellor of Mysore University. In fact we could not think of his coming home without Vallathol. This practice continued till the end of his life, even up to one year before his death. Vallathol used to stay in my uncle's house in Alleppey and of course in our ancestral home in Kavalam. But in Alleppey, at some point of time, when I started practising there as a lawyer and had my own home, he shifted from my uncle's house to my house.

At least on two occasions, even after Sardar Panikkar returned to Bikaner where he was the prime minister, Vallathol postponed his tour to stay with me and I had the rare privilege of taking him in my car to many places to sell his translation of the *Rig Veda*. His *Rig Veda* was very expensive and in those days difficult to sell. I remember a few interesting incidents from my association with him. From my childhood he used to correct my poems and would advise me how I should write poetry. I recollect one instance while he was staying with me. We went to the house of a very rich man—a prosperous cloth merchant—to sell the Rig Veda. He was a famous man; he who single-handedly conduct–the festival in the Alleppey temple, spending a lot of money. I took Vallathol there. In those days whoever wanted to communicate with Vallathol would write on his hand or on blank surfaces; he would immediately understand.

Udyan: Was he hard of hearing?

Panikkar: Yes. His poem *Badhira Vilaapam* was written after he lost his hearing in his fifties.

Udyan: So you were going into that rich man's house?

Panikkar: Yes, before entering the house I told him that he was a very rich man. I wrote on my hand, 'Will he give something? He is a rich man and may not be interested in purchasing such a book. What does it mean to him!' But then I thought there was no harm in trying and so we went in and he received us. I introduced Vallathol to him as the greatest poet living in Kerala. He was immensely pleased to receive such a great man in his home and when we were all seated, the cloth merchant ordered tea, fruits and snacks. Vallathol asked me to explain to him the purpose of our visit, so I did. After listening to me he said, 'Oh, but I do not read books!' I wrote on my hand for Vallathol: 'He says, he does not read books.' Vallathol laughed aloud and said, 'Tell him it is fine that he does not read books, let him only pay for it. I do not wish to give him double punishment!' I told him, 'See, he says that you do not have to suffer by both purchasing and then reading what you have paid for. You need not do both. You could select one. It is alright to not read, but please buy!' That was how Vallathol was!

On one occasion, while he was staying with me he suddenly fell ill. I called a doctor to examine him. I also asked him if I should inform his son. He said in his rough voice, 'There is no need for that. You are here, you are like my son. What is the need to give him cause for concern? As it is, I have given you reason to worry.' And so he stayed there and my wife looked after him.

Every night I would sit with him for some time and when his health improved he would happily tell us stories. He gave us a *shloka* which he recited from his memory. He told me, 'Write down this *shloka* [poem] and learn it by heart. It is a *shloka* which I composed long ago. No one knows this'. Three or four *shlokas* were recited. He had a habit of sniffing tobacco which he later gave up. But while he still had the habit, he even wrote a *shloka,* about how to get rid of it and how he got rid of it. I have unfortunately forgotten these *shlokas* and what was written down was also lost. However I could remember one on Lord Krishna of Guruvayur temple. And that I know by heart even today.

Udayan: Was that in Malayalam?

Panikkar: Yes. I remember his stature. His relationship with Nehru and every other thing was very well known. He was a towering personality. Sardar Panikkar was responsible for introducing Vallathol to Pandit Nehru and it was he who invited Nehru for the function in Kalamandalam, during its anniversary. When I was in high school, Sardar Panikkar came to Kavalam during summer vacations. My examinations were over and we were having a nice time, with Kathakali performances at home and other activities. When my uncle was about to go, Vallathol also prepared to leave. Vallathol proposed to my grandmother and my uncle that he would like to take *Kochu* (Small) Panikkar home. 'What do you say?' Vallathol asked Uncle and my uncle said, 'If he wants to go with you, fine. Did you consult him?' Vallathol said, 'Yes, yes! Yesterday when we went out for a walk I asked him to come with me. I told him I would take permission from his uncle, parents and grandmother. So if you allow it, I will take him and teach him something about art and literature.' My uncle was only too happy to send me off with him. And so I also went along and after seeing off my uncle in a train at Cochin, we took another train to Cheruthuruthy.

Nowadays it is called Vallathol Nagar. On the way he had to visit a friend. He asked me graciously, 'Would you have any objection, if we visit Parayath Raman Menon, a close friend of your uncle and mine? Would you find it interesting? You will be taken care of.' I agreed. We got off at Aluva and we went in a cart. He smoked a cigarette in my presence.

Udayan: Really!

Panikkar: Yes, he used to smoke. It so happened that at that young age I had also started to smoke. Strangely, much later, I found fault with my son smoking! Anyway, the bullock-cart had stopped at a railway crossing. I got off to have a smoke. When the train came, he asked, 'Where had you gone? It seems you wanted to smoke? Ha ha! My son also smokes!' All the while he was smoking too. 'My youngest son Balan smokes a lot,' he said. It was very interesting how he had such easy camaraderie with youngsters. We stayed there for a day and the next day again continued our train journey to Cheruthuruthy. It took us a few hours to reach his town. I stayed with him for a month. I met many of his friends who visited Vallathol's house. It was always full of visitors. I got introduced to Sankara Kurup, the poet, and to another poet Olappamanna. All these people could be seen there and he used to introduce me in such high terms: 'He belongs to that great tradition and he is a poet. You should all take note of him'.

Udayan: And were you also seeing some Kathakali?

Panikkar: Yes, his Kalamandalam was an abode of Kathakali. Vallathol used to take *kanji* (rice gruel) in the morning, which I shared, along with his daughter Vasanti and other members of the household. The poet used to go for his morning walk at 7 am and return in time for his *kanji*. Those days tea was not considered very essential nor was it very popular. We went for a walk almost every day. He would visit all *kalaris* and introduce me to the gurus and explain to me what Cholliattam was.

Udayan: What is Cholliattam?

Panikkar: Cholliattam is performing Kathakali without the elaborate costumes that go with it. It is just a rehearsal.

Udayan: And he would explain to you the story line of the performance too…

Panikkar: He explained it to me in all *kalaris*. There were two or three *kalaris* he visited everyday.

Udayan: And did they teach different styles?

Panikkar: Different personal styles as well as styles with regional variations. Later he would go to the office, sit there for a while and then we returned on foot. The office was very close by.

Udayan: Was he the one responsible for the rejuvenation and revitalisation of Kathakali?

Panikkar: Yes, he alone was responsible. You know, his letters addressed to

Sardar Panikkar are full of his ideas for the development of the Kalamandalam. I have published them because they were authentic documents. Whatever money he got in the name of the Kalamandalam, he utilised most meaningfully. He used to go to Bikaner as Sardar Panikkar's guest when he was the chief minister of Bikaner. He used to stay there; it was there that he got the opportunity to visit the Bikaner Library which had a rich collection of books. There he had the opportunity to translate *Karpoorcharitam* into Malayalam. Sardar Panikkar encouraged many writers including Vallathol, G. Sankara Kurup and Changampuzha Krishna Pillai and would send them English poems and anthologies of poetry from around the world.

Udayan: So your link to the performing arts was through Vallathol. You were connected to poetry of course, because you were writing poetry and you still do.

Panikkar: Sadly, all those early poems got lost.

Udayan: But you were already introduced to a great art form intimately. What were the other sources that you can think of, for your theatre, your link to the other performing arts?

Panikkar: While in Kavalam, I had a very limited opportunity to come into contact with art forms outside my district. We had Kathakali, Velakali and Thullal in our temple.

Udayan: What is Velakali?

Panikkar: Velakali is a martial art form. It brings out the body dynamics of the participating group of dancers. It is an artistic demonstration of the age old martial discipline popular in Kerala called Kalari. Thullal is another form, to which I was attracted.

Udayan: What kind of an artform is Thullal?

Panikkar: Thullal was a new form introduced, practised and written by Kunchan Nambiar. Nambiar belonged to the Nambiar caste or *Panivada*s (a *Panivada* is one who plays on the *mizhavu,* an accompanying percussion instrument in Kudiyattam). Nambiar was the court poet of the king of Ambalapuzha, near my town of Alleppey. Strangely enough, he was known as the king even though Ambalapuzha was only a very small principality. The King Devanarayana was a great patron of the arts. Kunchan Nambiar was punished by the king for creating Thullal in protest against the *Chakyar.*

There is a story that he was insulted on the Kudiyattam stage for having dozed off there. He was found napping while the *Chakyar* was relating an interesting story. The *Chakyar* made fun of him for sleeping on the stage when he should have been playing on the *mizhavu*. It was a practice in Kudiyattam that while acting, the *Chakyar* would poke fun at what was happening around him. So he made fun of Kunchan Nambiar, and Nambiar walked off the stage in a huff. In protest he started writing *Kaliyana Saugandhikam*. Then the story was enacted in the open courtyard of the same temple where the *Chakyar* was performing. A number of people were attracted by Nambiar's performance and they went to attend it. The *Chakyar* felt bad. The king was informed and as a result he punished Nambiar saying 'Don't enter here! I won't allow this art of Thullal to be performed in this temple premises'. Even today Thullal is not performed in the Ambalapuzha temple.

Udayan: And what is this Thullal form like?

Panikkar: It is a form of story-telling using music, with a lot of indigenous rhythms. Nambiar discovered Kerala's own rhythms inherent in many folk art forms. He went to the lowest rung of people and from them, learned various patterns of organic rhythms which belonged to the farmers who tilled the soil and developed them and gave them a very important place in his art. He composed stories from the Puranas. His works are very extensive. Apart from this, he himself was a performer.

Udayan: Who used to perform Kudiyattam?

Panikkar: No, Thullal is different from Attam. Thullal is like jumping, the movement is up and down, whereas in Attam it is a horizontal movement. In Thullal, story-telling is done by one actor in costume and another person standing behind him would sing while yet another would play the *toppimaddalam*, a percussion instrument. The performer recites poems and acts as he sang. He would sing two lines and enact them. Then the musicians would repeat those lines and the dancer would show *mudra*s (gestures) extensively. The art is known for its sharp satire. The *Chakyar's* approach is also satirical but in Nambiar's Thullal, it is a different kind of satire, equally, if not more powerful. His *Thullal Krithikal* became very popular. Now it has lost its popularity; but it is my Magna Carta for unearthing Kerala's music, the rhythms of Kerala, because they are practised even now in Theyyam and others forms. You will find these influences in my work.

Kunchan Nambiar e was a remarkably creative artist, writer and performer, who gave a new fillip to the cultural concepts of Kerala. He reestablished the old regional contribution to art and literature.

Udayan: And you have written a play on him.

Panikkar: Yes, it is called *Kunchan Nambiar*, his name itself. But I have portrayed his life only up to the point where his kingdom, Ambalapuzha, was subjugated by the Maharaja of Travancore. Ambalapuzha was taken over by Travancore and after that he was taken to Trivandrum by the king. I have written only up to that point. My approach to this myth was different. This story is a myth and is not accepted by all because people feel that it is not possible for a man to exit the stage and immediately create another form of art. All these points were questioned. The point which I stressed was that he was fed up with classical art and was not very interested in the story-telling of the *Chakyar*. From my angle, even his sleeping on stage was merely a pretense.

In my play, when the *Chakyar* criticises Nambiar showing how he slept, relating the context to the situation in the story, he very satirically comments, 'Look, the King is also sleeping, the whole audience is sleeping!' Nambiar then decides to work on a project. He works out the project and performs 'Kaliyana Saugandhikam' in the same premises. According to the story, Draupadi was once enchanted by a sweet-smelling flower and sent Bhima to fetch it for her. Bhima went to fetch the flower, crossing several hurdles on his path. While he was bringing the flower back to Draupadi, the king interfered, asking him to get out of the temple. Bhima had the flower in his hand and began searching for Draupadi to present it to her, to finish the story outside the temple.

However, there is yet another story that takes place much before all this. In the Ambalapuzha temple there is a custom of ladies bringing milk for preparing the *payasam* (sweet pudding) to be offered to the deity. Among them was Champakam, a beautiful girl. Now Ambalapuzha is also called Champakanaad or the Champaka country. Champaka is also a sweet-smelling flower. This girl Champakam also brought milk in the morning.

But the manager of the temple did not accept the milk because she was not willing to give herself to him. He unsuccessfully tried to molest her. According to the temple custom, if a vessel of milk was rejected, its contents were then not acceptable for the purpose of making *payasam* for the deity, Krishna. The milk she brought was turned down and she was very sad. She had brought the milk for Krishna and it was rejected, only because she did not agree to the wishes of the manager. She went to sleep heartbroken in the temple premises. In her sleep, she heard in a dream that Kunchan Nambiar was presenting his Thullal performance. Nambiar, who was not allowed to enter the temple and was not allowed to take his art to the temple, was now performing his art in the changed circumstances, in this democratic age.

Udayan: She saw that in her dream?

Panikkar: Yes, and she also joined in by acting as the character Draupadi and everything came through in her imagination. After fetching the fragrant flower, Nambiar who enacts Bhima is going out in search of Draupadi saying, 'Where is Draupadi? I have to hand this over to her'. And then Champakam comes with the milk; by that time the milk has almost become curd. Thus the love between Bhima and Draupadi becomes the love between Nambiar and Champakam.

Udayan: Oh, so that's there in your play?

Panikkar: Yes, when Ambalapuzha is subjugated by Marthanda Varma of Travancore, Nambiar leaves for Thiruvananthapuram on the invitation of the king to stay there as his court poet. So he takes leave of Ambalapuzha. He had to take leave of his Champakam too. As he walks away, she looks from behind and asks, 'Will you return?' With that parting scene the play ends.

Udayan: And what are other performing arts that you came in contact with in your formative days?

Panikkar: I had never seen Kudiyattam until I went to Thrissur accepting the job in Sangeetha Nataka Akademi as Secretary. I had the opportunity to see this art at the Vatakkumnatha temple. Before that I had no experience of Kudiyattam, but I had seen other forms which were all available around my district.

Udayan: And artists used to come to your home?

Panikkar: Only Kathakali artists would come to our home, otherwise these art forms were to be found performed in temples or near agricultural fields. I used to go there and see some of these forms.

Udayan: What was your childhood like?

Panikkar: I had many friends. We started 'Balajanasakhyam', a group of young boys.

Udayan: How old were you then?

Panikkar: I was in the fourth or fifth class, in my middle school years, I only spent my middle school time here in Kavalam. Those days we had the middle school course to be completed in four years after completing four years in the lower primary school. The middle school consisted of the preparatory, first, second, third; and then fourth, fifth, sixth. Eleven in all, and then college.

Udayan: Did you have some friends here in Kavalam?

Panikkar: Yes, there were some very close friends who lived around my home. Balakrishna Panikkar, Gopinatha Panikkar, Damodaran Nayar. All were of my age, we used to play together and also formed 'Balajanasakhyam', an organisation, and its meetings were held regularly. I was its chairman. During those times one elephant used to be brought to this small water logged village, crossing the Pampa River to participate in the temple festival. After that we would never go home. We used to be in the temple itself, seeing Kathakali, going after the elephant, asking the mahout to give us a lock of hair from the elephant's tail …. The hair from the elephant's tail is good for making a ring; you know, there is a belief that if you wear that ring it will cure you of fear!

Before the temple festival, there used to be a harvest festival in our village. We used to go around, see what happened on the fields, hear the farmers' songs and sing with them. This was also one of my hobbies during the summer vacation. With the holidays came the harvest festival and this was followed by the festival in the temple. That was my first schooling in art forms like Thullal and Velakali. We used to watch Thullal, without getting involved, watching from the periphery. The harvest songs attracted me very much; they still haunt me and have their influence in my writings. The characters in the village, the music that was heard then, the ever inspiring Pampa River, all these were attractive and inspiring.

Udayan: Even in your play *Theyyatheyyam*, this influence of harvest songs is evident.

Panikkar: Yes, it is there. In that play all the movements and choreography were designed based on the village experience.

Udayan: Ayyapa Paniker used to publish a magazine called *Kerala Kavita*. He published a text of yours. Ayyapa gave it a name. He called it a dramatic poem, *Sakshi*.

Panikkar: Yes it was *Sakshi*. It was in the format of a play…

Udayan: And Ayyapa Panikkar called it a dramatic poem?

Panikkar: Yes, it was a dramatic poem as well as a poetic drama. This type of play was not in vogue. Characters speak, but they speak in poetry. They speak as we worked in *Uttarramcharitam*; very interesting, very short. It is interesting to read also. The next issue of *Kerala Kavita* contained another similar play by G. Sankara Pillai; the name of that was *Kiratam*. I started rehearsing my play *Sakshi* in Alleppey.

I was not directing. Ayyapa Panikkar's younger brother, Keshav Panikkar, who has passed away, directed it. We did that as a work in progress, not a full-fledged production. It was presented at Kottayam. There were three centres where experimental work was going on, along similar lines—drama that was conceptually different from the popular dramas. It was going on in three places—one was by Sankara Pillai at Trivandrum and Sasthamcotta, nearby places where he belonged to, one was by Srikanthan Nair, a playwright, at Kottayam and the other was at Alleppey. I was at Alleppey at that time.

Udayan: Was K.K. Panikkar the one who directed *Sakshi*?

Panikkar: I wrote the play and K.K. Panikkar directed it.

Udayan: Which year was that?

Panikkar: Early 1970s or late 60s. It was not a turning point or a very important production, but we just started our new venture.

Udayan: And how was it received?

Panikkar: It was liked by a minority, but questioned and very strongly criticised by another section also, but still there was encouragement from many discerning critics and friends. They encouraged the attempt.

We decided this theatre should be taken up seriously and those days Kumara Varma had just returned from the National School of Drama completing his studies with Ebrahim Alkazi. Finding it difficult to exist in theatre, not knowing what to do, he had started to work on the production of a play

Saketam written by C.N. Srikanthan Nair. The play was a miserable failure. The style demanded by the text was realistic whereas Varma's treatment was different. I remember my youngest brother Velayudha Panikkar who in that production was doing the *sutradhara's* role, struggling to enact his *vachika* in the *Natyadharmi* way while the script was not written in a way that demanded the traditional style of rendering. So according to the director's demand the actor rendered this in the realistic style during rehearsals. The whole *vachika* of the play was in the hightened realistic tone which was C.N.'s forte. On the previous day during rehearsals, the author wanted a change in the rendering of the *sutradhara*; he was insisting that the rendering sould be in the traditional *Chakyar* style. My brother could easily deliver this with the permission of the director and some of our friends later commented positively on this. Despite such positive aspects the author did not like the work at all! Although Varma had proved his merit at the National School of Drama (NSD), he could not keep up that prestige. I suggested that he come to Alleppey, stay with me and do this play of mine, *Sakshi*. I recall that it was I who introduced Varma for his admission in NSD. He went there with my letter. I was, at that time, Secretary of the Kerala Sangeetha Nataka Akademi. When I offered to work with him on *Sakshi*, he was thrilled; we worked with a group of actors in Alleppey. This play was successfully presented in Trivandrum. In a newspaper called *Koumudi*, the play was severely criticised by a poet who was not known to me at that time. Later we became friends. This man wrote, Panikkar has written a poem, torn it into pieces and distributed it among a few friends, who were all reading it in meaningless ways, uttering lines which did not have any impact. One of my revered teachers in my Law College, a member of the Sangeetha Nataka Akademi where I was serving at that time, said to me without reservation, 'Panikkar what nonsense you are doing! How do you call it theatre?' He was none other than C.I. Parameswaran Pillai, one of our senior and talented stage actors!

Udayan: You mean to say that he did not like your literary work?

Panikkar: He used to appreciate my poems and songs. But being an actor on the realistic stage, deeply rooted in that tradition, he could not accept my experimentation in theatre. He was very close to me and so he came to watch with the feeling that he must see a play that I am doing. According to him, it was a terrible play. 'What is this?' he said, 'Is this a play? Panikkar, you can write songs and poems and that would be all right but don't try this!' I did not feel defeated nor did I feel that I did something wrong. I did all that with conviction and courage, so I did not want to stop it. I definitely felt that it would take time for people to realise what a play actually meant.

Udayan: But what were your days like when you were in the Kerala Sangeetha Nataka Akademi? They were very important years in your life, I think.

Panikkar: Yes they were important days because I was introduced to all forms of art in the Kannur, Kasarkod and Palakkad districts. These districts were rich in traditional art forms. For the first time I was introduced to Theyyam, Porattu Natakam, Kanyarkali, then Poothamkali, so many forms…

Udayan: You were inspired by Theyyam in writing your play, *Theyyatheyyam* …

Panikkar: It was much later that I wrote that play.

Udayan: But you also brought in Theyyam in your production *Urubhangam*…

Panikkar: Yes in *Urubhangam* I introduced Duryodhana's Theyyam coming out of him as a vertical growth when he falls in the battlefield with both his thighs broken.

Udayan: What was Theyyam to you, when you saw it for the first time?

Panikkar: I saw it in its habitat, *garbhagriha,* in its place where it is traditionally performed, not lifting it from its surroundings.

Udayan: And what was the impact it had? Do you remember that?

Panikkar: It was wonderful, colourful and without knowing even what Theyyam was, or the terms used (it was only later that I understood such things), even without all those details, just the appearance, the colourful costumes, the steps and the energy it created were all immenseley attractive. I was not clear about what the particular Theyyam meant, but the whole concept was attractive. Worship of the dead is the basic motif behind Theyyam, but of course there are *devata*s, mainly dead heroes who fought for the country, for the region, or even for the village.

Udayan: Mostly it will have only the *veera rasa.*

Panikkar: *Veera rasa* and *shringara* can be seen too and certain love themes combined with *Veera* are also present. *Kativanur Viran* is one such, based on a love theme. The story behind the Theyyam is that Mannappan, a young man dies in a war held in a neighbouring place. The girl whom he loved jumps into his funeral pyre. She also dies. Mannappan is celebrated as a god by the villagers. *Veera rasa* combined with love plays a very important role in this Theyyam.

Udayan: And you were quite taken aback?

Panikkar: Yes, I was moved by the theatre potential in this art form. The most important aspect was the transformation from actor to character. It is rudimentary theatre. Theyyam utters judgments and this works successfully in the social context. Even the cases which could not be settled by the Madras High Court were settled by Theyyam. Broken marriages were mended. These were made possible because people who were involved in such cases were staunch believers in Theyyam.

Udayan: And was this because it was believed that they were speaking from beyond death?

Panikkar: Yes, that's a very interesting phenomenon. And so is the whole drama, the way the actor, after finishing his make-up, gets transformed into the spirit; the final stage is when he looks into a mirror and is convinced that he is possessed by this spirit—he throws away the mirror. At several points, the transformation takes place in different ways. From the first day onwards when he decides to go through the penance in order to perform this impersonation, he is treated as God by the believers. The people of the village respect him, they respect not the artist, but the character he is going to enact and ultimately it is in the presence of the audience, which is the last point, that the transformation is complete.

Udayan: Transformation is the quintessence of Indian theatre. Did you find a link between this theory of transformation with the tenets of the *Natyashastra*?

Panikkar: The theory of transformation is essentially connected with the theory of *Rasa* in Natyashastra, which speaks of dominant *rasa*s and *sanchari bhava*s. We will have to relate it not only to the physical, which is there of course, I mean *angika* is very much there, but so too is *vachika*. Theyyam has wonderful *vachika* elements, pronouncing judgment etc., but when I pinpoint the transformation theory to put into practice, I must say that the relationship with *Natyashastra* is essentially through its *rasa* notion. There is a book written by one of our Theyyam artistes, Kannan Peruvannan, who now has passed away. I had written the introduction for that book. He writes that when a Theyyam artiste assumes a role, people may feel that he, does not require any mental acting. But there definitely is mental acting, even in a possessed state, which means that the spirit is within the artiste. He mentally prepares to invite the spirit, to give it space, to allow the spirit to make a visitation to his innermost being, and to convey the feeling that the real person is not the one the audience sees on the outside, but the one who occupies the inner core of the Theyyam artiste. This idea is evidently expressed in the Thottams, that is. songs which describe the various Theyyams. So it is something which relates the very mundane with a higher spiritual level. The artiste may have got himself immersed in the spirit but at the same time there is a distinct separation of the personality of the actor and the personality of the spirit. All this can be experienced only by actually doing it.

Udayan: Where one ends and other begins …

Panikkar: It is difficult to explain. Even while the actor is possessed by the Theyyam, he would also speak to you about mundane affairs, but in a very special way using stylised language. Once, when a devotee presented a two rupee note to the Theyyam, he looked at it and said, 'It seems that you have gone around the world to sell this but nobody took it, so you thought you would give it to your god.' We wonder who said this… the actor or the spirit?

Udayan: This was the one form that you experienced during your tenure as the Secretary of the State Akademi. What other forms really moved you from the inside, I mean those which really shook you, apart from Theyyam? You were talking about Kudiyattam also …

Panikkar: Kudiyattam and Theyyam were important. And I had the experience of Kathakali earlier.

Udayan: What was your earliest experience of the Kudiyattam?

Panikkar: I used to attend Kudiyattam performances at Vadakkumnatha temple in Trichur. I used to sit in Kuttampalam, the temple theatre, for hours in the beginning. I wanted to know what it was. I had a very good relationship with Chachu *Chakyar*, one of the masters who lived at that time. I had a wonderful time interviewing him. The interviews were for the Akademi, I still have a copy with me. I did such interviews with many famous

Kathakali and Kudiyattam artists. I interviewed the three *Chakyars*—Mani Madhava *Chakyar*, Chachu *Chakyar* and Madhava *Chakyar*, who recently passed away. In all the three interviews, I asked them 'When do you really become Duryodhana?' Chachu *Chakyar*, the oldest, in his ninety-fourth year when I interviewed him said, 'I am playing, I am only showing you what Duryodhana is, how Duryodhana is, only as a manipulator does in the puppet show.'

Udayan: Was he saying that he doesn't become Duryodhana at all, he only shows him and that is completely different from Theyyam?

Panikkar: Yes, so these are the two aspects in art. To what extent can you relate to each of them? In Theyyam too, the question is to what extent the artiste gets immersed in the character, although he is possessed.

Udayan: Even then he was identifying the two-rupee note …

Panikkar: The basic difference between the two is that the impersonator in a ritual art like Theyyam gets possessed, whereas in Kudiyattam, the actor never identifies completely with the role.

Udayan: Coming back to Chachu *Chakyar*, did you meet him regularly?

Panikkar: No. I will tell you about one of my experiences with him. When I was the Secretary of the Akademi we had taken a decision to honour Chachu *Chakyar* with the Akademi Award. He was never considered for a national award by the Central Akademi. I went to interview him in connection with the award. When I told him about the award, the artiste asked me. 'What is it, Panikkar?' I explained that it was recognition for his work and that he should come to receive it. 'I see. When is it?' he asked. I told him the date and time, which was at six o'clock. And he said, 'Six o'clock is difficult; I have my *sandhya vandanam* at that time. I can wait only up to five o'clock, no more. And to reach Irinjalakuda from Trichur it takes much time. So let it be. I won't come.'

I somehow managed to convince him. But he added that I must promise to leave him latest by 6.30, as the puja could not be delayed more than that. I promised and he did come. I sent the vehicle and he came very early and was heard impatiently asking: 'Where is Panikkar? It is already 4.30! Who is to give this? Come on and give it now. People are waiting!'

'The Minister has to come,' I said to him.

And he said, 'Ministers don't come on time! I have to leave now.'

'Sir, please don't leave.'

Then he asked me, 'How much longer? When will the Minister come?'

I said, 'He will come at five and we will start at five.' He waited from four-thirty to five and at five o' clock, he called for me again. When I went to him he said, 'Panikkar, it is five o' clock. I have to go. I can not postpone my puja'. His performance which had earlier been fixed had been cancelled, but I wanted this award to be given to him somehow.

Finally the Minister arrived at six o'clock. I went to the *Chakyar* and said, 'Sir, the award will be given to you first twing after the Minister's speech.' And he said, 'Ask him to speak less, I want to go.'

Udayan: Otherwise he would have missed his *sandhya vandana*?

Panikkar: Yes! He was least concerned about the award. So I took him to the stage and somehow completed the award ritual and arranged for his return home. He was very good in *vaak* (speech). He was brilliant in story-telling (*kooth*). Once while he was performing *kooth* at Trichur, a Minister came to attend his performance. The *Chakyar* was describing how Hanuman was putting up a bund to cross the ocean and reach Lanka where Sita was captive in Ravana's palace. When the Minister came, he was enacting how stones were carried by the monkeys. The Minister was accompanied by many sycophants. The *Chakyar* said: 'Oh! So many people are around, very good, we were expecting you. Your own people are engaged in carrying the stones, you can also join us! Come on! Come on! Don't waste time!' Everyone laughed aloud, but the Minister was not very happy. However he could not say anything! There was another interesting occasion when E.M.Shankaran Namboodiripad was the chief minister of Kerala in 1959. This happened after the dismissal of the Communist government of Kerala, which was led by him. Namboodiripad got the opportunity to attend Chachu *Chakyar*'s performance.

Udayan: He came there after he was dismissed …

Panikkar: The then Communist Party had a scheme of collecting a five lakh fund. It was not like the present day Communist Party. Those days they were very poor. They were collecting money in buckets. E.M. Shankaran was seated not in the front, but in the third row or fourth row, but Chachu noticed E.M.S.

At that moment he was talking about Brahma, Vishnu and Maheshwara. Brahma and Vishnu's stories were all very interestingly narrated and then Maheshwara's turn came. Shankara is another name for Maheshawara. Looking at E.M.Shankaran he started saying: 'Alas O Shankara, where were you sitting? What were you doing? You were sitting in that Kailasa with all power, and with all splendour and where are you now? Now you are just going around begging, "Give us gifts, give us this, give us that!"' Everybody laughed and E.M.Shankaran also laughed aloud.

There is yet another equally interesting story. Subramanya Iyer was the district judge of the Cochin High Court. It was his habit to doze off when advocates were arguing their cases. In the Vadakkumnatha temple, Trichur, when Chachu *Chakyar* was engaged in *koothu* every evening for a term, Subramanya Iyyer would attend the show regularly. One day a few advocates went to Chachu *Chakyar* during the day and told him they had a complaint. When he asked them what it was, they said, 'Actually this Judge, Subramanya Iyer goes to sleep when we argue. Only *Chakyar* can stop it'. 'How can I stop it? I have nothing to do with your court!' said the *Chakyar*. But the advocates insisted. The *Chakyar* agreed to try.

Subramanya Iyer never missed the *Chakyar's* performance of *koothu* and Kudiyattam. As always he came and sat in the front row. The advocates too were present. *Chakyar* began his performance and he said, 'Where are the Pandavas?' Duryodhana wanted to know and he had sent messengers to all places to find out where the Pandavas were. They were living incognito. Duryodhana's plan was to find them before the end of the stipulated term, so they would again have to go to the forest. So he sent *dootas* (messengers) everywhere. One of them came to report. Chachu said, 'Oh! Where is the messenger coming from?' King Duryodhana was very happy to know that he had brought some good news regarding the Pandavas. 'Come on! Come on! What news do you have? Have you gone to all places? Have you found out where the Pandavas are?' He started asking the messenger many questions. 'Yes, yes. Go ahead. What do you say? Have you seen them? Have you found them?' Then the messenger started narrating his experience. He said, 'At last I have been able to find out where they were.' After saying this *Chakyar* looked at Subramanya Iyer and said: 'Why are you not taking any interest? You asked me to go in search of Pandavas and now you don't feel like hearing what I say. Are you sleeping? This is not fair!'

All the advocates laughed and the Judge Subramanya Iyer also did not miss the point! Chachu *Chakyar* in his interview told me that Subramanya Iyer thereafter never slept in the court.

Udayan: Wonderful! What a way to do it!

Panikkar: Such were the strong influence and freedom *Chakyar*s used to enjoy! Now all that is lost. But we had occasions to get inspiration from such great actors to discuss with them about the subtle aspects of acting. Thus you find that the *Chakyar*s way of acting was much evolved, stylised and very advanced. Theyyam is very elemental, almost rudimentary. I had the occasion to compare these two and to derive energy from both. We cannot afford to neglect such tremendous potential from tradition. There is a feeling in our country that Vedas are the property of a privileged class, the elite class; that the others have nothing to do with it, it is Brahminical. This is wrong. No one can disown Veda, saying that it belongs only to one caste. It is wrong. It is bad for the country to turn its face from knowledge—it is our collective wealth, and no single community can appropriate knowledge as its own.

Udayan: Quite so. We left our discussion where you were talking about Ayyapa Panikkar's magazine, *Kerala Kavita* and your experience of reading poems in various public places. Let us talk about those days.

Panikkar: That was the time when this particular play *Sakshi* was written. It is included in my complete work of plays. One of my friends, an important writer in Malayalam, M.K. Sanu who had written the introduction to this work, made very positive and encouraging comments about this play. He said that of all my plays he liked *Sakshi* the most. Sanu was my school mate and college mate, a little older to me. I also take pride in hearing his comments although I don't believe it!

Udayan: Believe what?

Panikkkar: That it was my best play. To say that my first work was my best work, after having gained more experience in writing many plays and directing a number of them, one would naturally feel embarrassed! Being a knowledgeable critic, Sanu made this comment with sincerity and conviction and I love and respect him for it. That is why I felt proud. I must say that *Sakshi* was the springboard from which I took a leap and if the springboard itself is taken very seriously by someone, I am happy. Yesterday I was reminiscing about *Sakshi*. In that play, you know, the *vachika* is much shortened, very little as you used in our *Uttararamacharitam*. You remember, when I demanded something from you, you gave it but you made it so brief that once I had to say that you were stingy. But it has its own merit, when something is conveyed in lesser number of words. It is stronger.

So *Sakshi* was first published in Ayappa Paniker's *Kerala Kavita* and it was tried out by K.K. Panikkar as I told you. And then later Kumara Varma came. He was invited to do this play, and he did it. That was a great success for the movement that we represented. This was not for the supporters of realistic theatre or popular theatre. That's why they were very critical of it. They criticised it very strongly, because they could not conceive, of a play taking this sort of a structure.

Udayan: Their view is quite reasonable from their stand point.

Panikkar: Yes, at that time there was an unwritten belief about the structure a play: that it is supposed to be in a particular fashion. That rule had been broken.

Udayan: In the writing of *Sakshi,* what were, in a sense, the initial influences? Were there some plays that you had more of a liking for or were there some poems that you had liked more in those days?

Panikkar: That is only with regard to the style. I can say I was influenced, or I can now recollect that those days I was reading a lot of Tagore in translation, of course the English versions.

I read some of the plays of the Abbey Theatre people, you know the Irish playwrights.

Udayan: Synge, etc?

Panikkar: Synge and W.B. Yeats much more so. His *Calvary* … and then some other playwrights like Maeterlinck and western playwrights as well. When I read these plays I was enamoured, I was influenced by the change of style which I noticed in the modern playwrights.

Udayan: I see.

Panikkar: I admit those influences, which you cannot simply neglect. So these playwrights gave me an insight into the possibilities of structuring a play.

I came to the conclusion that a play need not be only a certain fixed thing. I mean it is all given even in *Panchasandhis* and yet no *Panchasandhi* is required. Bhasa has proved this especially in his short plays. But still there are some *sandhis* which are inevitable. You know, for instance, *Garbhasandhi* should be there, conflict should be there, but ultimately by the time I was writing *Sakshi* I had had some experience from life, some experience with certain individuals in real life situations who I transformed into my characters. I can not say openly who they were. I am thankful to them; but they looked different when they got transformed.

Udayan: Yes, that is how art should take from life.

Panikkar: But outwardly in deciding the structure, I was influenced by forms which I had come across, like the rudimentary theatre form of Theyyam and art forms like Kathakali where actors do not speak, but there is singing from behind. This is a different treatment of *vachika*. In theatre it is a general practice that the actors should themselves spell out the vocal. But Kathakali does not follow this; the *vachika* is taken care of by the singers. This change can be tried out in theatre on special occasions when it would help the thrust of *bhava*. The most important thing in theatre is how you convey the *avastha* through the technique of theatre. *Avasthanukritirnatyam* is a dictum which we should follow. *Natyam* is the *anukriti* or imitation of an *avastha* (state of being). It is not the *anukriti* of a story or *anukriti* of a situation outwardly, but it is the *anukriti* (mimesis) of *avastha* which is the inward situation, the inner essence of the thing. *Avasthanukritirnatyam* gave me a feeling that a thin story line would be alright to create a play.

It depends on how you treat it. In theatre the script cannot exist alone, it has to have a potential to communicate not only with reading. Reading of course will give you an idea about the *avastha*, but the reader should also have the imagination to create the *avastha* in its visual form.

Udayan: Yes. That's true.

Panikkar: It is true for a poem. There too you cannot simply assume that the thing is over. When I requested you to give me a line in *Uttararamacharitam*, you went into a trance. You were in search of how to express it through the medium of poetry. You know the idea comes to you only through the medium of poetry where you don't speak directly.

Udayan: Yes.

Panikkar: So why is that? Because you search for a way to communicate the *avastha*. This is how the *avastha* is communicated. When you are in the process, you are not worried about whom it is communicated to. Basically, it is communicated to you yourself. The difficulty arises when you look to the audience first. Your commitment to the *avastha* gives you sufficient confidence in communication. The quality of the audience may differ from place to place. You are not expected to create for all. At times some may say that they have not understood your creation and may say that unless they understand fully what you have said they are not prepared to call you a poet or artist. Of course it is not that we are not taking into consideration the receptive end of communication, but the standard of the receptive end has also to be fixed within ourselves.

Udayan: So that's how you came to write *Sakshi*.

Panikkar: This thought was not at the conscious level in me nor as an argument while I was working on *Sakshi*.

Udayan: I know.

Panikkar: But this consideration must have been there which I could identify only later.

Udayan: You were writing poems by then and you were part of a group which was also reading poems at public places and was received very well. Why at all did you then want to write a play?

Panikkar: I'll clarify this. One feels that writing a play and writing a poem are not the same. They are different because of the presence of the actor, through whom this poetry of the play is going to be realised. Whereas when you write a poem, the poetry gets realised not through anybody, but through the words directly. I mean the written play is addressed to the audience through the actor.

Udayan: What made you actually feel that you should write a play?

Panikkar: The medium, of course, is very important. It is different as well. Both the mediums have subtle differences, but generally the dynamics of the creative art is almost the same. The other day somebody asked me whether when I wrote poetry, drama, and film songs I had to engage different creative yardsticks. I said the medium was important but the creative dynamics were the same. You cannot differentiate dynamics in ritual and dynamics in theatre, it is the same, because in ritual there is a god or deity, the impersonator or *shaman* and the *bhakta*. These three elements are replaced in theatre by three other elememts. *Avastha* takes the place of god or deity, the actor replaces the *shaman* and the *prekshaka* (audience), the *bhakta*. Poetry in theatre should necessarily reflect the imagination and justify the vocation of the character. Poetry per se represents the poet's own imagination and personality. The poetic images in theatre always open areas of enactment which would suit *Lokdharmi* or *Natyadharmi* ways of acting. In the *dharmi* way we may have to treat *dhwani* differently. It is not in the same way as you experience it in life, which pertains to the *loukik* realm. Even in Realism what is heard in *loukik* is not just there, I mean it is not as if one is taking it out as a slice of life.

Udayan: You can't.

Panikkar: Exactly, you can't. So when you use a dialogue for a mahout, you need not sacrifice the poetry. Your poetic approach in presenting the mahout's character can also be influenced by the muse. That is why I say that the dynamics created in poetry have different sources, drawing from different areas.

You cannot divest it of rhythm. In theatre when a mahout makes his entry in curvature movement (non-linear movement), his entry is supported by instrumentation, mostly percussion in Indian theatre. This rhythmic treatment is essential in the *dharmi* way and this is absent in real life. So rhythm, music, and the way you render it, all these are there. Poetry cannot exist without these components.

Udayan: True.

Panikkar: Some people may find fault, for example, with the fact that Bashir uses certain Malayalam paradigms which are very much language bound and unusual even for many Malayalis. *My Grandfather had an Elephant* is one of Bashir's most important works. In all his writings you come across his unique way of story telling which is essentially down to earth. But even Malayalis do not speak the way he used to do it. So it is very realistic, very *Lokdharmi*, and very much bound to a tradition which is plebian, but that itself creates the poetic element in Bashir. You can use the same thing by rendering it into a more refined language, you can can lift it from its existing circumstance to a higher level. This is possible only by using the poetry in theatre which is visual poetry, the poetry which is heard and seen with the mind. This is all combined in the *sahitabhava* in theatre. Now *sahitabhava* (the experience of togetherness) in poetry is the togetherness of many things like *artha, vaak,* etc. In Sanskrit we come accross '*vagartha vivasampriktou vagartha pratipattaye*', that is a poem from Kalidasa's *Raghuvamsa*. Words and meanings have to be together. But will it be enough? No! *Bhava* should be there. Will *that* be enough? No! Imagery should be there. It goes like that. There should be *dhwani* also. You asked me about poetry and theatre. When you combine these elements with certain dynamics, poetry is created. It is significant how these elements are combined, the percentage of each component and this may differ from poem to poem. *Sahitabhava* in theatre, in theatrical poetry or in visual poetry differs from the *sahitabhava* which is in poetry.

Udayan: Yes.

Panikkar: We must understand that theatre becomes a *sahitya* with much more components as *sahita bhava*.

Udayan: Yes, that's true. You're absolutely right. Till the time of writing *Sakshi,* you had not directed any play.

Panikkar: No, even after that I did not direct for a few years. I directed a play only in 1978 when Ashok Vajpeyi asked me to direct a Sanskrit play. That was the first.

Udayan: But those days you were writing plays and poetry?

Panikkar: Yes. I would try to keep away and look at the whole work including direction in a very objective way and would give inputs to the directors. No director has refused my inputs, because we were all together in probing the state of theatre.

Udayan: Who were the people at that time you are referring to? I mean in the 1960s and 70s who were the people you were working with?

Panikkar: Kumara Varma, K.K. Panikkar and in the beginning some actors also. My actors were all very good like Nedumudi Venu. Venu is now very famous. Then there was Fazil who is now a very good filmmaker, who proved his worth as a film director. He too was my actor. Of course Fazil was an exception, he never believed in our kind of theatre. He tried to believe in it by working with me but he failed. He could not believe in it, he was out and out realistic. So he went away and started his films. He is himself a playwright, and has scripted his own plays. They were all very commercially successful, but others like Kumara Varma were different. Finally, I worked with Aravindan too, a celebrated filmmaker. There was also one Alacheri Mani, my childhood friend. He was younger to me. He died recently. Alacheri directed one of my plays after *Sakshi*, which was named *Tiruvazhithan*; it is an *itihasa* (historical) a character, character with *itihasa* dimensions.

Udayan: Mani directed your play?

Panikkar: I requested him to direct it. He was an actor. He himself was acting, and he directed as well. He was, of course, receiving ideas from me, and I was helping him. I was senior and was more involved in the creative field, writing poems, etc. They used to respect me, and I gave them freedom to think themselves, but then I would suggest certain things which they would readily accept and put into practice. Those days I used to look at these things only from a distance. And then there were my own disciples. One of them, Shiva Mohan Thampi, who worked with me on instruments, was directing a play, so I helped him. I remember once he and another youngster asking me, 'Sir shall I use something not usually done by you? May I try out cyclorama?'

Udayan: They were asking your permission to use a certain dramatic technique.

Panikkar: Yes. I said, 'You could try it out, but won't it be better to avoid it? I leave it to you.' He avoided it. And then later, he was able to find out, under my guidance, better ways of trying out the death of a character. It was about a man who was always trying to die, because he felt that after him, the deluge would come. He feels that after him nothing should exist. That is selfishness. This being the man's attitude he wants to fake his death. He is that classic character Tiruvazhithan. He tries out many methods of dying. To convey this, the director wanted to show him as tied and his picture shown on cyclorama. I told him, 'Why do you want such a contrivance? You can show it directly, that would be better. But then, I leave it to you to decide'. He tried it out, and then told me, 'Sir, I tried this, but I accept your opinion on this.' In this manner, creative work went on where I was at the same time present and absent! And ultimately it was only when I came to Sanskrit drama that I started directing. Even in the beginning, I used to help Kumara Varma.

Kumara Varma was requested by the State Sangeetha Nataka Akademi, when I was its Secretary to do a play for the National Festival organised in Trichur. And this was *Bhagavadajjukiyam*, which I had translated into Malayalam. This was after Kumar's failure in *Saketa*. After that he did *Sakshi*. I invited him to do a play, which I had translated and that was the *Bhagavadajjukiyam*.

For *Bhagavadajjukiyam* I had support for research to collect all the different aspects of the play. I was doing the research, and Kumara Varma also joined me. He joined me not for his work but earlier, while I was writing the play.

Udayan: I see.

Panikkar: The largest, the biggest available *attaprakaram* and *kramadeepika*, that is the theatre manual of the *Chakyar*s, is for *Bhagavadajjukiyam*……

All the rites, the rituals after death are there because there is a statement in *Bhagavadajjukiyam* that Shandilya has been going from hermitage to hermitage in search of physical happiness … what he wanted was good food. In that connection he makes a comment that in his family there is *shraddha* (last rites). These are widely discussed in the *attaprakaram* and *kramdipika*. But the *Chakyar*s were not performing the play until recently. It was Rama *Chakyar* who had prepared this play taking inspiration from the theatre manuals. I happened to go through this manual with help from a great person, a great scholar, Narayana Pisharody.

Udayan: Pisharody, the Sanskrit scholar?

Panikkar: Yes. He had this. Later that *attaprakaram* was published by the Akademi. But this was much earlier. I came to know that he had this wonderful collection so I used to go to him, sit before him as a student.

Udayan: Before Mr Pisharody …

Panikkar: Yes and I used to take down notes. I told him I was going to do Bodhayana's *Bhagavadajjukiyam* which I translated into Malayalam.

Udayan: Pisharody also did the translation?

Panikkar: He also did it. His translation is there. But I gave my translation to Varma. And then Pisharody said, 'I am also doing it; it is very good that you have done it, I want to see it'. He came for the show, too.

Udayan: So you studied *attaprakaram* and the *kramadeepika*, etc. and went into the details of all that and you discussed it with Kumara Varma.

Panikkar: Yes, with Kumara Varma, for example, the entry of Shandilya. He was involved even from the very inception of the translation. He was also very much interested in my doing the translation. There was a Hindi translation which was also referred. Then there was the Sanskrit and we were also struggling about how to translate it into Malayalam. Both he and I were not that knowledgeable in Sanskrit. But the hurdles in understanding the original could easily be overcome. Ultimately I could do justice to the original in my translation and it was published. It was selected as a text for tenth class by Calicut University.

Udayan: The translation of *Bhagavadajjukiyam* brought you some money.

Panikkar: Yes but more than the money the work itself was gratifying! It was published with my production notes. In the second phase of its production, Gopi and Nedumudi Venu, famous actors in my theatre as well as in films had their masterpiece performances as Shandilya and Guru respectively.

Udayan: Did Kumara Varma, after coming back from NSD, have any notion of the kind of traditional ways of doing theatre in Malayalam or in Kerala? Was that kind of knowledge available? *Attaprakaram* and all that?

Panikkar: He had the tradition of seeing indigenous theatres. He belonged to a big family where tradition was respected. What he had learnt was the theatre of Alkazi—English western theatre. When he came he was full of enthusiasm, full of Alkazi and his methodology of direction which was questioned by the Trivandrum actors and even by people like Srikanthan Nair. That was why he was a failure in *Saketam*. I already told you that.

Udayan: Yes, you did.

Panikkar: His production *Saketam* was criticised severely the day after its presentation. And he used to behave like Alkazi, he would clap his hands and say 'Come on!' to all senior people and actors. He used to treat them as his students. He would say, 'Come on! Tomorrow you must all come on time! I don't want anybody to be late!' All this was not tolerated. I told this to Kumara at the request of Ayyapa Paniker. The organisers were worried. They said, 'You are very close to him, you tell him that this is not the way a director should treat the actors. He is not Alkazi. Alkazi is an institution'. That was Alkazi's method of direction, where there was one man making decisions perhaps because he was a teacher and he never wanted to consult any one. When I started working with Kumara Varma that was my turning point. A feeling of ensemble acting and direction came to me and that ultimately sprouted with all its vigour, and with all its meaning in my work with Aravindan. Now I can refer to the work with Aravindan with great creative joy.

Udayan: Yes.

Panikkar: This is what I feel about my work with Aravindan. Aravindan met with a terrible failure in producing one play of Srikanthan Nair at Kottayam. It was called *Kali. Kali* was a meaningful change in Srikanthan Nair's career, a mark of his love for indigenous theatre practices.He was a strong protagonist of this idea. He had taken it as a mission to speak on the nessesity to introduce Indianness in our theatre and he gave a nomenclature to the drama in his dream, *tanatu nataka*. Earlier to this all his plays were written in the realistic mould, except his three celebrated Ramayana plays, *Saketam, Lankalakshmi* and *Kanchana Sita*. Of the above three palys *Kanchana Sita* was made into a film by G. Arvindan. This was one of Arvinda's much discussed work all over India. The Ramayana plays worked as a significant change in C.N.'s theatre life.

Udayan: You were saying about Arvidan's failure in the production of *Saketam*?

Panikkar: *Saketam* was a play with a difference it was difficult to interpret. On the stage there is an effigy which is growing.

Udayan: So it is like Ionesco's *Amaedie*?

Panikkar: I wouldn't say it is absurd. He was definitely introducing the Indian technique of *Natyadharmi*.

Udayan: Was the failure due to lack of proper understanding of *Natyadharmi*?

Panikkar: This was not the only difficulty. On the whole this happened at a time when new sensibility in theatre just started evolving.

Udayan: You have discussed this with Srikanthan Nair?

Panikkar: Yes. When I met Srikanthan, he asked me, 'Why can't you try your hand in producing *Kali*?' I went through the full script of the play. Then the next time I met him, I said, 'I'll do it but there's one thing … I'd like to change the locale.' The locale in the play was precisely stated as a 'satra' where there were several rooms. In one room resided Vilasini the heroine, and in other rooms there were the other characters in front of which there was the effigy. I told him that I would not take this precise naming or rather direction of the locale 'satra' and that I would like this to happen nowhere or rather anywhere. He heard me out but did not allow that. He said, 'No, Panikkar, you have to stick to what I have written.' This was a major point of difference about the autonomy of the playwright and the autonomy of the director when these two ideas come at loggerheads. This opened up a very serious discussion. You see C.N. Srikanthan Nair never allowed any change in his script. Just see what we are doing with the original of *Uttararamacharitam*!

Udayan: He couldn't have imagined it?

Panikkar: He could not imagine such a thing and yet his *Kanchana Sita* was allowed to be produced as a film by Aravindan. And it was fortunate for Aravindan and for Srikanthan Nair that *Kanchana Sita,* the film, was released only after Srikanthan Nair passed away. I am sure he would not have tolerated this.

Udayan: Was there so much deviation?

Panikkar: Aravindan had taken only twenty sentences from the whole play!

Udayan: That's all?

Panikkar: Yes. Only twenty sentences. He wrote somewhere that Sita is *prakriti*. This was enough for Aravindan. And even that sentence was not taken as it was, it was shown. Wherever there was a reference to Sita, he would immediately take the camera to the wide and vivacious nature, the rich foliage and the wonderful dance movement of nature. *Kanchana Sita* was terribly criticised. You know I remember we were all supporters of that film; I was in full support of *Kanchana Sita*. C. Achutha Menon, the well known Communist leader and former Chief Minister strongly criticised the film. He was an important thinker and writer.

Menon was thinking in the right way, also on many matters, except this! He read a lot of books and wrote not only on Marxism but on many other subjects. Naturally, he wrote on art also. He strongly criticised Aravindan and the point he raised was—and this point I had to very strongly rebut—why Aravindan has not done justice to Srikanthan Nair's play. It was as if he was arguing on behalf of Srikanthan Nair himself.

Udayan: And Srikanthan Nair was not there …

Panikkar: He was not there. He wrote: why did he show this outer *prakriti* (nature) to represent Sita? It seems he has not understood about inner *prakriti,* outer *prakriti* cannot represent the inner *prakriti.* Then he quoted Damodaran, another Communist, as saying that outer *prakriti* and inner *prakriti* need not be the same and all that. I wrote against this in the same magazine in which that article was published.

Udayan: Which magazine?

Panikar: *Janayuga,* a Communist magazine. I wrote in response that I happened to see this article and I respect Mr Menon as a writer, but since he has quoted K. Damodaran, I would like to quote another source which amply justifies Aravindan's position. And I then quoted Sir John Woodroffe. Woodroffe was not an Indian, but he is someone who has gone deep into the Tantrik tradition of India and he says that outer *prakriti* is nothing but inner *prakriti,* the outer and the inner structure should necessarily coincide. Otherwise what else is *prakriti*? I wrote extensively quoting from Woodruffe. And then Menon wrote another reply to that. And then I wrote that I did not wish to continue this argument. But he wrote again, saying that Woodroffe need not be correct, who was Woodroffe after all?

Udayan: But tell me one thing. With Srikanthan Nair, this debate of yours about the relationship of the theatre director and the playwright came to the central stage. And with the making of *Kanchana Sita* it was further dramatised but as I understand, that debate was still continuing in your mind?

Panikkar: This debate was there in my mind, but it was not taken as a regular debate in the circles of theatre, because Srikanthan Nair was respected by all and he was one with us. He was writing about me, in praise of my *Daivathar,* etc. And he was part of our movement. So this matter was not taken seriously. Except for holding the sensitivity of the written word and that too in his own text, C.N. was exemplary in all that he preached and achieved. Inspite of the wordy exuberance, his Ramayana trilogy made a lasting impression in Malyalam theatre and literature. My relationship with him was cordial and he supported my theatre sincerely and eloquently. His dream about the theatre of roots remained unrealised; but as I would often say, his best plays, according to his own conviction remain yet to be written. He had two themes nurtured in his mind and probably designed well also about which he once referred in our conversation. One of these, named *Chirukandan Tira,* had an autobiographical undertone. As the name suggests the story line was fully charged with the energy that he had mustered from an art like Theyyam. The other plot was about a downtrodden worker in the agricultural field.

Udayan: The reason for Aravindan's failure in the production of *Kali* is not discussed.

Panikkar: I have not seen the production, so I am not in a position to explain this. But I presume he failed in the the *Saketam* production because he tried to strictly follow what was written.

Udayan: He might have tried to be totally faithful to the script.

Panikkar: Maybe. I did not even discuss this with Aravindan. But even then I wanted Aravindan to do my play. I knew that Aravindan was not at all vocal. He never used to argue as to why he did certain things in his film. In filmmaking, he was like Alkazi; his was a one man show. He would decide everything, because he was in a possessed state when he directed films. I saw that in a film which was scripted by me which he was doing. Even I could not go and speak to him because he was so deeply engrossed in his work. He was maintaining his autonomy as a director and if anybody asked him why something was so, he would get upset, because he didn't care to explain. That was also one of the reasons, to be very frank, that I loved him. We were together, but he could not argue his position and convince the actor. He could not face the situation of an argument.

Udayan: But when he was directing a play he was somebody else.

Panikkar: He was completely different. That is what I want to say. I am sure he might have done *Kali* mechanically as a director under the supervision of Srikanthan Nair. Probably that was the reason whyhe failed. But my presence as a playwright in a creative endeavour was such that I never used to interfere with the director. I would encourage him. And if at all there was anything to be stated or discussed, at the end of the day we would talk. I would not directly interfere at all, because I did not want to thrust my autonomy on others. In fact I was very much there in their minds, I was very much influencing them without interfering.

Udayan: What was the play that Aravindan was doing?

Panikkar: *Avanavan Kadamba.* It took 90 days but we will come to that later. In filmmaking there was probably only one actor who created problems for Aravindan and that was Gopi. In Chidambaram when he was acting, Gopi would ask, 'Why should I show that Aravindan? Tell me?' Arvindan would reply, 'No, no Gopi you just show that.' And Gopi would say, 'But I want to know from the director what you mean by it'. Then Gopi would be sympathetic to Aravindan's helplessness and try to argue for Aravindan.

Udayan: Let me tell you something. Hitchcock was once asked what actors were to him. And he said: They are cattle. They are actually cattle in cinema! Theatre is a different thing. In cinema, the camera is the medium and the sound recorder.

Panikkar: Aravindan knew all the subtleties by virtue of his talent. He was different from Adoor Gopalakrishnan. Both of them were important filmmakers with their own methods. Aravindan never followed any directorial notes or diagrams. It was all spontaneous. Gopalakrishnan, as far as I know, was very meticulous in doing his homework. He had a say in the fixing of the frame and every such thing that was important. Gopalakrishnan was more concerned with the perfection of the frame and all that. He was brilliant. Arvindan's flight of imagination was the brilliant thing about him.

Udayan: That's true.

Panikkar: Both are different and both are great. So with Aravindan, I kept away, I decided not to interfere even in the script written by me. I never used to interfere. Even if I had a feeling that this was my play and that it was not going the way I imagined it, I still would not interfere.

Udayan: You were talking about *Avanavan Kadamba*.

Panikkar: Aravindan was roped in to do this play in spite of the fact that Aravindan's style of working was not very well known to me. Earlier of course, he had taken *Kanchana Sita*, which I liked. My elder brother Keshav Panikkar was acting as Valmiki. He told me how he did his casting. It was a very peculiar way of casting; he had a wonderful deviation from other people in casting itself. He cast Lambadas (tribals near Vijayawada) marked by small pox as Rama and Lakshmana. When some one asked him, Why small pox marks? he replied, 'Why can't Lakshmana also have this disease? And why should Rama look like a prince, a romantic hero of the Ravi Varma painting?' So it was the repudiation of the existing concept of the calendar heroes. Aravindan did that. That was really a revolution. It opened up a very strong, very reasonable argument and threw up questions about how and why heroes should look a certain way. It was there, you know, the concept about heroes itself had changed in films. Otherwise Venu and Gopi, who were my actors, could never have come in films unless this change had worked in the minds of the audience as well as creators of films. Even now this calendar hero concept is still there in the commercial films. It has not really changed.

Udayan: You were saying the casting was revolutionised by Arvindan.

Panikkar: I was aware of only this thing about Aravindan. That means only the result, only the product was seen. I could gauge through the product of what Aravindan did, his contribution. So when he came to Trivandrum and I too shifted my residence from Alleppey to Trivandrum in 1974, I had come with a rough script of *Avanavan Kadamba* with me. After reaching there I met him. I had some friends there earlier, because I used to come there and join them in Srikanthan Nair's and Sankara Pillai's productions and then there was *Kerala Kavita*. *Kerala Kavita* was a common ground and it created a good background. So I got some friends who were ready to work with me on my script. Natarajan came who was a very good manager. He was good at management in theatre as well as acting and was a sensible man. He and I jointly worked and I told Natarajan, 'We should rope in Arvindan. I have come to know that he has failed at Kottayam in his theatre production of Srikanthan Nair's *Kali* and yet we should get him to do this play.' I had Venu with me in Alleppey for whom I had arranged a job in Bal Bhavan. But because I shifted to Trivandrum, I wanted to shift him to Trivandrum to work with us. He finally came down and stayed with me. So then, when we started the work of our *Avanavan Kadamba,* I met Aravindan with Natrajan and met Gopi. Gopi was already my friend. He started coming to me while I was at Alleppey. He was enamoured by my theatre. He very much wanted to work in my plays. Those days he was with Sankara Pillai and he openly told him that he wanted to come to my theatre. He said, 'I want to work with Panikkar Chettan.' And he came to me. When he came, I made this offer to him, 'Stay with us at Alleppey and do this (Velichaped) shaman's role in *Daivathar.*' It was a landmark production. After doing *Sakshi* and *Tiruvazhithan* and some other plays when we reached *Daivathar,* it turned out to be a different experience.

Udayan: How beautifully people move and create new possibilities … I am talking about Gopi.

Panikkar: And when I shifted my residence to Trivandrum with the *Avanvan Kadamba* script partly done, I wanted all my friends to join me. Venu got a job in a local magazine as a representative; he had to write for it. He used to write well, he had to take and publish interviews. Venu started staying in Trivandrum with Paramshivam, a dancer. He started classes in dance, in Bharatnatyam, but I wanted him to switch to Mohiniyattam because I knew that Bharatnatyam had been thrust upon him. It was not in his psyche. Actually he belonged to a family of Thullal artistes. And so I wanted him to unlearn whatever he had learnt in Bharatanatyam for the purpose of working in Mohiniyattam.

Udayan: Thullal, in which Paramashivam was an expert, is a very different dance form from Bharatnatyam which I presume goes well with Mohiniyattam?

Panikkar: Yes, I could use his services for Mohiniyattam. So I wanted him to do this work and I had already started my work in Mohiniyattam in those days. I found Paramshivam to be a very interesting person, a guru who could teach, who could switch to Mohiniyattam because he knew the basics of this dance form through his Thullal background. His place became a meeting ground for all of us. He had a home and a small thatched shed for dancing. We used to meet there but then that was not enough for us to do the rehearsals. Venu was staying there which was helpful for us to assemble for rehearsals in spite of the insufficieny of space. We started rehearsals in earnest in 1975 with Aravindan and Gopi. Aravindan was doing the direction. Fortunately we got a space at Swathi Thirunaal's Ammaveedu, a place of historical value, where his compositions in Mohiniyattam were practised. It was a palace, given by Swathi Thirunaal to his wife, who was a Mohiniyattam dancer and therefore it came to be called Ammaveedu. Ammaveedu was usually where the queen stayed. It had a beautiful quadrangle, an open space and also an inner space which was good only for dancing. The outer space was best suited for our rehearsals. We rehearsed for ninety days to prepare the play *Avanavan Kadamba.* And many people used to come for rehearsals. Aravindan had many friends who visited regularly. And all these people—from the film industry and other art lovers—would come to Trivandrum from all over, and they would come to the rehearsals if they were staying on. In fact Aravindan was free at that time after finishing his film *Kanchana Sita*. He had only to attend to his duties in the Rubber Board where he worked as an officer. He was fully engaged in these rehearsals and through the rehearsals we were trying to inculcate in the actors a sense of freedom using the autonomy of each component in theatre. This was very alien to Aravindan's way of working in cinema. What he lost in cinema, he gained in theatre: his own freedom. Lots of people used to come and watch the rehearsals everyday and a few youngsters made a veritable celebration out of them singing the songs from the production. People like Ayyapa Paniker were, of course, with us in all our endeavours. It was total enjoyment and creativity. Aravindan was not an autocratic director and suggestions from any quarters were tolerated, but he had the final say. While others implicitly obeyed Aravindan's directions, Gopi used to question him on the whys and hows of acting. The others would not dare. But Aravindan was not very vocal in helping Gopi sort out his problems. Slowly, all of us became friends and everyone felt approachable. All that had resulted from ninety days of rehearsals. We put up the show in a school compound, in the open air, which was a vast space, because the play demanded such a space. Local theatre people, the so called realistic theatre people attended. They had their own reservations. I still remember that on the first day of the show we were praying to Ganapati that no rain would come. Three coconuts were broken at the Ganapati temple, one in my name, one in Aravindan's name and one in the Monger Natarajan's (the manager's) name to ward off rain. And while coming back after breaking coconuts, one close relative of mine, who was a very good actor, said: 'It seems it may rain.' Natarajan got offended and said: 'What are you saying? It won't rain. We have all done everything required, and there is nothing to worry about.' It finally did not rain, but it did drizzle a little. In the case of all other productions, it would always rain, and people would wait until the rain receded and wait till the whole premises was cleaned before the play resumed. Even now this is the case. On my seventieth birthday the same play was done a second time after a long gap. Gopi could not act in it because by then he had had the paralytic stroke. But Venu was there and so was the rain. We did it again on my eightieth birthday. This play has grown with time …

Udayan: When the play was done for the first time, what was the reaction of the people?

Panikkar: It was wonderful. It was received with a standing ovation by the audience, and that was significant for a play which was against the taste of the so-called realistic theatre lovers. They too had to admit its worth, not officially, but through their actions. And it was accepted wholeheartedly by many. There were a lot of things discussed about this play. There was a wonderful discussion on the play and the production in Malyalam, which has not yet been translated into any other language. The discussion on one of my plays, *Ottayam,* has been translated into English by my son Harikrishnan. There are other very extensive discussions with many participants, scholars and theatre practitioners like Ayyapa Paniker, Sankara Pillai, C.N. Srikanthan Nair, etc. It was published along with the plays *Avanavan Kadamba, Daivathar* and *Ottayan.*

Udayan: What was the main thrust of these discussions?

Panikkar: Every dimension of theatre was discussed starting from the script. For example Srikanthan Nair was asked to speak on the topic of whether the autonomy of the playwright should prevail in the production of the play. This was a significant point that was extensively discussed and debated.

Udayan: And didn't C. N. Srikanthan Nair change even then?

Panikkar: Srikanthan Nair did not budge. He remained where he was.

Udayan: These discussions should be translated.

Panikkar: Ayyapa Paniker took the initiative in organising all these discussions on the performance of plays.

Udayan: Were they held together?

Panikkar: No, they took place at different times. He wanted this one particularly and he even insisted that C.N. should be there. He took the upper hand in the first discussion on *Daivathar* also. He was very much enamoured by *Daivathar.*

Udayan: We were discussing G. Aravindan's contribution and his style of working and you said that he initially failed with his first play very miserably and then you offered him your play.

Panikkar: Yes I offered him *Avanavan Kadamba.* And he was very happy and told me, 'If Panikkar Chettan is with me, I have the confidence, and I said, 'I will be behind you, I have never directed any play, but I have given enough material to all those who have directed my plays, similarly I will be there with you.' Arvindan was an ardent lover of music, but he did not create music for his films. It was Hariprasad Chaurasia who did the music for his film, *Pokkuveyil* ('Twilight'). And for his other films also, music directors were engaged. In this case, I mean for *Avanvan Kadamba,* I did all the songs and music. When I was writing the play the tunes for its songs also came to my mind. It is another aspect of writing: those writers who can inter relate *vaak* (language) with music are called *vaggeyakaras*.

Udayan: I think these writers have the capability of imagining music in *vaak* (language). And I am aware you definitely are one such *vaggeyakara.*

Panikkar: I don't think so! But one should also be capable of visualising the word with its musical potential, especially when one is engaged in theatre because theatre is a space-time continuum. Language, music and the visual, all three go hand in hand. They should be treated holistically. For *Uttararamacharitam* whenever you write your couplets and your single lines and give them to me, I immediately sing them. One is able to feel the music in the words. You know, the words have an outer and an inner music. And when suddenly you catch both, it is magical, because even if the meaning of the words is not open to you, no meaning is known to you of the words of whichever language, from the sound of words you do get the thread of the tune. If you know the meaning along with the formation of the tune, then you catch both the inner and the outer music of the *Vaak* (language). *Vaak* and *geya* (music) need to be combined with the visual. This is essential for theatre and this of course was discussed with Aravindan while discussing with him the theme of the play during rehearsals and even in the pre-rehearsal period. Aravindan never asked anything, he only heard and accepted everything. But while carrying it out, he maintained his personal views and judgement.

Udayan: We digress here slightly. I just want to ask you from where this *vaggeyakara* in your case might have come? In other words, what are the sources of the *vaggeyakara* in you?

Panikkar: Let me humbly submit that I don't deserve that big qualification. Shall I say, I have discovered myself in this regard; whenever I come to Kavalam, the village where we are now, I discover this. Earlier, when I was here, I used to go to the fields and I think that I had gathered this *vaggeyakara* spirit only from our workers in the paddy fields. The harvest here is done to the accompaniment of music. During the harvesting of an area, they (harvesters) move backwards in a line while cutting the crops. It looks beautiful, very interesting to see. They come backward with the sickle cutting and then tying and keeping it aside. When they did this movement in groups, they sang. Singing was essential for them. Similarly singing was essential for measuring out paddy in large quantities, there were hills, small heaps of paddy and they would start measuring from one corner of it. One man would put paddy into the *paraa*, a standard measuring pot.

There is an iron stick, with which they let out the paddy heaped above the iron bridge attached to its mouth. Three such measures of paddy are put into a bigger *kutta* (basket) that is made of bamboo splinters, strong enough for three such *paraas*.

So when he starts putting the paddy in the basket, the timing is such that he starts singing the word 'onne' or 'one'. This singing would go on until this measuring in the *paraa* was over and the measured paddy was put into that bigger basket. Then he would sing 'rande', or 'two'. Then he goes on with the music till he reaches 'moonne', or 'three'. This way he goes on until the count reaches hundred. At that point he would sing 'dharana' which means, 'Keep in mind (that I have reached hundred).' This way the person who measured would communicate the idea to the person overseeing the whole thing that is, to the representative or the owner to have 'dharana' (knowledge) about the fact that he has covered one hundred *paraas*. And then this man would take a stalk of coconut leaf and bend it to mark it.

Udayan: Which means hundred *paraas* of paddy is measured?

Panikkar: Yes. And then he would go to the next hundred. These cultivation activities were all supported by music. Without music these activities would be tiresome and boring. This is the way music comes into the practical aspects of life. Like when you push the cart, you tend to sing. There is air thrust in the production of sound.

Udayan: This way the body gets energised.

Panikkar: Yes. This was there in every activity in the village. You could hear the music from the *vallam* (the boat) from which people were selling fish. They would call people to come out to purchase fish. They would call meen which means fish. This word *meen* was, in a way, sung. At night when you go in a *vallam*, on a village stream and you come across a bend you would call out '*vallam* ….' Which means this: 'Here comes the *vallam*, take care, come by the left'. So everything in village was conveyed through music.

Udayan: You were internalising all that, maybe, in your childhood.

Panikkar: Yes, communication of signals was there; life itself was lived like that. Even in the household, the communication by the old women was like the practice of the theory of suggestion. Suggestion is what Anandwardhan calls *dhwani.* In the household the old woman would tell the daughter or granddaughter something like *pashune kettu* (tie the cow), or 'bring the clothes from outside'. Such sentences were spoken to communicate some other meaning as well. In the above cases it meant that it was getting dark. When something was said it often meant some thing else. It could contain some other meaning also. This is *dhwani.* So *dhwani* and the use of language, using time and space by making the signal, all these happen in life, especially in rural or agrarian life. Then these are raw; raw because they are applied without any formal learning. It comes naturally. When we go to the temple after harvesting we go with the first ear of corn cut in the harvest as an offering to the deity of the village temple.

Every Kuttanad village is like that and from then on the activities of the village shift from the fields to the temple, immediately after the harvest. Harvest itself is an *utsav* (festival). In the temple *utsav* there is the *utsav* Bali, ritual offerings to the associates of the main deity, which is the most important ritual connected with the festival. It is attended by men and women with great devotion. My mother used to take us—it was mandatory to attend this ritual—but we were more interested in seeing art forms or following the elephant. *Utsav* Bali takes place within the inner chamber of the temple. The temple would be closed and there would be offerings of food to the *bhutagana*s which was done to the accompaniment of rhythm on percussion instruments.

Udayan: Yes, there are stones there, around the parikrama, I saw them, and I could not understand why they were there …

Panikkar: They are all *bhutagana*s (spirits) and they are offered holy water and rice and they would take a round of the temple, first inner and then outer, after finishing the inner *parikrama*, they would come out and take the outer *parikrama.*

Udayan: And *bhutaganas* are supposed to be inside and outside also?

Panikkar: Outside the temple is present the major sacrificial stone *ballikallu.* It is a big stone placed in front of the temple.

Udayan: Is it a major spirit?

Panikkar: A major sacrificial stone is just in front of the flagstaff and inside the front door that opens to the inner chamber.

Udayan: The big stone?

Panikkar: Yes, the big one, and little stones are around it. Rice and water are offered. During the offering of the sacrificial food and water, the percussionist follows the *poojari* (priest). While the *poojari* does the offering, at particular point, he takes water and sprinkles it. There is a special grass, the bunch of which is used for these rituals, called *darbha* grass, used for sprinkling water on the stones for all this, and there is an assitant to help the *poojari.*

Udayan: There is one question that I wanted to ask you. You were saying that when he is offering the sacrificial food, the percussionist does something following him. What's his function?

Panikkar: He interprets or supports what the *tantri* does. He knows this works as the signalling for the ceremony. It's inter-related.

Udayan: Are you trying to say that the food offering ceremony is accompanied by the percussionist with a meaning?

Panikkar: Yes, the offering is accompanied by the percussionist and whenever there is a change required by the *poojari* in his action, he shows it in a particular way, by raising the *darbha* grass as an indication.

Udayan: Which means that the *poojari* makes a certain kind of signal…?

Panikkar: Yes. Then the percussionist takes this signal and changes the rhythm. I have discussed all this with the *poojari* at length. The indication for the change over is made by the movements of the grass. This signalling was incorporated by the *Chakyar*s in Kudiyattam. They call it *kouttuvilakkuka.* It is a composite word, made of two parts: *kottu* which means playing and *vilakku* which means stop. Till the percussion begins on the *mizhavu* the *vachika* (enunciation of the text) cannot be done. In the *Natyashastra* it is suggested that only when the *Bhandavadya* stops, the *vachika* comes, not while it goes on. This is what *kottuvilakkuka* means in Kudiyattam. The actor signals to stop playing the *mizhavu* and this is officially done for entering into the next passage of *vachika*.

This particular movement has come from nowhere but the ritual. The technical word for the grass is *koorcham*. The *Chakyar*s do this the same way in Kudiyattam and stop the percussion to take to the *vachika* acting.

Udayan: That becomes the signal for the entry into the text …

Panikkar: Yes, and then the *vachika* begins. This is the inter-relationship of the visual and the auditory parts. Here they combine very well for proceeding with the text.

Udayan: This was a nice journey that we had, going into temple with the *tantri* and then trying to understand the relationship of theatrical movements with ritualistic procedures, but in the process we have digressed a lot from what you were saying about G. Aravindan. You were talking about Aravindan in relation to theatre music.

Panikkar: He was good in music. He would even ask me to change the music when he felt uncomfortable with a tune.

Udayan: Oh, that was all there. But he couldn't do the music.

Panikkar: He had done the music in a film that was Shaji Karun's *Piravi*. Ours was a united work in which togetherness was there. Aravindan was very sharp. His understanding about the script, his worries about how to go with the script, they were all very much there. But inner confidence was also there. He would try to solve issues by himself and then one could see it on his face. But then, he would not express it. Sometimes, I would go to his rescue. I would understand what he meant, what he was struggling with.

Udayan: Yes.

Panikkar: And then Gopi would interfere. Gopi was very free. Even Venu was not so free. He would not take that liberty. Gopi's approach was different. His interference was such that if he decided something, he would do it. He joined the BJP officially. Many actors, many of his friends really wondered why Gopi did that. But he did not care. His decision was his own, for which he was not liked by some. But even then, he was respected by all. In his relation with Arvindan, Gopi used to interfere while working in films, as well as in theatre. In theatre, his interference was soft; I was the only person with whom Gopi had really been soft. He always used to put his ideas respectfully to me; he would never enforce them, because I could easily convince him.

Udayan: In *Avanavan Kadamba* while Aravindan was doing it, did he make some changes in it or not?

Panikkar: Yes. I did make changes, when the play was being rehearsed. For example, there was one character, Mantri Makan, meaning son of the Minister. This was changed, I was not happy with a character being so blatantly named. I wanted to change that. A relative of mine, a prominent actor Sukumaran Nair, whom I used to call Sukumaran Chettan, used to attend the rehearsals of *Avanavan Kadamba*. He cautioned me against this and advised that I should change this but his reason was not the one I had thought of. It was the days of Emergency and this could have a reference to…

Udayan: Some particular Minister?

Panikkar: No, to Indira Gandhi's son …

Udayan: Ah! That was Sanjay Gandhi's time!

Panikkar: So he felt that it would be better to change it but then I was reluctant, precisely because of that. Then we—Gopi, Aravindan, Venu and I—thought of finding better names. I gave the name Vadivellavan to this character. Gopi was the one taking that role. A few more similar changes were made and we also added some lines as we did to the *Uttararamacharitam*, as it was demanded by Aravindan. And then I used to create songs. Once I would create a song, then they'd all sing together and then those who'd come to watch the rehearsal like Bharatan, the filmmaker, would also enjoy them. These songs were very popular amongst a group of people.

Udayan: They became popular even while the rehearsals were going on?

Panikkar: These songs were loved by many.

Udayan: You did the same play at many places …

Panikkar: It was presented in Kerala and in Delhi. It was a Malayalam play and was received very well here. And it was selected as text book by the university. It was first produced in 1975. Even after 35 years, it is still being done.

Udayan: And you did the same play with the repertory of Bharat Bhavan.

Panikkar: Bharatratna Bhargava translated the play into Hindi and I directed it.

Udayan: Did you make any changes from the way the play was done by Arvindan?

Panikkar: Yes, I did make some changes, because the language demanded it. I was not sure about the language quality, but still I felt that changes needed to be done. I made Bhargavaji make changes to my satisfaction.

Udayan: I mean, did you also change the way the play was being done?

Panikkar: I made slight changes, but interpretation-wise, there was practically no change. Even then, it was not exactly as Aravindan did it. It is not possible to avoid making slight changes because a play grows with each production.

Udayan: Yes, that is also how I feel.

Panikkar: I tried to keep my sub-text to that version. I did not want to disturb that quality, which was established by Aravindan's directorial style, because in his production my contribution was also there. It had contributions from all of us. It was the result of group work, ensemble acting, because everybody contributed and felt that the play was his own; that shared feeling was there. I didn't want to disturb that. If I wanted to do it differently, I could have done so, but that would have been a forced thing. I could do it with other plays. But this play, I thought should remain in the original style, because in this play the form and content are quite interrelated. It is only with great difficulty that one could separate them and then think in a different style. Somebody else might be able to do it differently. Not me, because I was part and parcel of the whole process of creation, of Arvindan's production.

Udayan: In this play and in all your plays as well, the practice of rhythm is very central. I mean, in you the rhythm almost flows, one rhythm after the other, like what you were saying about the temple. Where did you learn such variety of rhythms, were there some particular teachers you went to and learnt from, or you just imbibed them from your surroundings?

Panikkar: One should not say that one had no guru. Art cannot be learnt just like that. There has to be a guru. In my case, my own mother was my guru. She was not a musician, but she got me enthused with her native folk leaning. She used to do Thiruvatira. My father has also contributed very much to the sense of rhythm in my life. Being a member of the matrilineal family, everything related to the mundane affairs were managed by the *karanavar* of the matriarchal family (manager) who was the uncle. My father had taken up a very significant responsibility in moulding his character on a highly spiritual level, introducing all of us children to the spiritual texts like the *Bhagavad Gita, Bhagavatam*, etc. We had music lessons also. So they were my first gurus. My uncles, parents and my elder brothers Kesava Panikkar and Ramakrishna Panikkar were all my gurus. I had many gurus in my village life. There was a guru belonging to the community of *Kaniyan*s, you know the community of *jyotishi*s or astrologers. One great *Kaniyan* was my guru in Sanskrit. His name was Govinda Ganakan. I learnt *Sriramodantam* and such *kavya*s during my childhood days itself from this guru. And then there was another guru of music who lived with us. We used to call him Bhagavatar sir. His name was Parameswaran Pillai. He taught my wife Sharadamani, my youngest brother Velayudha Panikkar, my sons Hari and Sree, my brother's son Padmanabhan, my sister Saraswathy—all of us. He was our family. He was my first guru in music. My father was also learning under him. My eldest brother was also my guru, who taught me *mridangam*. This learning process helped to perfect my rhythmic sense. I learned rhythm received from ordinary life activities in our village, from agriculture and from other sources. Lessons in *sahitya* as well as music, all learned in a much unstructured fashion. I was not taking music lessons or lessons in literature from any one. Often I used to sing and my brother would play the *mridangam* and one of my cousins, my wife's eldest brother Ramachandran Nair whom I called Ramachandran *machoon* (cousin), would play the violin. They were all non-professionals, but my brother had almost reached a professional level.

Udayan: What was it that you were saying about your mother?

Panikkar: My mother organised Thiruvatira in different family homes: in Ayyapa Paniker's home for a season, in our own house for another season of Thiruvatira. Thiruvatira is a women's festival. And a few days ahead of the festival, they would start practising. And I would play the *mridangam,* which usually was not an accompaniment for the Thiruvatira. Thiruvatira is known by the name *Kaikottikkali* in north Kerala. *Kali* means play, *kaikotti* is clapping the hands and they danced in a circle. You know, this was the folk forerunner to Mohiniyattam. My mother was very good at Thiruvatira. It is a free style dance. So grandmother used to say to younger girls, 'Why don't you join?' And if someone said, 'Grandma, I don't know how to dance it' she would say, 'What is there to know? You only have to join in!' And then they would join and learn. They'd do as the others did. And then they would go around saying, 'See! Now I know this art!'

Udayan: And you would play.

Panikkar: No. I used to play a percussion to encourage them. My mother used to call me to Ayyapa Paniker's home. I was quite young. My brother did not live in the Kavalam village. He was in Alleppey. But I was bound to the village. And these are my impressions of my village life. These were all routine here in Kavalam. Art was a part of our life. It was through life that the soul of art would come to you and influence you, and get you absorbed.

Udayan: That is true. You were also talking about your *Daivattar* yesterday, the way it was written and the way it was done ...

Panikkar: Many of the characters in *Daivathar* are from the village life. There are four to five important characters in *Daivathar*, like Mannathi who is the village washerwoman. On the whole it has a village setting. There's Kaniyan, the astrologer ... The astrologer's character was performed by Venu. You could still find astrologers but you don't find them everywhere anymore. That was a society which was different and was work-oriented...

Udayan: Functional ...

Panikkar: Yes, functional. The art forms were also related with such functions. This probably was inherited from the earlier Dravidian *thina* culture where each *thina* had its work orientation based on the geography of the region, the *thinas* were *mullai* (forest), *kurinchi* (hills), *palai* (desert), *neytal* (sea shore) and *marutam* (plains). Apart from this division, the land was mainly divided into the main units—the sea shore and the high land. There is belief that the sea shore was safeguarded by Amman and high land by Ayyan. There are many art forms connected with their worship. There are many lively performance forms dedicated to Amman. One such is *Padayani*.

Udayan: *Padayani?*

Panikkar: *Padayani* is a common man's art-form, in which all the village community participates, making their contributions. It is an ensemble of ritualistic dance, in which many spirits make their entry and perform their vivacious dance to the accompaniment of lively percussion on an instrument called *tappu*. Bhairavi, Kalan, Sundara Yakshi, Sukumara Yakshi are some of the spirits. Kalan, one of the main spirits represents time. Yama, the god of death, chases the epic character Markandeya who is destined to die at the young age of sixteen. He takes refuge at the feet of Lord Shiva who kills the god of death and saves his devotee. He represents the Great Time, the god of death, the destroyer of time or the incarnation of the Great Time. The death of Smaller Time or Yama creates problem for all living beings. Life comes to a standstill—a very interesting theme for all times.

Udayan: You were saying that it is a popular art in which many communities participate.

Panikkar: Yes, the village communities belonging to different vocations are engaged in the preparation and organisation of the art. For instance, Mannathi brings the fresh cloth to be worn by the performers; the Mannan gets the cloth, etc. I hence introduced the character Mannathi in my play *Daivathar*. Mannathi would bring the cloth. Mannathi's (or Mannan's) work was to clean dirty clothes. She would wash and make them spotless white. Making her entry in *Daivathar*, my Mannathi character says:

> *Here comes Mannathi, I am born low*
> *I collect the dirty clothes of the household*
> *And make a bundle of them*
> *I come before the village audience*
> *To pay my respects to you.*

That's how she enters. When she enters, the Kaniyan or the astrologer, who is already there in front of the temple, is seen. Now after her entry, she looks around and finds a man sitting in the front row. She goes to him and says, 'Oh, *Tamburan!*' A person higher in social status is called *Tambura* by the lower classes. So she says, '*Tamburan*, you've put on a very good dress. Oh! It is very white! And you look very smart! Do you know who has whitened this? Who has done this washing? Who has brought this freshness to your dress? Do you know that? It is I, this Mannathi! And you wear this and feel proud of your dress.' Let me rinse your mind. Then from behind the stage, Kalankaniyan says, 'Mannathi! Don't pick up quarrels with him. They're all big people! Come back! Come back!'

Udayan: Who is Kalankaniyan? Please explain further.

Panikkar: Kalankaniyan is a *jyotishi*. He's the one who controls every other character through his rhythm. He has the *udukku,* a small rhythm instrument. And whenever a character transgresses his limits, he will give a *muthaippu.* *Muthaippu* means *tihai* (three cycles of beats indicating the completion of a rhythm). Once that is played, the character cannot move. Even to the character Shaktan, one with immense physical strength, Kalan would give a *muthaippu.* Then there is Buddhan, the intellectual. Buddhan just sits in the temple, always meditating. He doesn't speak anything. And there is Komali, the jester. All these are characters of *Daivathar.*

Next is the Velichapad, a role which Gopi did. Gopi came as a guest to perform this role. Velichapad is the oracle of the temple. In the beginning, all characters enter the temple premises and then suddenly the oracle appears, possessed. Assuming the role of the goddess Manakkattam, he curses the village. The curse is very significant. 'The whole village with all its cultivable land should go dry this year, without water, without getting a drop of water and all sorts of maladies will happen!' And then the Kalankaniyan, Mannathi, Shaktan, they all come and say, 'What is this, O Mother!' (Addressing the character of Velichapad) And Buddhan just sits there, concentrating. 'What did you say? The whole village will suffer! Then how will we live?' When Velichapad returns to the normal state, Shaktan asks, (in an intimidating voice) 'What did you say? Who are you to say all this? It's all your creation! There's no goddess in you! I don't believe in it!' Hearing this Kalankaniyan says, 'Oh! No, no, no! Don't say that! The village is going to be destroyed! And Amma, the mother goddess, is against the village! And did you not hear that diseases would spread?'

'So be careful! We have to do something! We must act in the interest of the village!' Kalankaniyan is very much for it, because his name itself is Kala that is, time; the astrologer is one who deals with time. And then he asks Shaktan, What should we do? Tell us!' and Shaktan says, 'I will decide' Then Velichapad says, 'No, no! How will you decide, not you!' Now that the possession is over, he has once again become an ordinary man. He does not know what has happened.

Udayan: Now he could also participate in the discussion like the others.

Panikkar: Yes. 'I don't remember what I've just said', he says. He asks Shaktan, 'Shaktan, what is the problem?' He doesn't know how to suggest a way out.

A way out is suggested by the most intelligent man, i.e., the astrologer. The astrologer says, 'We have to make someone the God of the land. Someone should be made God to deal with these problems'.

Udayan: What does that mean? Making someone God?

Panikkar: It meant choosing someone to be some kind of leader or *devata*. It was decided, 'We should make a god, whom we should all obey and offer unconditional leadership. Everybody should accept him; otherwise we'll all have to suffer. We'll have to find a saviour who will overcome this oracle: Someone from amongst us or from anywhere!' Shaktan would like to become the God but he does not say that openly. And Kalankaniyan tries to find the person who could be made God, even from this small group. And then he goes around with his rhythm looking at each. Whenever he looks at someone, he/she feels, 'I'm going to be the God'. Shaktan is almost certain. At first he touches Velichapad. He looks at him. Seeing this Shaktan says, 'Leave him! He will be a bad God! He cannot do justice to the role. He has already done what he could. And what has happened? He's only cursed this village! He has nothing to say. So you leave that fellow!' Then he goes to Mannathi, the washerwoman.

Udayan: She may be a good choice?

Panikkar: 'Oh, you! What do you say, Washerwoman? Can you become the Goddess?' and she says, 'No, no, no *Tambura*! How can I? I'm a poor Mannathi and I know only this laundry work!' and the Kalankaniyan says, 'But that is also good work! That is enough, if you accept this.'

And she says, 'I'm not bold enough to lead!' Like that Kalankaniyan goes around. And then Komali comes. Komali's entry is very interesting. Komali means the jester, you know like circus Komali.

He is dressed like a jester. Whatever he finds along the way, he makes it his attire.

He says, 'Why don't you spell out my name? I feel that I'm the only person who can save this land!' And then Shaktan interferes, because Shaktan wants to become the God, while only he is not mentioned.

Udayan: And he's only thwarting others' chances!

Panikkar: Shaktan says, 'How can this Komali, who has no purpose in life, and just roams around, become a God? He should not be our God!'

But Kalankaniyan has to take the final decision. And Shaktan would like Kalankaniyan to take a decision in his favour, which of course, never happens. And then finally Kalankaniyan goes to the Buddhan. Buddhan is always in meditation. He's only an ordinary person spending most of his time sitting in the corner of the temple. He doesn't look at Kalankaniyan, does not open his eyes. And then Kalankaniyan goes around him. And then he says, 'He is the right person!' and Shaktan asks, 'How? What can that fellow do? He's always meditating with closed eyes. He has not proved that he's alive at all!' Kalankaniyan hearing this, says, 'No, no, no! I'm the one to decide who will be the God!' He declares that he was the best suited to be God and says, 'Please open your eyes!' And then Buddhan opens his eyes, looks at everybody and closes his eyes. And then Shaktan says, 'See! How can you make him a God? He's not even uttering a word. A person who cannot speak, how can you make him the God? Now I don't want to waste anymore time! If you feel someone should be the God, you should be able to find the proper person! Since you have not been able to do that, I assume myself, to be the God!' Thus finally Shaktan himself makes the verdict.

Udayan: Like many other self-proclaimed gods of our times ….

Panikkar: He gets into the interior of the temple, assuming himself to be the God. That's the first act. In the second act we see that in spite of Shaktan becoming the God, nothing changes. On the other hand, a terrible time follows. And then the whole Manikhem village turns dry with no food and water. There is not even a drop of water anywhere. In the second act we see they're all suffering. Even when the most hilarious comedian tries his hand at comedy it only fails miserably because of his weakness. Actually it could even be worked out further to create an interesting sub text. And then, it is all because of this fellow, who got into the interior of the temple, who's never been seen since. Nobody knows whether he is inside the temple or has escaped from the back side. So they decide, 'We don't care about this Shaktan, because he's unfit. So let us decide for others and make a real God out of this Buddhan, who is best suited'. And they make Buddhan their God in the second act. While Buddhan walks in a very somber way, they sing along, moving in a procession.

Udayan: Around the village?

Panikkar: Yes. And at the end of the act, Shaktan comes out of the temple. He's always got a *chaatta* (whip).

Udayan: Or a leash?

Panikkar: Yes, a leash. With the sound produced by the leash, he threatens all with his physical power. He comes out and says, 'What nonsense! That bloody fellow has been made God? I'm not going to stand this insult!' With this the act ends. Later Buddhan is not found anywhere and the villagers search for their missing God.

Udayan: He has disappeared without leaving a trace.

Panikkar: They search everywhere. When Shaktan was made God he went inside the temple and when Buddhan was made God he had disappeared! 'Where has he gone? We want him, because our village is not yet free from danger! We must make him sit down and we must offer him *puja*, but he cannot be found! What do we do?' they lament. Then Kalankaniyan finds a way out. He finds a stone. 'Why don't we make this stone our God? Why don't we attribute Buddha in this stone, since he is not seen?' And they agree to offer prayers to the stone. And while the prayers are going on, Shaktan watches. 'What nonsense! Is there no human being in this country to offer prayers?' When the *bhajan* is in full swing, the real Buddhan comes in a totally tired state. 'I'll die if you don't give me a little water! I can't move an inch. Please give me some water!' he says. And Shaktan consoles, 'You're fortunate that you are being propitiated. I will ask them to give you water'. And he goes to those singing *bhajan*s. 'Hey Kalankaniyan! Your God is waiting here! He is hungry and thirsty. Give him something! Give him at least some water, otherwise he will die!' And Kalankaniyan replies, 'Huh! Let the *bhajan* be over! Ask him to wait until the *bhajan* is over!' When the *bhajan* reaches a crescendo, Buddhan the God dies. As he dies, he asks, 'Who are they propitiating?' Shaktan explains: 'They are worshipping only you, you are fortunate, you are being propitiated!' and Buddhan says sadly, 'But I want water. Water … water …!' And he dies. When the *bhajan* is over and the *prasad* is brought, the god is found dead.

Udayan: But was that a questioning of the conventions? Or a satire on creation of human gods?

Panikkar: It is a critique of the fact that without seeing the man, without seeing the Shiva in the *shava* (corpse), people make god out of *shava,* people make god out of stone. A stone cannot be a god unless it has Shiva in it. And nobody realises that it is the real man who suffers at the cost of a stone. Without seeing this real man, the Shiva in man, there's no point in performing any sort of *bhajan* (prayer). This is one of the experiences of Sree Narayana Guru. There is a story that once Narayana Gurudevan was visiting a place where his bhajan was going on. His photo was kept there and was being worshipped by his followers. Hungry and thirsty, Narayana Gurudevan waited outside. And at last he said, 'What is being done! When I'm here, you don't give me attention, you don't care about me! But you're worshipping my photo!' This gave me the idea that this has a much wider significance.

Udayan: Who directed this play?

Panikkar: This was done by Kumara Varma. It was a very different production, a path-breaker.

Udayan: In what sense? In the performance aspect?

Panikkar: Not only the performance. Also in the structure of the play and all else that goes with it and in the way it was presented. It was so interesting and gripping; people liked the music, the theme and the message that was hidden in it. I remember Ananthamurthy saw it in Calicut. He was introduced to me only after this show. He was there in the audience in Sahitya Parishad in the 1970s. He came to me and said that this was a new experience and that they all enjoyed it. It was very gratifying to me.

Udayan: This was done with Gopi?

Panikkar: With Gopi and with my active involvement not only as a playwright, but also as a musician. I used to sing. And there was a dialogue between me and Venu in the beginning. I was sitting there to support the music. There is a dialogue between Venu and I on the same instrument, the *udukku.* That was the beginning of the play.

Udayan: It was like a *manglacharan.* The *taal mangala.*

Panikkar: Yes. And then throughout I was there, playing this instrument.

Udayan: Till then, you never had this desire to direct your play yourself?

Panikkar: I always felt that I too was directing it. Although I was not officially the director, my contribution was there. And I was not trying to project my position. I was only writing. I wanted to see things done. I was interested in seeing how the director would do it. How would the *Rasika* see it? Of course, all my directors were efficient and competent, and I had full confidence in them. I did not want to interfere with them but still I would always communicate with the director. We discussed it behind the curtains. When I took up directorial work in *Madhyamavyayogam* later in the 1970s, I wanted to give freedom to everyone to contribute. We established this ensemble work, which was ultimately useful to me: to think aloud, discuss and then to change, the readiness to change even the script. But this kind of training made it possible for me to be able to change the script if the need arose. It involved so much: doing, making it, seeing that it is being done by a director, making changes according to the director's wish, thinking with the director, making him think along with the script, making textual changes … All such interaction between actors helped me a lot to take to direction. It is not like Alkazi's way of directing. It is a method of understanding the actor, having a process of give and take with intelligent actors, discovering the quality of the actor and making necessary changes. The experience I gained by making other directors direct my plays also helped in the resolution of these psychological questions.

Udayan: Yes. And then comes the year 1978, I think when you directed your first play *Madhyamavyayogamm*. You were asked by Ashok Vajpeyi to direct a Sanskrit play.

Panikkar: The entry into *Madhyamavyayogamm* was not straight and simple. There was a curvature in the entry. It was not a linear entry.

Udayan: What was that?

Panikkar: I entered the play through *Ottayan* which essentially dealt with the art of acting itself; the art of the actor, the presence of the actor on the stage, the presence of the actor in life; this inter-relationship and also the theory of transformation, which was very important in my theatre career. Transformation is the basis, you know, the basic ingredient of theatre. What is theatre? I would say, basically it is transformation. So that transformation theory worked in *Ottayan,* while it was written. Firstly, it was directed by Kumara Varma, and later it was directed by me with changes. That was my first directorial venture, not this Sanskrit one. I did it with changes and with Gopi as the *Ottayan,* as the *Chakyar,* as the actor. Earlier, when Kumara

Varma did it, he was true to the text. He used only two woodsmen and one *Chakyar* Jagannathan who enacted the *Chakyar's* role pretty well. We were strongly criticised by both literary men like the the playwright—respected by all of us—and Appukuttan Nair, who was a known spokesperson of the art of Kudiyattam.

Udayan: I know he was doing a lot of services to Kudiyattam.

Panikkar: He was a Kudiyattam specialist. Both of them criticised the production. Kumara Pillai said that he could not accept it as a piece of literature, but the acting and everything else were alright. And Appakuttan Nair said, 'As a piece of literature, it is wonderful but the acting was very bad'! But this did not upset me or Kumara Varma. Later he left and I had to do the same play with Gopi. Then I wanted to give it a different colour. Thus I redid my own play. I changed the play introducing the group and the theme became the individual versus the group. The group is dull-headed. It is from the group that the individual comes out. An individual has the feeling that he creates for the group; that he is the creative spirit of the group. So he has to move away. The group comes after him. He tries to escape from the group. These elements were introduced while I did this with Gopi and the group. All the subtleties of the problem were there which gave me an insight into the play, which I had written. In doing that play, I was trying to discover myself as a playwright as well as a director, as well as, you know, as the audience, as a *Rasika*. It was really a great experience, doing that play with Gopi.

Udayan: Can you just very briefly say what it was like when Kumara Varma did it?

Panikkar: Kumara Varma did *Ottayan* as an experience of a *Chakyar*. The *Chakyar* saves himself from a dangerous situation when he encounters a few woodsmen in the forest who were about to kill him. He saves himself by using his magical acting talents. All these aspects were there in the written script as well but they constituted only the peripheral storyline. What was missing in that production was taken up by me. It was not against what Kumara Varma did. Kumara Varma gave the fillip, the impetus to me to go further with this probing into the inner structure of the play. The outer structure was very well established and the inner structure too was probed slightly. But then I found so much while working with a great artist like Gopi, who was ready to spend any amount of time, any number of hours with me discussing and trying, testing and probing jointly into the possibilities of the script as well as the areas which are offered by the script as non-sound areas. Then the whole idea of *Ottayan* got illuminated, where the lone tusker or the lone man, who feels totally alone even while he is in a group. All these philosophical levels could be worked out. And then madly he, Ottayan, wants to escape from the public, from the group with his creative urge but the group is always behind him not allowing him to escape. The whole group is only woodsmen. No creativity is possible by a group. In the interest of the group, we are all working alone. This had not been exploited to this extent in Kumara Varma's production. I had the rare privilege of working with Gopi in a very creative context. He had come leaving all his assignments in films, sacrificing a lot of money. He spent about 20-25 days for the play; concentrating on just this from morning onwards. Instrumentalists too would be there. We'd forget everything. We took another house and spent the whole time there concentrating on nothing else but this. And we presented this production in 'East Meets West' in Mumbai. It was a very great success.

It was organised there in NCPA. And Gopi, after coming back from Mumbai, returned to films to do his work, which he could not complete in time. And then he had to do very heavy work … even at the cost of his health.

Udayan: What did the direction of *Ottayan* do to you?

Panikkar: Through *Ottayan*, I entered into my own concept of direction, which was quite different from the way things were done by others. Even in my theatre career, this was an eye-opener. From then on, there was this question of the group and the individual. You know the group work in Greek chorus? I don't claim to have introduced the group; the group was already there.

A group works in many ways. The same group can transform to perform different roles. In a written work like *Pashugayatri*, the group works as Nagas who give the Tantrik the wealth pot. Initially the wealth pot is kept away from the Tantrik. The Tantrik wants to take it from the Earth, but the guardians of the Earth protest. They are against such an act. So the group works as Nagas and the same group, at the end of the story becomes the people at large, where the boy gets drowned. You know, the group has a quality of having the same face because they have to behave in the same manner. The boy in *Pashugayatri*, a born idiot, becomes intelligent. It is a story of the Indian youth which realises its powers. He realises and he becomes one with the group. Becoming one with the group represents the attainment of social consciousness that is derived from the individual-group relationship. This as a principle, as an interpretative device, was introduced in many plays like Kalidasa's *Shakuntala*.

From *Ottayan* to Kalidasa's *Shakuntala*, it was a long way, because I had to pass through *Madhyamavyayogam*, *Karnabharam* and *Urubhangam* to reach Kalidasa. Doing Bhasa's plays, I reached the point of interpretation where I found out a way, a *marga*, to reach Kalidasa's *Shakuntala*. In *Madhyamavyayoga* the group is very limited: three Brahmin boys, their father and mother; but when I came to *Karnabharam*, it was different. In *Karnabharam* the group plays a much more important role. There, you know, the philosophy of group versus individual had already been developed from *Ottayan*. And it reached out when a play like *Shakuntala* was attempted; there Dushyanta is being helped by the group only, the group is stirring the forest and creating the opportunity for the king to do *mrigaya*, hunting. And then once the hunting is done, then it turns out to be the *mrigaya*, the hunt for the girl; the hunt for animals becoming the hunt for a human being, a poor girl of the hermitage. And he lives with this girl to his satisfaction. That too is reflected in the group. The group first finds fault with the king. It says: *mrigaya vihari parthivo Dushyanta*. The king's *mrigaya* has taken a very unwanted turn. They find fault with the king but the king refuses to listen to the opinion of his people, his *prajas*. *Prakriti hitaya parthiva, praja hitaya parthiva* is the final. So *praja hitaya* is not cared for. He proceeds further, going deeper and deeper into his commitment with Shakuntala.

At the end of the third act, the same line is repeated: *mrigaya vihari parthivo Dushyanta*. The first time when the people, find fault with the king, it is through Shakuntala's pose that it is expressed. He then decides to go with her and not with the group. *Chinaamshuka miva keto*, my mind is like *Chinaanshuka* (Chinese silk), flowing in the wind this side and that. And then he decides to go with the girl. In the third act, this line is repeated again, when he has reached almost the cessation point in his love pursuits. And then when the *mrigaya vihari* is heard from behind, he opts to choose his duty, leaving Shakuntala behind. So, there was a whole process through which the group was put to use. And then, in my production of *Shakuntala*, you find that in the final stage too, the group had to agree with the reunion of Dushyanta and Shakuntala after seeing the ring. The ring is taken by Vidushaka and shown to everyone. It comes from of the fisherman who found it while fishing. When the ring reached the King through Vidushaka, it awakened his memory. So the ring works as a strong image which is the crux of the theme of *Shakuntala* as the nomenclature *Abhijnana Shakuntala* reveals. *Abhijnana* denotes the awakening of memory or *pratyabhijna* of the King. The awakening of the King's memory was possible only with the involvement of the people who were responsible for regaining this symbol. It is only then that Dushyanta accepts Shakuntala. That is why I conclude this play, probably unlike how Kalidasa wanted, but as the time demanded and the group worked as the catalyst. This is only my interpretation, my subtext. But, you know, regarding the way the group is used, this is very important. Here too, in *Uttararamacharitam*, the group will have to definitely play a big role, which is not envisaged anywhere in the text. There is, of course, the sound of the roaring from behind of the *sainik*s (soldiers). But the presence of the group in taking the story through, that has come to my production from the *Ottayan* experience. Before that, in *Sakshi*, in *Tiruvazhithan*, or in *Daivathar*, the group was not very live, except that in *Daivathar*, of course, there is a group … four-five people but then they are all individuals. They have their own names, their own qualities—theirs is not the group quality. It's not a total mind, a social mind, a *samooh chetana*. For me the social mind working as a group has become a phenomenon, a very important aspect in theatre, which I find very much relevant in the present day democratic setup or life. These are the days of democracy and when a king is to be viewed in the present context, he cannot be seen in the same way as was during the time of Kalidasa or Dushyanta. It is different. The role, the approach, the relationship, is all different. And to me it is as significant as a philosophy.

Udayan: Do you think that theatre plays a role without consciously trying to do so to make people aware of various relationships? I mean relationships like those of the ruler and the ruled and all that. Theatre is a very physical activity unlike poetry. In theatre you can actually say, 'This is Dushyanta and this is Ram,' for instance.

Panikkar: Ideas become characters through images in theatre and hence *drishyakavya,* or visual poetry.

Udayan: Did you envisage that the audience should become more aware of these new social relationships which are coming into being in India? Did such a thought come to you?

When you do theatre, do you think that theatre also makes people aware of the new social relationships that have come into being in a particular society?

Panikkar: Theatre definitely presents certain social relationships. On the textual level, theatre (which is the *vachika,* the text is to be made into *vachika*) has a definite relationship with the social context. The social context is very much there, because the characters are there, precisely named. Now whether it is a king or an epic character like Karna, they are more than just characters, they also represent the 'social' feel. They are juxtaposed against the social context in the text, because the text is very much social, very much down to earth, very much in touch with reality. That is how it becomes a springboard. Only in its treatment do we try to create these definite characters that belong to everyday life, but they may not be directly referred to as such. But they have their semblance with day-to-day life characters. For instance in the case of Karna, though the character and the sequence of events are as per the epic, the character was story-based and the story is essentially related to your earthliness. And it is from there only in theatre that these characters which emanated from life with assumed dimensions are taken to realms which are go beyond like the *Natyadharmi* and *Manodharmi* levels of the representational art. Again, the representation is there, but they represent *guna,* they represent qualities. And they sometimes go beyond the personal level. The personality which represents life will create a depersonalised level. What I say is supportive to the great philosophy of ours.

Udayan: What kind of relationship do you find that the epics have with our life in India? How important do you think these epics like *Mahabharata* or *Ramayana* are for every day life in our country?

Panikkar: Epics are created by man. It is only a creation of man's imagination and experience and they cannot be totally unrelated to life. They have definite moorings, they have definite roots in the life of the country, and the life of the people, whether present, past or future. You cannot bifurcate; you cannot separate the epic characters from the life situation. Karna cannot behave like Oedipus; he cannot behave like another character of a western epic. His behaviour, his *Dharmasastra*, his ideals, everything is rooted, and that rootedness is nothing but rootedness in Indian life. At the same time Karna represents a situation that is universal and hence depersonalised.

Udayan: So it is a reflection of and on life.

Panikkar: It is a reflectionof a kind of life; whichever kind is lived. That life was lived here. It relates, essentially to the concepts of sages like Valmiki, or at other times authors like Vaikom Mohammad Bashir as the case may be. In your case, you create characters and these are not characters for the present alone. You may take characters from this time, but they are not for this time alone. They can transcend your own time; otherwise the whole thing has no relationship with the fleeting life. Their relationship of the characters with life is proved only by the power of these characters to transcend time.

Udayan: That's true. That's why these characters live in the time of their own. The theatre director has to bring them into his or her specific time for the sake of the play. When an actor enters the character, they take their idea or the director's idea of time into it and thus make a transcendental character living in a specific time and space and create a new possibility of transcendence. After *Ottayan* came the offer for the *Madhyamavyayogam.*

Panikkar: Yes.

Udayan: How did you take it? I mean here was somebody asking you not to do your own play in Malayalam, which you had already started doing, with *Ottayan.* And suddenly an offer for doing a Sanskrit play comes to you. What was your initial reaction to that? I mean, your life was going to take a new turn with that!

Panikkar: I didn't know that! I was searching out traditional texts and I could find the same creativity there. Its dynamics applies to all times. So when I happened to read Bhasa, it came to me easily. I read translations of Bhasa's *Madhyamavyayogam* and *Urubhangam,* not the original. I was attracted to Vallathol's translation of them. When I read *Madhyamavyayogam,* I thought, it is a story which could well have happened at any time. It happened long ago and yet it can well happen even now, not just time-wise, I mean it is ubiquitous. You know, this relationship can happen anywhere. The family relationship is an ideal. This ideal family relationship, the familial bond, still exists in India. We have nurtured this wonderful bond of family. Even Engels has expressed the idea of family as distinct from the rudimentary stage of coming together as heads of culture. So there was this concept of family and also the *pavitrata* (sacredness) of family relationships. There is a *laxman rekha* (limit) for each member in the family which is set by dharma. I feel each one enacts a role in family life. The father enacts a role and has the sensibility to understand and treat each relationship in a particular manner. The father cannot behave in the same way with his son, daughter and wife. Certain yard sticks are to be maintained for the well-being of the family.

In *Madhyamavyayogam,* father Bhima and son Ghatotkacha try to identify each other. The relationship of father, son and mother is very significant and the *madhyata* (middleness) was created by Bhasa in a family situation. I feel that in family life one should be prepared to sacrifice. If one wishes to avoid quarrels in a family, one should learn to adjust. That person who is prepared to adjust for the well-being of the family is the *madhyama* (the middle one). In every Indian family, you will be able to find this. When a question or a difference of opinion arises, one should eschew adamance and be balanced. The one who plays the role of being *objective* is the *madhyama* (the middle one). Of course he may have to suffer. But he happily undergoes such suffering. He accepts it with a sense of *ananda* (pleasure) or a sense of duty. All the subtle elements of Indian family system which prevail even now were there in those days and were very much discussed by Bhasa in *Madhyamavyayogam.*

Udayan: What were your apprehensions when you were going to stage Sanskrit plays, because till then you had worked in and done your own plays and you could have taken all kinds of liberties in doing them. But what about doing these classics which were being done, as you knew, by the *Chakyar*s and others? With what kind of attitude did you approach this play of Bhasa's, *Madhyamavyayogam?*

Panikkar: I had my apprehensions about who would help me by providing the text and its ramified meanings. The same apprehensions which I face in *Uttararamacharitam*, when you return to Bhopal and when I do the rehearsals in your absence, in the absence of script writer! Because I cannot add a single line in Hindi. Now it will not be fair because it will not go well with the other parts of the text. So this is a problem. How the would the text become amenable to one's work and interpretation? This is the main problem. Then there is of course, the problem of Sanskrit language. But this we solved easily because I had already translated the work. Unfortunately, we had to learn Sanskrit through English. So, there is always this English guide. And of course, there were guides like Narayana Pisharody and when difficult questions arose we could consult such people; but there were very few like him. The script was to be interpreted. And you know *vyakhyana* (interpretation) was not that difficult, because *vyakhyana* was free *vyakhyana*. It was not *vyakhyana* for the literary *patha* (text) alone. The literary *patha* (text) would give you an input to create a *drishya patha* (visual text). Thus the language problem could be sorted out. But trouble was to edit the script because it was very difficult with Bhasa! I will tell you a very good example of how I tried to edit and failed. In *Madhyamavyayogam*, when the middle son was taken away, the old man cries out with the whole family. And I took only the portion where they say: 'We are bereft of everything!' But there was a beautiful *shloka* (poem) which I deleted, edited, which was stupid on my part, because it was so meaningful!

Yastrishringo mama tvaseen manojno vamshparvataha

Sa madhyashringabhangena manastpati me bhrisham

'My *vanshparvat* (Family Mountain) had three *shringa*s, or peaks and the *madhya shringa* (the middle peak) has been broken.'

This is what the old father laments when the middle son was taken away by Ghatotkacha. While I was editing the text *manastapati me bhrisham* was deleted but I had to take it back. Initially I only took *Parimushitha smoh bhoh parimushitahah*, 'we are bereft, we are bereft' and thought that it was enough but it was not enough for theatrical justice. That's why when you work on the performance text of *Uttararamacharitam*, I always ask you for more! 'Give me two more lines!' If the lines are worthy to be translated into action, then more lines will not be an impediment in theatre. But the fact is that if it is just poetry then there is a problem. Poetry is to be viewed in two ways; one is as poetry itself, good poetry, thought-provoking poetry. But if it is lacking in the possibility of visual interpretation, then such poetic text becomes a *bhara* (load) for theatre.

Udayan: An unneccessary weight on theatrical action ....

Panikkar: Yes. It would become *bhara*. There lies the problem of editing. We can use our sensibility and editing has to be done with a visual sense. Holding on to your interpretative vision, but adding again when the author is not with you, is very difficult in the case of a Sanskrit play. But since it is an epic, it is possible because we have similar works or those which inspired this particular work, even at the risk of breaking the chronology. For example Vyasa's lines were used to embellish Bhasa. The entry of Kunti in *Karnabharam* and her dialogues with Karna all belong to Vyasa who was the source of inspiration to Bhasa also.

Udayan: You can go back to the original source and bring lines or images from there. In this way you, in a way of saying, also show the geneology of the Bhasa's text.

Panikkar: Yes. For example in *Karnbharam* I wanted the fight between Surya and Indra, which is not evidently in the script. The script does not give enough material in *Karnabharam* for the introduction of Surya and Indra. Similarly, when we were working on *Uttararamacharitam*, we were discussing how Rama should be introduced in the performance. The entry of the character is very important in the Indian theatre ... in any theatre for that matter. This is true in Japanese theatre also. 'My name is Kiyoyori', says the actor to the audience in a *kyogan* which we are doing for children. The translation of this *kyogan* was done by Dr Ayyapa Paniker.

Udayan: *Kyogan*? What kind of theatre it is?

Panikkar: *Kyogan* is a light, comic type of skit which is done in between serious plays.

Udayan: I see. The introduction of the character, you were saying, is very important.

Panikkar: Introducing a character is very important in Sanskrit theatre. How Ghatotkacha looks, how he enters, etc. He enters as the Brahmin family is passing through the forest. So in the beginning, when I first did Sanskrit theatre that was worked out in detail. He is described by Bhima as '*simhasya* *simhadamntro madhunibhanayanah',* which means he has honeyed eyes. He probably has got them from his father, whereas *simhasya, simhadamntro*—lionlike face and canines, have come from his mother. This *shloka* (poem) describes two aspects of Ghatotkacha. I remember how Ghatotkacha was introduced as showing both sympathy towards human beings, which he got from his father, as well as the trait of cruelty he inherited from his mother, implied in the *simha bhava.* He was not made to look like that, he could not look like that in his outfits. These details are not there. So you have to use your imagination by reading the text. In the text, the description is given by one character about another, but you should not take it in the literal sense. You have to be creative in designing even the outfits and makeup of the character in such a way that he does not seem a visual translation of the literal. You have to recreate what is stated by that character by *abhinaya* about that character. All this is highly imaginative and gives freedom to the director, to the reader and ultimately to the audience to imagine Ghatotkacha by reading this text.

Panikkar: These are aspects I had faced. Very important problems while producing a play.

Udayan: Whenever you have done any Sanskrit play like *Shakuntala* or *Vikramorvashiyam, Malavikagnimitram,* or any of Bhasa's plays, you always create a sub-text which you finally perform. I mean, there is a sub-text lying in every play for you. You believe this, and then you unearth that and then perform that. What was that sub-text like? As your early plays were concerned they were your own; so the text itself was a sub-text in a sense. But in this case, you might have done it for the first time. So what was it like?

Panikkar: This change can easily be explained by our own experiences these days when we are working on *Uttararamacharitam* to create a text to be performed. What you have created from *Uttararamacharitam* is a sub-text. In the re-creative process, what is emerging out of the greater text is the sub-text. The text becomes a raw material. Even the text which you have written, is a sub-textual material, which creates in practice, another third text. Because everything cannot be written! You can only give, you can write a lullaby but how that lullaby is to be enacted, how that lullaby is to be sung, all these are what *Chakyar*s used to discuss in their theatre manuals, the *attaprakaram* and *kramadeepika. Attaprakaram* speaks about how it should be enacted on the stage; *kramdeepika* says how the make-up should be done, for instance how the *gopi* (the mark on the fore head) should be, all this is to be found in *kramdeepika*. When both are combined they give you an idea about the whole sub-text. Now, what you have written as *Uttararamacharitam* is a sub-text which is further to be put into practice on the stage.

Udayan: And thereby it will again change.

Panikkar: Once again it has to, if not change then at least its details have to be worked out. *How* and *why* should come in the way; so let me answer that earlier question that was raised in reference to *Karnabharam* as to how the text was embellished. The text was embellished by acting, by body-acting, by mental-acting. And more than that by introducing Surya, who was not there in the text. I wanted to show strife between the celestials: Surya and Indra, for which Karna had to suffer. So this was my own interpretation, for which new textual material was required. So I had to introduce Veda mantras for presenting Surya and Indra. This worked as non textual text.I lacked text. Kunti had to be present here, she had to enter, for which there was one *shloka* (poem). The rest of it I introduced from the Mahabharata, the scene of Kunti meeting Karna. She had met him ealier and that is recollected, recapitulated on the stage, for which there was no text except the statement Karna makes when he remembers: 'my arrows are not working probably because of what my mother has stated.'.

Udayan: Yes, he has to go against the wish of his mother that he should not fight against the Pandavas, especially Arjuna, because they are his brothers. This is only indicated in the text of *Karnabharam* but its details are not given. Logically so, because Bhasa is writing or doing a play for an audience which is well informed about the connotations of such a statement.

Panikkar: Therefore, Kunti was made to enter but: where is the text for Kunti? And just making an entry in a very broad way, in dim light she comes and goes. All that was okay, I thought, but something should be communicated. There was no text. And what was Karna's attitude? He was moved by his mother's presence: he embraced her. But while embracing his mother, he suddenly remembers her cruelty in abanding him. Here Kunti says, '*Kaunteya tvam*' 'You are my son, you are Kunti's son'. This is from the *Mahabharata*— 'You are not Radha's son, you are my son. Your father is not Atiratha. I was living in my father's house, and then you were born.'

All this is stated using two *shloka*s from the *Mahabharata*. Then she requests him, 'Don't kill Arjuna,' and Karna replies, 'You will have five sons, either me or Arjun will die'. This is not in Bhasa's text. Or probably he envisaged the whole scene as I did it. Thus the short script of *Karnabharam* could accommodate additional non-textual text and it only strengthened the dramatic impact.

Udayan: You were talking about *Madhyamavyayogam*, how you decided to direct the original.

Panikkar: Yes, we have already discussed the Indian family issue. It has natural tendency of holding together, coming together. Now it has become difficult for us to practice this with the concept of the nuclear family being dominant. When this concept dominates, all of us become small islands.

Udayan: That's true. My question is, how did you come to a certain notion of the treatment of that play? I mean till now you were doing different plays. Plays that you have written were much closer to the times that you were living in, but here was a play that was distinct in time, but also timeless.

Panikkar: I had the experience of partition in my family, as well as my wife's family, with disputes over land and property. In my wife's family, the division was to be done after the death of my uncle. The smallest portion was given to her. Everybody was demanding too much and tensions were high. Nobody was prepared to compromise even an inch. Thus one had to do the role of the middle one (*madhyama*).

Arjuna is supposed to be *madhayama* Pandava (the middle one among the Pandavas), but Bhasa wanted Bhima to be the *madhayamapandava*. Why? This is not stated there, it is outside the purview of the text. It is not directly stated, but usually the *madhayama* Pandava is Arjuna because he is the middle one. Arjuna is known as *madhayama* Pandava, Bhima is not known to be that. Bhima is elder to Arjuna. Then why did Bhasa make Bhima the middle one? Because Bhima had suffered a lot.

Udayan: And the poor fellow does everything for Draupadi but Draupadi loves only Arjuna.

Panikkar: The main thing is that Bhima suffered for others. There is an element of sacrifice involved. This is treated by Bhasa in a very subtle way, which is very much *Natyadharmi*; it is not a realistic situation. The first son offers himself saying he will go with Ghatatkocha. The father says, 'No, don't go!' Then the second son says, 'No don't go, I will go!' Then the third chimes in, 'No, both the brothers should remain, I will go!' Everybody is offering to go! This is another point which Manmathan Nair Sir always used to say; in a family system you should always be ready to sacrifice for others, you should control your own appetite for the sake of others when there is a scarcity of food. This readiness to sacrifice is very important on the part of a person who is passionate about the welfare of others.

Udayan: Yes, the readiness to sacrifice is important for a culture as well.

Panikkar: When the first son offers, the second son says 'no' when the second son also offers, the father comes and says, 'I offer myself'. Then the mother comes. All five members of the family offer his or her life for the well being of others. It's a wonderful situation. But Bhasa wanted to smile at the selfishness of man in this context and that is why the father owns the elder son. When Ghatotkacha is about to take the elder son, the father cries out, 'Oh, I can't bear this, he is too dear to me! He is the first born. If he goes, who will do my last rites?' He is only stating a fact and that does not mean that he doesn't want the other sons. But he stresses this point because at that moment he faces the stark reality that the first son is being taken away. So he interrupts saying, 'Don't take him please'. Ghatotkacha then takes hold of the last son. This time the mother comes and says, 'Don't take him. He is my dearest.' But there is no one to speak up for the middle one!

Udayan: Even the father's little selfishness is a reason.

Panikkar: There is good reason. But he does not want others to be killed.

Udayan: When he says that he doesn't want the eldest son to be killed, he's the one to perform his last rites, he means that he's the one who would associate him to that other great family of ancestors waiting for him to join them. In fact, he is also saying this for a certain notion of family itself.

Panikkar: That is all there but then Bhasa also wanted to show a tinge of selfishness in the parents even at that moment. So that is why I introduced a stage picture in which the father embraces the first son on one end and the mother, the youngest son on the other end and the middle one is all alone in the centre …

Udayan: … expecting something?

Panikkar: Expecting what is to happen next dramatically. Who will own me? Ghatotkacha goes and looks closely at the father and mother and then laughs. That is what is called *Bhasohasa* (humour of Bhasa). Bhasa has created a situation like this in which everyone can laugh, because if you are put in such a situation, as you said, none of them could be blamed. This is a very serious situation where anybody would probably act like this. Even Ghatotkacha has sympathy for the middle one. In this situation the middle one says, 'Who is there for me?' 'I am there,' Ghatotkacha holds him. 'I am there,' he says and people laugh, 'I am there.' But for what?

Udayan: To be killed.

Panikkar: That is a dramatic moment!

Udayan: And also I was reminded at that point of the *Kathopanishad* when the father tells his son, 'I give you to death.' That connection is there. And Nachiketa is the one who raises all the big questions. So, the middle one is, in a sense, a coincidental Nachiketa in this place, suddenly finding himself in a similar position. What I was also interested in knowing was that when you saw that Sanskrit play by Bhasa and you had seen Bhasa being performed by the *Chakyar*s in so wonderful a way, what did you think you should do with it?

Panikkar: The moment the question came for me to do this play, it was already translated into Malayalam. But the offer came from Ashok Vajpeyi to do it in the original Sanskrit. Only then more serious problems came. Otherwise I had made up my mind to do this in Malayalam. The moment I thought of doing it, a very good image came to my mind, the image of 'three-ness'. The three-ness that is created by Bhasa in the play is very important. Three-ness suggests the middle one, unless two on both sides are there, there cannot be the middle one and the middleness always creates three-ness. Another aspect is that there are two families, and in both these families there are three-nesses. I created a stage picture in mind where there must be something which makes the audience count the three-ness.

Udayan: It is interesting to know that you started thinking about *Madhyamavyayogam* through these three-nesses.

Panikkar: Three-ness was very important. And three-ness gave the whole concept about the play. Three-ness: three sons of the Brahmin; Ghatotkacha, Bhima and Hidimba.

It's a very balanced three-ness. And three-ness or rather *madhayama,* the middle one is the theme of the play too. *Madhyama* is the theme of the play. *Madhayama* creates a sense of duty to be fulfilled to a family and that has been done. The entire family relationship—with father, with mother—all works through it. When Bhima identifies Ghatotkacha as his son, it's a very dramatic moment. The whole thing comes to his mind through music that we used as a stronge signifier.

Udayan: In fact, at the end of the play both the three-nessess are restored.

Panikkar: All is restored. A very peculiar aspect about the play is that I was confused and I wondered whether we should start with Hidimba's entry. I even discussed it with Ayyapa Paniker. Then I came to the conclusion, which I told Ayyapa Paniker. Bhasa had done a wonderful challenging change by not starting the play with the *sutradhara,* which was always the practice. Normally the *Sutradhara* enters in the beginning of every play. But here the *sutradhara* works through Hidimba who comes at the end. Ayyapa Paniker said, 'You have done very well in that wonderful passage where Hidimba says in the end, 'Why is this? What is this happening? How did it happen? It is all my design". She doesn't speak like that however… there is no direct speech, '*Idisham vi ah*', (It is like that). That is all she says.'

Udayan: It's an indirect speech.

Panikkar: Which means, 'This is how it should be', that is, this is my doing; I managed to bring you here by my son. So the *sutradhara* quality of this character comes only in the final moment.

Udayan: Yes, through the figure of Hidimba.

Panikkar: Yes and that too at the finale, I wonder whether *pratyabhijna* works there. I took it this way. Sometimes we imagine something would happen and it actually happens. In Hidimba's case she knew that the Pandavas were somewhere in the forest. By sending her son to bring a human being as food for her, she fancied that her son would come across Bhima and thereby an opportunity could be created to put an end to her separation from Bhima and to introduce her son Ghatotkacha to his father. The finale of the play is this dream come true.

Udayan: Oh! Because you were planning the play differently, incorporating the idea of *pratyabhijna* that works in Hidimba's mind!

Panikkar: I just wondered why not it like that, but then the question was how? That was a difficult problem to solve!

Udayan: Is *Madhyamavyayog* done in Kudiyattam also?

Panikkar: No. *Karnabharam* and *Madhyamavyayoga* are not done in Kudiyattam. One scene from the fourth act of *Swapnavasavadattam*'s is done. *Dutavakyam is* also there. There are commentaries and all that. *Abhisheka Natakam* is there too.

Udayan: What was your notion regarding the movement of actors on the stage? Like in music, for example, the modulation principle works in the way that if you place *shadaj* at a point and *gandhar* at another point and if you change the *shadaj* and also the *gandhar*, then this slight change will bring about an emotional resonance in you. But if you fix it, like for example, on the harmonium or the piano, then you can't produce the emotional quality of the raaga music of India. And I think on the stage you do not fix the movement of the actors once and for all. They are continuously fluid, they are continuously agile and they move in relation to each other.

Panikkar: Yes, in relation to each other, in justification of the text. The text is the point. It is the *shadaj,* and it is from there that the *gandhar, madhyam,* etc., changeable *swaras* (notes) are planned. When a character makes his or her vocalisation to another, you have to plan it ahead. When Shakuntala is to be thrown out by Dushyanta or he throws out Sarngavara or Gautami, they have to be placed in an appropriate position before that. The positioning of character is, very important, because he hears everyone and then he rejects. Therefore it should be in juxtaposition only—the whole thing has to be planned, choreographed. The planning will be such that motivational working and the placement of characters will naturally come as dictated by the textual context, by the *bhava*, and through the relationship with the characters. You cannot fix that this character moves 40 degrees in relation to other then the other character moves 30 degrees. It cannot be drawn on paper like a picture and reproduced in the performance space. This is something that happens as part of the performance flow, in the performing space itself and in the *vachika* design too. It cannot be laid out on paper.

Udayan: It is said that the well known realistic actor Manohar Singh could not speak his dialogue without cues. This is possible, but in your theatre it is out of the question.

Panikkar: Absolutely. Out of the question.

Udayan: Alkazi used to do that. He would draw.

Panikkar: Sankara Pillai used to do that also, Kumara Varma would do it in the beginning but then he gave it up. He would go to the area where we would enact and then would plan. Movement cannot be restricted like that even by marking earlier on paper. You know, *manodharma* (improvisation) works. Once the actors were thorough with the portion, they were all on the stage. In the said context in Shakuntala there are only four people. There are four people on the stage and Dushyanta is singled out. He is the lone man there who rejects the others approachs by which what I meant is, they proceed against, him idea, wise and movement, wise and he gets singled out. And he resists, but ultimately has to throw them out.

Udayan: There is also the relationship with the group and the individual. He throws her out and what happens? The group comes and takes her in its embrace.

Panikkar: Movement, choreography and everything is motivated. But motivation cannot be drawn; it is dependent upon the rendering. The motivational reaction can be built up only vis-à-vis the interaction from the other side. So thereafter, learning the whole situation well, intelligent actors can go from *Natyadharmi* to *Manodharmi*. The travelling from *Natyadharmi* to *Manodharmi* happens only in advanced levels of acting and then there is no need for 40 degrees or 30 degrees drawing! They cannot but behave like that. Even if there is a slight change between right and left, they still know where to throw the body, to throw the voice. Similarly, in the fourth act of Shakuntala, this is a very important act according to scholars. It is not that important from the viewpoint of acting, but from the literary viewpoint it is important. Here too, the movement to the character is not linear: first she goes to that plant, then she goes to the deer—it cannot be like that. It is a going around through the path towards their destination, in a curvature movement leading to the gate of the ashram. This is converted into virtual space in the circumambulatory direction. First is the fireplace, where Shakuntala is asked to give obeisance to the fire by going round it. There you first have Gautami, then Shakuntala, Sharngarava Vaikhanasa, and Kanva going round the fire. That is the first movement which creates the going around. And then they come across the *lata* (creeper) which is dear to her. All this comes in the round, and the whole thing has to be designed in such a way that it happens one after the other, at the final moment, the deer called Dirghapanga appears. In the first scene we see the deer is pulling her sari; then the same Dirghapanga is seen in a very sad situation when Shakuntala leaves the hermitage. After that Kanva, her father, shares his sorrow with the deer.

Udayan: It is a very moving moment. In your theatre the geometry of your movements is fluid, it's not fixed, it keeps on changing.

Panikkar: We have planned the exit through the front, through the side of the audience. And the rhythm is taken to *tihai* or *Kalasham*.

Udayan: In music, there is the concept of the *nyaas*; where you're going to do the *nyaas* is decided, for example, you will do the *nyaas* on *gandhar*. But how you create a *chhand*, a kind of form is up to you. It is possible that you may not actually end up in *gandhar*, you may end up in the absence of *gandhar*, but *gandhar* will be there, that is decided. And something very similar takes place in your theatre, because in your theatre …

Panikkar: Music and rhythm, especially rhythm is there, and of course *alapa* also comes in, but rhythm leads it, always controling the movements. There are two components: *alapa* and rhythm. Rhythm is dominant. By this I mean sometimes rhythm may be tying and untying an idea and it is a constant process.

Udayan: Because it is through that that you create temporality, a sense of time …

Panikkar: Yes, and also the tempo. Temporality and the tempo …

Udayan: The pace, that's true. That's *laya* …

Panikkar: Yes, that is *laya*. And the space that is virtual.

Udayan: What was the response like for *Madhyamavyayog*'s production in Ujjain?

Panikkar: Oh, it was tremendous! It was very well received and they gave us a standing ovation. Ujjain was festive with a lot of crackers being heard all around because of Deepavali. But the lights went off for some time when the *sutradhara* entered (at first Nedumudi Venu was the *Sutradhar*). Then suddenly the stage seemed lit. I wondered how that happened! Then I noticed a few vehicles were quickly arranged close to the stage thus lighting it up! Venu, the *sutradhara* sat there alone, there was no mike, and there was this light from the vehicles. Soon after, everything went back to normal. Venu was confused about what to do, and finally when he was about to speak out, the lights came back along with the mike.

Udayan: And what was the reaction like?

Panikkar: The show was greatly appreciated. They were seeing something totally new. They hadn't seen anything like this, not only in Sanskrit theatre, but also in contemporary theatre! Soon after the show which was on November 2, 1978 we were invited to Delhi by Kamaladevi Chattopadhyaya in February, after she read about the success of the play. We were invited to Delhi twice, once in February and then again in the end of March. The first show was at the Sri Ram Centre and a lot of people from the theatre world attended it!

Udayan: You mean Alkazi, etc.

Panikkar: Alkazi, Avasthi, Nemi ji, etc.

Udayan: Habib Tanvir?

Panikkar: Habib Tanvir was not there. He saw it elsewhere.

Udayan: Yes, I asked because I know he has seen it, he told me so.

Panikkar: Many others like Kapila Vatsyayan, Kamaladevi Chattopadhyaya and many others were there, and a number of theatre critics. After the show, only Kapila*ji* didn't come and meet me. She remained behind but she met Padmanabhan my nephew who was doing percussion and said, 'Please tell your uncle that tomorrow I must meet him. Please request him to meet me.' So I went to see her the next day. She was full of praise for the performance. And Alkazi came to me in the theatre. Alkazi wanted to see what the headgear was made of. Ghatotkacha's headgear was Aravindan's design.

Udayan: Was Aravindan there?

Panikkar: No, he was not there. Ghatotkacha's headgear was made of grass with which we make brooms. And Bhima's headgear was made from the palm leaf. This play was staged in Calcutta also. Shambhu Mitra came for the show. I met him before the show. I was very happy to see him and after the show he came to the green room. He wanted to see the costumes: How Aravindan had made the costumes. He congratulated the artists, embraced me; he was very moved.

Udayan: What kind of discussion took place between you and Aravindan about the costumes? Because the costumes were very special, and Aravindan by then had already done *Kanchana Sita*.

Panikkar: Yes, the play was done after *Kanchana Sita*.

Udayan: So what kind of discussion was there between you and him?

Panikkar: We were all enamoured of natural materials.

Udayan: Was it Aravindan's decision?

Panikkar: Yes, it was Aravindan's decision and he decided the materials also. He was in charge of *aharyam* in all our productions until *Theyyatheyyam*, even in *Theyyatheyyam* he made some suggestions… some decisions were taken and they were passed onto our actors, but then he could not complete it…

Udayan: Because he died …

Panikkar: But *Theyyatheyyam*'s costumes were almost as he desired.

Udayan: So did he use these natural materials?

Panikkar: Yes, mostly.

Udayan: With the use of natural materials he brought a certain kind of time quality also to it. I mean Ghatotkach and all characters wearing such costumes made of natural materials.

Panikkar: I don't think a time factor could be associated with natural materials because this story, the characters and the natural materials are beyond the limitations of time. Characters are ideas and they represent ideas, so naturally costumes also with their texture, colour, quality, etc. add to the idea. Natural materials enhance the folk quality, for example, the grass used to make Ghatotkacha's headgear or the palm leaf used to make Bhima's headgear; all qualify the characteristics on a suggestive level.

Udayan: Was the decision about costumes taken solely by him on this basis?

Panikkar: He discussed these matters at length, he watched the rehearsals… he did not decide too soon because he wanted to see the rehearsals, he wanted to see the movement patterns. Of course he wouldn't interfere, but he would watch from a distance, because he had directed theatre before. I had good rapport with him. He just sat there and in some cases he would even make suggestions.

Udayan: He was very gentle.

Panikkar: He was. And then he would discuss these things with whoever was to execute them like, for instance, Pankajakshan Nair who was with us then but left us later. But now there are actors like Murali, Saji S.L. and Komalan. Murali was doing the costumes, paintings, etc. He did them for *Vikramorvashiyam*. He was very good in painting as well as in making costumes.

Udayan: When was your repertory made? When you did *Madhyamavyayogam* did you have a group of actors?

Panikkar: Yes, I had a repertory from the time we started *Avanavan Kadamba* with Aravindan. Those days they were not paid. We started regular group work from the very beginning. There was a set of 10-15 people and they got some support from Government of India later. We started getting support. The first support that we got was very meagre. It was from the Ford Foundation. It was only five lakh rupees. It was a very small amount. Later the Ford Foundation started 'spoiling' many of our actors and directors by giving 20 lakhs and such huge amounts of money. They didn't know what to do with that kind of money! Govindan's son Manavendrannath, Jose who passed away and Raghu—all these four, five people were given twenty lakhs each with which they could not do anything!

Udayan: And what was the idea of actor's training in your mind in the beginning?

Panikkar: Before *Avanavan Kadamba* I did some training in Alleppey. There was a Kalari Guru from Vaikom. He used to come and do massage for all of us. It was from him that I first learnt Kalari. While the oil massages were going on, he used to teach me some of the *adavus*, that is, Kalari movements, but of course, those were just rudimentary and beginning lessons. During *Madhayamavyayogam* also, we had trained people. Balakrishnan was doing Bhima's role. He was a good Kathakali artiste but had the rare privilege of participating in our theatre, after unlearning Kathakali through non-usage. He could unlearn Kathakali but at the same time its energy was with him.

Udayan: Do you mean Kathakali was kept away like a costume so he could wear it again.

Panikkar: No, we strictly wanted to avoid the Kathakali grammar, but retain its energy. When I worked with him and requested him to do movements like Bhima's climbing the mountain, he could very easily do it. He was a short man, but due to his acting ability, he could become big on the stage. Jagannathan was doing Ghatotkacha's role. He is a brilliant actor who has learnt many art forms and is very thorough at rhythm.

Udayan: He is also a beautiful dancer.

Panikkar: He is. He was doing Ghatotkacha. Now he's in films and in television serials.

Udayan: Were they all trained in different ways?

Panikkar: That gave me a feeling that actors can learn some style but retain its energy and thus keep it neutral.

Udayan: What is neutral?

Panikkar: I thought that Kalari, of which I had got a taste in Alleppey, would be the right thing for them to learn. I went to the C.V.N Kalari Gurukkal and I too joined them to do the exercises. Earlier, Sankara Pillai and Ayyapa Paniker used to conduct workshops where they had introduced the western drill, because actors didn't have any idea of how to use the body. So they made it a matter of routine to keep the drill.

Udayan: For the actors.

Panikkar: And then *vachik* exercises. Vocal exercises were done by trying out all kinds of voices. I visited one of these camps and had discussions with them, and also with Ayyapa Panikkar. Of course he knew that I did not approve of the western drill method. I told Ayyapa Paniker that the drill was not the right thing; a drill would not teach us body control. Only Kalari could give that kind of complete body control. I told him that we had started Kalari. Even now our actors are sent for Kalari training regularly. We have two new actors now, you'll find them here. I have requested Kalari Gurukkal to give them special training.

Udayan: What kind of training is given?

Panikkar: The training is quite different from the western drill method.

What is achieved here is what the Gurukkal calls the *sharira bhava*. *Bhava* happens in the mind. And *sharira* expresses this *bhava*. He calls air thrust, *vayu sthobha*. He has taught us many poses like the cat's pose, the horse pose etc. That is why I told you we can have a human horse! Human horse can be brought to the stage only if you can behave like a horse, if you can create a *mudra*, (gesture) with your body. T.R. Sukumaran Nair was a very senior actor in the realistic stage. He was realistic as well as he used to act in plays like C.V. Raman Pillai's *Martandavarma* (stage adaptation), epic themes etc. His rendering was very melodramatic … and like Shambhu Mitra he had a good voice. But when it comes to *sharira bhava*, such great actors were missing the point because their style did not call for this. He was the son of a great Kathakali actor and in his acting he tried certain subtle applications of body language like a character becoming big by raising himself on his toes, etc. That was only applicable in his case and not in the case of everyone in realistic theatre. But even he could not imagine an actor coming as an elephant to the stage in my play *Karimkutty*. He came to me privately and said, 'Why don't we avoid the elephant being brought to the stage? It looks very awkward. Instead why can't the character say that he had come on an elephant which is left outside?'

I said to him, 'Chettan, this may not seem good to you, this is the Indian theatre concept which is essentially *Natyadharmi* in which one can assume the role of an elephant by bringing out the 'elephantness' of the elephant… this is something that is not there in realistic theatre. He agreed and he tried to believe, saying that if a human elephant is introduced it might create a *hasya* feeling.

Udayan: But wasn't he an ardent lover of Kathakali?

Panikkar: Yes. But the belief was strong that Kathakali and theatre were different. I also believe that theatre is not Kathakali. But we should agree that Kathakali is theatre. Theatre can learn many things from the rudimentary theatre forms like Theyyam, Mudiyettu and the like.

Udayan: You told me how he stood on his toes …

Panikkar: Yes. He told me he tried this in the role of Ravana in Srikanthan Nair's *Lankalakshmi* …

Udayan: He taught you how to become Ravana.

Panikkar: No, how to represent might and greatness. His belief was interesting. But realistic theatre had nothing to fall back upon unlike us who have the *Natyashastra*. It was not even our *Lokdharmi*. Some people like Sukumaran Nair were able to come out of realistic theatre and imagine how they could use the dharma in *Natyashastra* by virtue of their intelligence and inborn talent …

Udayan: Were you with him in theatre too?

Panikkar: No, I just used to visit him and also enjoy his acting. When the subject of theatre was introduced in the School of Drama at Calicut University during its formative period, I was also in the syllabus committee.

Udayan: In Trivandrum?

Panikkar: No, here in Thrissur. Sankara Pillai was the director. Even he was just planning what was to be taught. I don't claim that I had something special to offer! Rather, it was a slow evolution for all of us. I was in the committee, Karanth was there and Sukuraman Nair and N. Krishna Pillai were there too. Krishna Pillai was an author and was known for his powerful plays like *Bhagnabhavanam*, *Balabalam*, *Kanyaka*, etc. He was influenced by the western realistic structure of playwriting. Rightly or wrongly he was called Kerala's Ibsen, which I don't think he ever relished! But this was common among many of our writers in regional languages, be it novels or drama

Udayan: Are you talking about the time a drama institute was being made in Thrissur?

Panikkar: Yes. Krishna Pillai was very nice to me; Sukuraman Nair too. They were, in fact, interested in my work and were my well wishers but they were strong believers in realism and they deserve all our respect in that regard. The situation I am going to tell you about is very interesting. The syllabus was being discussed (Narayana Pisharody, the famous Sanskrit teacher and scholar was also a member, but he could not come) and Sanakara Pillai was presiding. There was a question and it was Sankara Pillai who brought it in the open: 'What form should we teach?' He asked me and Karanth and then added: 'Each year we can select different forms; shall we select Mudiyettu this year?'

Udayan: What is Mudiyettu?

Panikkar: It is a ritual drama in which *dharma* fights *adharma*. The Godess

Kali the daughter of Lord Shiva represents *dharma* and the demon Darika is the embodiment of *adharma*. The fight takes place in the open courtyard of the temple. Kulis or *bhutagana* are the supporters of Kali. Darika has his brother Danava also on his side. There is another interesting character Koimpidar a soldier representing society who is with Kali. The fight between these two groups happens at many places in the open. The Kali gets possessed and furious and finally the antagonist Darika is annihilated (when she is about to kill Darika). Mudiyettu is a form of Kalinatakam where Kali and Darika are engaged in battle and there are specific steps. *Mudi* means crown. When the crown is put on the actor performing the role of Kali, he gets possessed and when she is about to kill Darika, the *mudi* (headgear of Kali) is removed and he comes back to normalcy. It goes on like that. Sankara Pillai's idea was that each art form should be taught. Sukurman Nair's opinion was that some indigenous theatre form should be taught. They were to select each form for each year. They even selected Kathakali. But they didn't know what purpose that would serve. But before we could make any comment Krishna Pillai said, 'Sukumaran Nair, why should these people insist that students should learn a form?' This was partly correct and partly wrong because for theatre performance, a definite art-form need not be learnt as such. That is why I was arguing for Kalari which is not an art form.

Udayan: It's a norm and you can learn a certain norm. The form has to be created by you.

Panikkar: Kalari is an offence and defense mechanism which is very neutral. There were two opinions within the context of indigenous theatre. Sankara Pillai believed that a form should be learnt. He did not realise that learning one form meant learning a certain grammar and that grammar could not be taken to theatre. But Krishna Pillai meant something else. Why learn a form at all?

Udayan: What did he mean?

Panikkar: Krishna Pillai asked Sukumaran Nair, 'Why is Sankara Pillai insisting that students should learn a form of theatre or a form of dance or something. Why should we introduce such a thing?' At that point Karanth and I wanted to support Sankara Pillai in a general way. We thought we had to support him. Karanth and I were there as supporters of indigenous theatre and these two were very staunch supporters of realistic theatre, which also needed to be learnt, ought to be studied as part of the curriculum. So then I did not say anything on this matter. 'We have to think about whether it should be learnt or not,' I said. Karanth agreed with it and we looked at each other … what I meant and he meant was different.

Udayan: Which year was this?

Panikkar: Somewhere around the end of the 80's.

Panikkar: Sankara Pillai was the Founder Director of the drama school. Later in the meeting, he said: 'Let it be shelved, we will decide about the form later. If any particular form is not required to be taught, we won't discuss it. But Narayana Pisharody has suggested that *Urubhangam* may be prescribed as a text.' At that point I interfered and said that between *Urubhangam* and *Madhayamavyayogam* Pisharody should not have chosen the former. I would suggest *Madhayamavyayogam* as this was a very simple text. *Urubhangam* could be slightly difficult, structure-wise.

Udayan: Or even at the level of consciousness.

Panikkar: Yes and they agreed. Krishna Pillai was immediately in favour of my suggestion. He said 'Yes, yes what you said is correct, we decide *Madhayamavyayogam*. Sankara Pillai, take note of this and write, *Madhayamavyayogam*.'

I had great respect for Krishna Pillai Sir. And he also liked me. Once in one of the university committees, he suggested that I include the study of *Avanvan Kadamba*. There was a personal relationship. Then I said, addressing Krishna Pillai: 'Sir, Sankara Pillai has suggested that we teach a form like Mudiyettu and I think what he said is partly correct.' And he asked, 'Why? It has nothing to do with this, this is drama. *Mudiyettu* is only an art form; *Madhayamavyayogam* is drama,' and then I asked 'So if you agree that *Madhayamavyayogam* is a drama then I would like to know how Ghatotkacha would lift the tree and beat Bhima with that tree?'

Udayan: So you put your idea across in an indirect way?

Panikkar: Yes. And he said to Sukumaran Nair, 'What he says is correct. How can Ghatotkacha beat Bhima with the tree unless he learns how to lift the tree?'

Udayan: And that demands physical action.

Panikkar: Sukumaran Nair's acting methodology or Krishna Pillai's writing methodology never came anywhere near Bhasa's idea of Ghatotkacha uprooting a tree or uprooting a mountain. According to his methodology it would not be possible at all.

Udayan: So you asked him how it could be done.

Panikkar: 'How will that be done unless some form or some dance movement or body movement or body kinetics is known? These are very essential.' Krishna Pillai then agreed to introduce Mudiyettu. Since they didn't know all this, the students were put through a system of learning, which was Macaulay's legacy, even in schools and colleges. When *Avanvan Kadamba* was taught, teachers found it difficult; but now teachers have also changed. In many colleges now, teachers feel they should see *Avanavan Kadamba* to understand it or at least to develop a certain sensibility to interpret a script through the angle of production. This has come about very late. But we have digressed!

Udayan: We were talking about the introduction of Kalari for your actors.

Panikkar: Yes, so now there was the question why Mudiyettu and why Kalari? At that time I was not very efficient in dealing with this subject, because I too was in the process of thinking and evolving. But by that time I had started Kalari and I was beginning to understand a few things. I started Kalari in the 1980s, but I always wondered if a form like Kathakali would be of help too. Balakrishnan, who did the role of Bhima, had learnt Kathakali from a senior Kathakali guru, though he was not into performance. But he had learnt its basics. The reason I said he was useful for me was because he was able to forget the Kathakali he had learnt. He unlearned all the Kathakali lessons gradually so he could meet my requirements easily. And this is precisely the reason I say a neutral form like Kalari will be of great help in the creation of an actor. An established form with an established grammar as in the case of Kathakali or even a folk or a ritual form like Mudiyettu will not be helpful in theatre if you learn and try to imitate it. Learning is all right, but learning should be followed by an intelligent unlearning process which the teachers should also be aware of... but then that was not the case! And how to put these forms to use is still a difficult proposition. The NSD is now facing the same problem. You know they bring in many forms, for instance, they invite many Chhau artists, etc. who present physically strong forms. And the students are all taken aback seeing the Chhau movements. Gopi, who knows Kalari and has the correct methodology goes there too and he gives classes to the actors, but he's very unhappy because there is no one there who would use this. They just learn it for the sake of learning. And after some time, some students get bored and start asking, 'Why should we learn this?' Similarly about vocalisation; once during the time when Mohan Maharishi was the Director, he came here and recorded Vedic music and we went to Panniyar. We collected the *Rig Veda*, the *Sama Veda* and the *Yajur Veda* chants from the original Vedic chanters.

Udayan: From which city?

Panikkar: This is near Thrissur. Panjal is the village, about which Fritz Staal wrote a book on *Atiratram Yajna*. He has also documented Vedic chanting. I went there and collected the whole thing for NSD but now where is all that material? Nobody knows. On a subsequent occasion when Kirti Jain was the Director, she wanted to collect it again, so she sent Ratna, Kavalam Padmanabhan's wife. She took me to Panjal, and other places. Fortunately even at that time the senior Vedic chanters were alive, some of them were in their nineties. One person was 94-years old. They sang the Sama Veda. Now they have all passed away. The oldest man living is a 70-year old. Now Sangeet Natak Akademi is planning to take the recording again, but then all the stalwarts have already gone! I had asked the Akademi to expedite this work. But nothing has happened so far.

Udayan: What did you have in mind?

Panikkar: Not me! Kirti *ji* wanted to record and keep it there and Ratna was sent and it was done. But now nothing is being done with that recording.

Udayan: How do you teach your actors vocalisation? How do you do neutral training in vocalisation?

Panikkar: You know, this is a question which I have been handling for a very long time. Are we doing our vocalisation by imitating the *Chakyars*? No. Just imitating will not help. Articulation and mere rendering are different things. Articulating the passage is possible only by using air thrust or *vayusthobha*. Now *vayusthobha* in theatre should depend on the thrust of the words, the thrust on the *bhava*, the demand of the *bhava* in the text. This is only in relation to the language used. The syntax of the language is involved; it should go well with the genius of the language … like you said, in Hindi it was possible, you could say such a thing because you feel what is acceptable. It was accepted in Kerala too. Even Sanskrit pronunciation while doing a Sanskrit play should be made acceptable to the quality if the language. It was accepted in the case of *Chakyar*s. Can you extend the sound after a *visarga* for instance? I feel we could. How? For example let us take the case of the *Visargam* in *Ramaha*. *Ramaha* and *Ramah*, both ways of pronunciation are correct. Brahmins from Chennai will pronounce it *Ramaha*, while we pronounce it *Ramah* or sometimes in both ways. The sound of *ha* is there. When you conclude a musical rendering, a sing-song dialogue rendering of *Ramahaaaa*, the *'aaaa'* comes only after the *visarga*. *Chakyar*s sometimes go wrong, you could say it is wrong, the pundits might say so, but still it is allowed. Why is it allowed? Because the *bhava* has to flow. It is called *pracharanam*, which means the *bhava* should reverberate; the idea should take its origin from the pre-acting to the acting with vocal to the post-acting. These are the three points or three different areas of acting. If you take one unit of acting, it should have that pre-acting phase, like for example, to take a stone is pre-acting, throwing it at a dog is acting and then you throw with the thrust and along with the thrust, sometimes the *vachika* also comes and then after that…

Udayan: … you look at it …

Panikkar: Yes, you look at it and enact, 'Oh! It has gone away.' That is post acting. So this way in each unit of action you have pre-acting, acting and post acting.

Udayan: Which could also be pre-verbal, verbal and post verbal…

Panikkar: It could be. Sometimes the verbal itself may come in the beginning as pre-acting.

It could be pre-acting or even post acting. The gestures develop into a situation and then the *vachik* may come, it is also possible. Vocalisation has all these aspects. What I did in vocalisation was this: I would tell myself, 'This is my text; this is its potential, its requirement.' And I would think of the style in which music was to be put into the *alapana* or in the rhythm.'

This is what we have done in *Uttararamacharitam* where you have given me the freedom to untie or tie the rhythm. Sometimes when I'm about to untie it, you get it tied. All this depends upon the situation, the moment and the audio-visual combination. And I have taken from traditional Vedic chanting. I have also been inspired by the traditional folk and tribal vocalisation. They have relations which are very interesting to find out.

Udayan: You mean to say that you have taken from folk rendering and Vedic chanting?

Panikkar: Yes, and tribal too, you remember how Rama calls aloud to Sita in the wilderness? So that was my source of vocalisation. The first source is the text, the demands of the text, the *bhava* of the text. For bringing this *bhava* and its demands, I have the material with which I go back to the earliest source from where even *Chakyar*s got their inspiration. *Chakyar*s had also received inspiration only from 'oathu', the Vedic chants. That is why the Brahmins used to say *oathu pizhachu koothayi* meaning you have taken from our *oathu* and went wrong and that is *koothu* or your dramatic rendering. When the Vedic rendering went wrong, it became *Chakyar*'s rendering. We need all these precursors. We must travel as far back as possible irrespective of whether it is Arya or Dravida, patrician or plebian. Thus we take all this because all things belong to us. The second source is Vedic chanting. The use of air thrust to express *bhava*s is common to us as well as *Chakyar*s. We try to make it stronger to interrelate it with the body language and thereby create the time-space continuum.

Udayan: And the *bhava* part that you were referring to in relation to the text, should actually come with that *prana* and *vayustobh,* breath and air thrust.

Panikkar: *Prana* and *vayusthobha.*

Udayan: Now in Vedic chanting also this *vayusthobh* is very much there.

Panikkar: Very much. Even in enunciating the mantra.

Udayan: In the movement also …

Panikkar: It relates to the movement also and is used to correctly interpret the word.

Udayan: Like what you said about Kalari that it has neutrality of a kind, can you tell me about the neutrality of vocalisation?

Panikkar: The actors learn the *shloka* by heart. For example in *Urubhangam* there is a *shloka*:

> *shrimaansamyuga chandanena rudhirena ardraanuliptachchhavih,*
>
> *bhoosansarpana renu patalbhujo baalavritam graahitah,*
>
> *nirvritte amritamanthane kshitidharanmukta ....*

He gives a graphic description of Duryodhana's appearance. Duryodhana crawls like a snake.

Udayan: His body has blood smeared on it like *chandana* (sandalwood).

Panikkar: And it is very *aardram* which means it is wet. And the *chhavi* (his image) is effulgent. To each word the body of the actor should react: *bhoosamsarpana renu patalbhujo* 'While crawling on the earth the dust on the blood...'

Udayan: ... seems like *parag,* pollen grains.

Panikkar: Yes, and then *amritmanthane suraa asuraa,* etc, like the snake abandoned by the gods and demons after the *amritmanthana*...

Like the snake he crawls. For the entire rendering of the *shloka* the basis of vocalisation is the working of the voice to suit the *sanchari*s (fleeting emotions) and keep to the *sthayi* (stable emotion). For example, when Duryodhan says *Bheemenabhitva,* 'Oh! That Bhima has hit me!' when he utters the word 'Bhima,' he should evoke the maximum ...

Udayan: Disregard ... hatred ...

Panikkar: He should say: *bhe e me e na bhi tvaaa.*

Udayan: And thus a sense of sarcasm and hatred.

Panikkar: *Samayvyavastha.* Then breaking all rules, here there is an emotion of wonder (*adbhut rasa*) as well. *Gadaabhighaatakshatajarjaroruh...* 'Both my thighs are broken!' This is very, very sad and so there is *karunam* as well ...

Udayan: So through such vocalisation all these sequences of *rasa*s and *sanchari*s would come through.

Panikkar: Yes, and then at last he, Duryodhan, is nevertheless indomitable and that is the basic *rasa, veera.* All this you have to design in the dialogue rendering, in the subtle movements of the body and ultimately the *sthayi bhava* should be maintained in the vocalisation. We have looked into all this. I sit with the actor; engage in their way of rendering. This exercise has been done. Now, of course, Girishan can do it by himself, I need not worry.

Udayan: How do you actually choose your actors, what is it that you see in a person you take in your repertory?

Panikkar: Casting is a really difficult work. When I work with groups other than mine, I engage one Kalari artist; usually Gopi is sent for that preliminary job. His report on each group member is one of the main guidelines for casting. There are other considerations also, like voice quality, taste in music, etc. I did the casting like this in NSD while I did *Urubhangam* in Sanskrit with second-year students in 1991. One student called Shelka was cast as Duryodhana. I remember my experience there. It was very interesting. During the first week of the reharsals, the actors who were made available to me for reharsal sessions in the evening, one raised a question under the leadership of Shelka like this: why do you teach us these movements? Why do you insist that Duryodhana, with both thighs broken, should dance? How could it be possible? My immediate reaction was that I take this doubt with all seriousness and definitely request the Director of NSD to hospitalise Shelka and provide me with another actor, whom I would cast! Aravindan also was with me at that time working in the costumes of the production.

Udayan: It is interesting that you wanted to recommend the actor to be hospitalised.

Panikkar: This question is an eye opener to the whole theory of *Natyam* in the Indian sense. How was Duryodhana made to move? He could safely occupy a convenient space in the stage and enact the role always as a person hit on the thighs. But Indian concept of *rasa* demanded that he could not remain static in the main *Karuna rasa*. This *sthayi* or dominant *rasa* is to be embellished by *sanchari* with their transitory emotions and this would necessarily call for movements.

Udayan: So the actors whom you select should have an overall view on matters related to Indian aesthetics.

Panikkar: Certainly this requires proper orientation. Availability of actors is a great problem but the available person should be useful also.

Udayan: Yes, that's what I am saying.

Panikkar: Actors should be available as well as useful. They should have conviction also. But these boys who came are educated. One is an advocate; his mother came in with the other one. Both are very good. For the roles of Lava and Kusha they are very good. They have a sense of rhythm.

Udayan: Do you ask them to perform something before you select them?

Panikkar: Yes, I am concerned with *swara, suswara* which means they should be able to sing *Sa Pa Sa Sa Pa Sa.* If one can do this, it is sufficient. They can build up on that. Once I had no other option but to take in a girl. She was from Sankara Pillai's School of Drama. She had done the School of Drama course. She is very good now. But at the outset she had no sense of *swara*… she performs very well now, but when she came, she could never keep to the *shruti* and had a problem with rhythm but then she got it. When I see aspiring actors I get the feeling that it is possible to improve upon them and bring them to *shruti* and rhythm.

Udayan: On seeing a boy or girl can you decide whether he/she could do it?

Panikkar: I can make out if she or he would work out or not. I mean, whether they have the passion for this work. In the old days, very young boys would be taken to the Kathakali *asan* (teacher) and he would be able to make out if they had the capability to become Kathakali dancers from their body language and facial expressions. Recently we got a girl who at first glance, did not seem to be good. Still I said this girl was had potential seeing her readiness, her dedication. She had learnt *chenda* (musical instrument) and she has a wonderful sense of rhythm and precision in rhythm. The only defect is again that *Sa Pa Sa shruti* won't come! Her name is Parvati… I asked Sarita to work with her, to bring out whatever is there in her. She worked hard and showed the same result. One can't exactly say how the selection ultimately works. In theatre, one need not be thrown out like that. Everybody can fit in, any one who works hard in the whole scheme.

One could be used in the group for, instance and you see the group is not unimportant. The group is very important, but the actors should not feel that they are doing something less important. In *Malavikagnimitram*, it is the group which creates the tree and the tree is central in the production.

Udayan: Yes. It is important, almost a character in your production.

Panikkar: When I visited the Soviet Union I had a discussion with a theatre director called Tobakov who I met at the Indian Embassy. I asked him how he makes a selection of actors. He promptly replied, 'Oh, I select only talented people!' Then he asked me how I select and I said, 'For me talent is necessary! But how could you discover it when it lays hidden deep in him or her like ember (*Kanmadam*) in the stone?

Udayan: What is that?

Panikkar: *Kanmadam.* It is the black thing within the rock which flows out and is used as a medicine.

The point is that you cannot make out the tastes and talents of men from the outer appearance alone. I raised my point to him and asked, 'How do you arrive at the decision that an individual has no taste? Only God could know where He has placed talent!' In the case of the rock the whole outer thing is hard rock, but inside there is *Kanmadam.* You'll have to search; you'll have to travel through difficult rock. You may also find an Ahaliya in the rock! The only thing is you should chisel away the unnecessary portions and an Ahaliya might emerge! If you know how to chisel, if you know how to sculpt, you might find her.' Well, the Soviet director Tobakov didn't have anything to say.

Udayan: His method might be choosing well prepared, already trained people. But in India you can't actually do it, because the so called trained people are actually untrained, especially for theatre.

Panikkar: Availability is one thing, but so is opportunity. It is only when someone is given an opportunity that he or she can flower. Like our girl Malu. She now shines very well in any character. Malu is going to be cast in *Kalivesham* as the wife of the actor. And in *Theyyatheyyam* she did Amma's role very well. Have you seen *Theyyatheyyam*?

Udayan: I have. It was performed on your eightieth birthday. What is the role of your study of the *Natyashastra* in all these productions that we are talking about? What role did it play in your theatre?

Panikkar: Actually we created a *Natyashastra* only to ultimately find that it corroborated with the old *Natyashastra.* We would create a movement and the *Natyashastra* would corroborate it. Thus when we discovered that what we did was as per the *Natyashastra*, I requested my group too to join me in my enquiry. It started with *angika abhinaya.* We were not graduates in the Natyashastra but we found the relevance of the *Natyashastra*, and we found the Natyashastric principles being put into practice unknowingly by virtue of our association with other art forms and also because of the possibilities of the human body. When we found that whatever we tried out coincided with the Natyashastric principles to some extent, we started taking interest in the *Chari* chapter of *angika abhinaya*. Kalaripayattu also gave us an insight into the *angika abhinaya* and *sattvika abhinaya* in *Natyashatra*. Gopi was an actor well-versed in the art of Kalari and I started doing experiments with him. I also took my group to the Kalari. There are certain practices in Kalari like the animal stances, like the *matsya vadivu* (pose of the fish), *marjar vadivu* (pose of the cat), *kukkura vadivu* (pose of the dog), *gaja vadivu* (pose of the elephant), *and ashva vadivu* (pose of the horse), etc. There are eight *vadivus* and these are all similar to the *angika abhinaya* chapters of the *Natyashastra*. We tried to link the two and also to extend the possibilities of Kalari and introduce certain new things in Kalari. Kalari gurus articulate their instructions in a rhythm. There is no rhythm set as such, but there is a rhythm of the body, and instruction is also carried out rhythmically. I introduced rhythm into the movements of Kalari and also enlarged its scope. I introduced the various *charees* too into the style. *Bhava* was added—*bhava* was already there at a very rudimentary level because the Kalari guru used to tell us about *sharir bhava*. When *Narsimha vadivu* was shown, guru would say that one should have *narsimha* in one's mind and should meditate on *Narsimha*. It's a very rudimentary way of applying the mind. But we made it more expressive by bringing in all the different *bhavas* added to the Kalari practice and the possibility of Kalari practice was also extended. With the result we have now laid down a basic teaching methodology to teach an actor about how to use his body. In Kalari there is a saying that you should have eyes all over the body. That means that you should be alert and watch out for enemy from any side and be capable of quick reaction and retaliation. The significant factor was not the arrival of the enemy but one's own conscious awareness of one's body and quick, reflex action. These things were followed in structuring a methodology for preparing actors and then we combined it with *vachika* and *sattvika*.

Our actors were given the opportunity to attend classes … in fact recently there were a number of workshops. Either we would organise workshops or when some other organisations like the Kudiyattam Kendra would organise them I would insist that the actors attend. This time we organised a Kudiyattam workshop where I specifically invited students and practitioners of theatre and our actors were also present and I asked all of them to get involved. The main thrust of the workshop understood *angika, vachika, sattvika* and *aharya*. There was one very interesting paper which I suggested because the person who had made a film on the life of a Kudiyattam artiste asked me, 'I am interested in studying your efforts to know about the efficacy of Cholliattam as a training process. It is as you say: I would like to see only the real person.' There is some validity in his argument that *aharya abhinaya* sometimes takes away the originality of art in Kathakali and Kudiyattam. This was his opinion. He said the human body could be so expressive in Kalari and if Anjaneya (Hanuman) appears in a heavy costume or for that matter if any character appears in heavy costumes, it would take away the inner *shobha*, or the attractiveness and communicative ability of *angika abhinaya*. He gave a reason that when he filmed Nottam, where Nedumudi Venu wanted to smile and then laugh in the costumes of Bali, he could not express those with the ordinary expressions that he normally used in theatre. He had to make it doubly forceful, otherwise it would not have reached the audience. I don't believe that logic is correct because it is only for someone like Nedumudi Venu that the costumes become a burden. For an established Kudiyattam actor or Kathakali actor like Krishnan Nair, *aharya* is not a burden because they are used to acting with costumes. I do not agree with his argument that a contemporary film or theatre actor may find their particular costumes a burden but his approach to the subject on an academic level is interesting.

There is a work which deals with this very idea. It is called the *Natankusha* and it was written by an unknown author. The above mentioned paper was very relevant in the light of the serious arguments raised by the *Natankusha*. The major argument raised by the *Natankusha* is meaningful on academic level and stupid at the same time; meaningful because it quotes the instance of Hanuman. When Hanuman in a heavy costume appears as Hanuman, we are able to accept that this is Hanuman but during the course of his narration of his experience with Sita to Rama he becomes Sita which looks terrible! That is what the Natankushkar says. This creates *rasavichchhitti*. With all the costumes he wears we have to imagine that he is Sita, which is unbelievable and this creates an impediment or obstruction in *rasa*. But it is stupid or absurd because it cuts the very branch on which art sits on. Art is but a transformation methodology; without that there is no theatre. If you cannot transform into another character, with that character's feelings, then how can *sancharis* (transient emotions) work? In the case of Hanuman becoming Sita, it is only the *sanchari bhava* ... . In story telling, you cannot have a linear way of telling the story. This is the point. Story telling does not follow a graphic line. It is the curvature that makes the Indian method of story telling interesting. When you, in Hanuman's costume, want to communicate that you have met Sita and she told you something, then you quote Sita's words. By doing that you become Sita or you assume Sita's emotions. You do it in the outfit of Hanuman. Are you stopped from doing that in real life? You try to imitate another person or you try to transform into that persona. This is the basic qualification, quality of art—the art of transformation, the art of representation—which is unknowingly done even by common people. Even the common vendors who sit in the market place, when they relate a story, when they narrate what had happened in their neighbourhood, they impersonate characters, for instance someone who picked up a quarrel, the way he spoke, behaved, etc. This is a basic tendency of man. We find it even in children, and that is the quality of theatre also.

Udayan: We saw the way you did *Madhyamavyayogam* in great detail. Then the second play of Bhasa you took was *Karnabharam.* Why *Karnabharam?*

Panikkar: Initially I wanted to do all the plays of Bhasa because his plays are unique in representing the quintessence of Indian theatre concepts and practices. Ayyapa Paniker also was always instigating me do all 13 plays. But then I started wondering whether I should search out other sources also and said we could try *Ashcharyachudamani* too. The author of *Ashcharyachudamani,* Saktibhadra, was also a rare and gifted playwright of the caliber of Bhasa. I thought I should not overlook Saktibhadra even while giving due credit to the genius of Bhasa. Saktibhadra belonged to Kerala and his real name was Bhuvanabhooti. He belonged to a place called Pathanamthitta and his work, the *Ashcharyachudamani,* consisted of seven acts, all seven equally rich in theatrical potential. Seven wonders of the *Ashcharyachudamani* out of which I did only *Swapnankam* which still remains a wonder along with the others. I wanted to do one more at least. If I were to cover Bhasa alone, then I couldn't do all this. I told Ayyapa Paniker, 'Let others do Bhasa, why should I?' And he said, 'You can do *Ashcharyachudamani* also but while doing Bhasa you are creating a practical *Natyashastra*. *Natyashastra* might have dealt with all these but there are areas where you can contribute. For example, in *Madhyamavyavoyam*, Ghatotkacha lifts a tree and beats Bhima with that. How do you meet this challenge in acting? How do you register this in an *attaprakara*? You cannot, there are such situations which prove beyond doubt, which establish the quality of Indian theatre and this becomes evident when you do Bhasa's plays.' I said to him, 'These are areas related to theatre practice and such situations are available in Saktibhadra also. That is why I find this author worthy to be tried out. In *Ashcharyachudamani* there is the Ravana with ten heads. He drinks Sita's beauty with all his twenty eyes and with twenty hands, he tries to embrace her. How does one show this in theatre! *Maya Sitankam* is wonderful! There are other instances also in *Maya Sitankam* where the necessity of innovating such theatre practices becomes inevitable. *Ashcharyachudamani* has been translated by Dr V. Raghavan. The theatre world must take essential note of this wonderful play called *Wondrous Crest*. Apart from *Uttararamacharitam* I wanted to request you to translate one of these seven wonders.

Udayan: We'll do that after *Uttararamacharitam*.

Panikkar: I have done *Maya Sita* in Malayalam and not in Sanskrit. Saktibhadra's Sanskrit is not like Bhasa's. I like Bhasa's Sanskrit the most, it is very simple. Another significant fact about *Ashcharyachudamani* should not be left unsaid. Each *ankam* is known by a separate name like *Parnasalankam, Surpanakhankam, Asokavanikankam* and the like. This represents a very interesting dramatic culture peculiar to Kerala and to *Chakyar*s. Each *ankam* is done with all the necessary requisites which would constitute a play, I mean, with all the required *sandhi*s. So this enables the play to be done over seven days or seven sections, each having its own structured build up.

Udayan: That means you value the structural brilliance of play, however short it is, or however segmented it is. Then why did you select *Karnabharam* which is said to be unfinished amongst some scholars?

Panikkar: The opinion of the scholars is well taken care of, but while doing it, I wanted to make it a well structured play with a proper beginning and end. Probably the scholars were led by the argument that the play never ends with Karna's death and that may be the reason why it is considered unfinished. But I felt that the play was very different in its structure. It starts with the words of Karna, 'O Shalyaraja! Take my chariot to where Arjuna stands!' The play ends with the same words. It might sound absurd, but there is a lot of transformation that takes place between which creates the entire drama. We tried out the transformation methodology to its fullest possible extent in the production. It demaded it, it was inevitable. *Karnabharam* can be divided into two parts. The first part happens before Karna enters the battle field. He happens to see his mother Kunti and comes to know from her the reality that he is her son. It is after he has this knowledge that he enters. I made some changes to his state of mind when he makes his entry. It was slightly different in the earlier productions. Now after the *sutradhar's* part we go straight to the character. The mental conflict of the character is represented and a voice comes from behind saying 'Surya *putra*' and Karna looks up towards Surya. And then we hear: *suta putra* Karna, *Kaunteya* Karna, *Radheya* Karna. It is a huge conflict in his mind and he falls down. But then he again musters all his energy and jumps up and the emotion of *veera* (valour) is evoked. But the *veera* (valour) is suffused with *shoka,* sorrow, *sashokamupaiti.* There are two parts here too. In the first part, Karna is trying his arrow. His failure begins when he thinks, 'Why has this *astra* (weapon) failed? Is it because of my mother's words?' His mother enters in his imagination and he is tormented by these thoughts. Finally he is able to dismiss her from his thoughts and he tries his arrow again. Then again a voice is heard and that is his guru Parashurama cursing him that at the required time, his knowledge of archery would fail him. And he falls down saying, 'This is the reason why this *astra* (weapon) is not working!' Here I have used Kalari. This is how I placed these events.

Then we go back to the first part that is, Parshurama's curse. Karna recapitulates what had happened, his experience with Parashurama. He wants to tell it to someone. He says, 'Shalyaraja, listen to me about my *astras's* (weapon's) story.' Shalyaraja is ready and in my production transforms himself to be Parashurama. He comes from within Karna. He transforms into Karna's mind and from his mind, he asks, 'What happened then?' Shalya enacts the role of Parashurama created in Karna's imagination. The

transformation takes place there and then he says, 'I went to Parshurama.'
'Then what happened?' Shalya asks from behind. In the process of describing
this, Shalya himself helps Karna by assuming the role of Parashurama. This
is what transformation is. And he enacts the role which is slightly difficult
to communicate. I introduced this because this story is known to the whole
of Bharatvarsh. Then the question is why Karna is stating it to Shalya who
already knows it. He wanted to recapitulate and analyse the story in detail.
It is the analysis of an idea, an experience, because it is something that has
already happened earlier. So he relates and shares it with Shalya and while
sharing Shalya becomes Karna's own *antahkaran* (conscience.) At the same
time, according to Karna's wish, he also becomes Parashurama. This is very
tricky. He enacts the role of Parashurama and everything about the curse.
Until the story of the curse is communicated, Shalyaraja is Parashurama.
This transformation from Shalya to Parashurama and back to Shalya is
achieved with a very special theatre practice. A clockwise movement from
within transforms Shalya into Parashurama, and while he returns to being
Shalya it is an anti clockwise movement. Thus the story is finished, being
completely enacted.

That is the first half. Before the actual situation of the war, comes the
moment of taking the decision and then he enters the battlefield and the
play starts with Shalyaraja being addressed by Karna as mentioned earlier
with the words,

Shalyaraja, yatra asav arjunah tatraiva chodyataam mama rathah,

'O Shalyaraja! Take my chariot to where Arjun stands.'

This sentence is present in the beginning, the middle and also in the end.
That's why it never ends with a *Bharatvakya* or anything like that. So some
scholars believed that this was an unfinished work, which I don't believe.
The play itself stands unique in its structure. In the second half suddenly
as the battle is on, Indra comes there and a Brahmin emerges out of Indra
asking for *mahattaram bhiksha* or a great gift. Here too there is a theatrical
possibility which was exploited by the method of transformation. In ordinary
conversations you could say something like, 'I have these gifts. If you want
you can take what you like.' But then why did Bhasa write about the cows,
horses, elephants, etc in detail? Karna offers many gifts to the Brahmin and the

chorus enters as cows, horses and elephants, etc. So this transformation leads to a celebration of gift giving, known as *danaveera* as Karna was known for his charity. The first was the detailed analysis of his experience with Parashuram and the second was his detailed celebration of charity. Both are a celebration of ideas. His giving of alms to Indra disguised as a Brahmin culminates in his saying, 'I will give you my life.' 'No no no!' says Indra and then Karna asks, 'Then what is it you want? I know what you want … you want my *kavach* and *kundal*.' And becomes consumed, or possessed withmaking this possible. During the first production, the actor did not want to be possessed but he was ultimately convinced.

Udayan: Who was the actor?

Panikkar: Kaladharan. He enacted the role first and he was not willing to get possessed. He told me that it was not possible for him because he was not an actor belonging to that tribal tradition. I said, 'It is your tradition, you probe within you I was rather firm with him. 'If you can't discover your tradition within your self then I can't work with you, I am sorry. I don't want to teach you. If I teach you then it will become very artificial. So you sleep over the idea, probe sincerely, and think about these aspects about Karna.'

I told him, 'Imagine you are in Karna's position. You are asked to give away something very close to your heart which cannot easily be given away,; it is not like giving an earring or a garland. It is something equal to your life itself. When it is asked of you and when you have no other choice but to give it, what would be your reaction? Think about it and come tomorrow or day after and inform me.' The actor also has to contribute and imagine. I cannot get into his mind and imagine for him. I had imagined the situation and I felt it could not be done unless the actor got possessed. In normal circumstances, a man cannot cut off things which are dear to him, your body and your very existence where sacrifice is required. How is such a sacrifice done? What is the medium for sacrifice? You have to go beyond yourself.

The next day Kaladharan told me that he couldn't sleep the whole night. Early that morning he telephoned me, 'requesting a meeting'. We used to meet in Guru Gopinath's Viswa Kalakendra for rehearsals. He said, 'Today, I am ready to try. Let me see'. 'That is enough', I said, 'You are ready. Your readiness is enough for me. If you have become ready that means you believe the inevitability. Otherwise, you tell me any device with which you can remove these *kavach* and *kundal* and give them away as alms. So preparation is required, this pre-action is required. For the pre-act, you come ready, and I will work with you.' When he came there, I said, 'Possession is possible. When I told you that possession is possible it was only in theory. Now you work up the rhythm which I will give you. You cannot simply paint a big wall without having anything to stand on.' I worked out the rhythm. I took the idea from tradition. It began slowly, and then got faster and faster in arithmetic progression. Finally the rhythm mounted to climax by that time the actor was to get possessed. Rhythm can only help but it can't create.

Udayan: Rhythm can serve only as scaffolding.

Panikkar: *Dhyana* should be there, his own concentration should be there. But only by practice will *dhyana* come. He did that scene successfully.

Udayan: Why is it that the *veera rasa* interests you so much? As far as I know the very two basic *rasas* are *veera* and *shringara*. You moved to *shringara* only later but *veera* was always there. I ask this question in light of what I was trying to say earlier that Gandhi felt that Indians don't have a sense of *shaurya* (valour) in them that they have started lacking in *veera*. Why is it that it interests you so much? Does it have something to do with your own life or your own surroundings or the lethargy of this country? I mean it is so lethargic intellectually and otherwise, the *veera* or *veerata* (valour) is missing here. We are no more *veera* people; we are no more a people with *utsaah* which is the *sthayi bhava* of *veera rasa*. I must say we were so once!

Panikkar: Yes, that is the reason why we should inject, instill, *veera* into our audience also. They should see the play with *utsaah*. From *veera* you can enter into *shringara,* then we can enter into *karuna*. This is what we are going to do in our presentation of *Uttararamacharitam*. It cannot be the other way round. If you start with *Karuna*, your theatre will be done away with in the beginning itself. From *veera* I could go to all the three plays of Kalidasa. I could bring variety to them although there are so many things which are common in all of them unlike the case with Bhasa. Each play of Bhasa's is different. In all the three plays of Kalidasa the heroines are nothing but Nature.

Udayan: You have in fact highlighted that dimension of the heroines of Kalidasa.

Panikkar: The sub-textual spirit of Nature is very much there.

Udayan: Do you think there is no variety as far as this dimension is concerned?

Panikkar: Of course, there is variety but outwardly many similarities are also present. To enter into *shingara*, which is the *rasaraja* (king of the rasas), and *karuna* is something to be tried out. Whether we will fail or succeed, it is only possible if we start with *veera*. And like you said *veera* is a thing which is lacking in our life, in our politics, everywhere. *Veera* demands sincerity, all *rasas* demand sincerity. *Veera* means to fight and *veera* keeps you alive, its *sthayi bhava* is *utsaah*, it keeps you always living. Your existence is proved in *veera*.

Udayan: … and self-respect as well.

Panikkar: *Shringara* is alright. Personally I am not very romantic. Romanticism is good, but with *veera* only. I would like to take up even romanticism with a purpose. Romanticism for the sake of romanticism is no good for me.

Udayan: Was *veera* the reason you were attracted to Bhasa initially?

Panikkar: At first it was not because of that. I was attracted to his way of writing, the way he structured his plays and all that. Till then I had not read all his plays. I had read only *Madhyamavyayogam* in translation, and *Urubhangam*.

Udayan: Both are plays of *veera rasa*.

Panikkar: Yes, I read *Karnabharam* later. I was attracted to these plays because of reasons other than the presence of *veera*. They were eminently actable; they had the possibility of developing visuals, etc.; all these were factors which attracted me. But of all the *rasas* the percentage of the possibility of winning the audience is much higher in *veera*. The audience should come. At least the willing audience should come with us. You shouldn't have to go after the audience. They should be attracted.

P.K. Balakrishanan once said referring to my plays that I was trying to go on a *yatra* (journey) where I take my audience with me from one play to the other. He said that I have a select audience that travels with me. I want the audiences with whom I communicate, whether by reading or by presenting plays, to be specially prepared, for the show no matter how many or few constitute the audience. I always have keep in that I have a minority audiences. Minority audience would be alright but that minority could create a majority at some time. But presently they are a minority. I should travel with them; I should take them on a journey with me.

So one person's work is different from another's. There might be slight differences as well as similarities. Audiences should be able to identify that. They should be able to take it. They might say, 'This is the same rhythm he used in the previous production.' Some people ask such questions. I have to reply, 'The rhythm may be the same but the situation has changed.' You may find the same rhythms and instruments. How many instruments can you change from production to production? Kudiyattam has only *mizhavu* and Kathakali has only *chenda* and *maddalam* as main instruments and that is it. So that is not the important thing. You must give your eyes, your ears, your minds to the variety which is created within my story telling and in details, in nuances. Then you will find the difference.

Udayan: Were there some other Malayalam plays to which you were attracted, which had valour as the central motif?

Have you read or loved any such Malayali play, or poetry or novel with *veera* or valour?

Pannikar: There are many such; poems, stories and forms like Kathakali. There was a Kathakali play that resulted in my play called *Kalivesham*.

Udayan: Because *Kalivesham* has also *veera* in it.

Pannikar: Yes, *veera*, *roudra*, *karuna* and *shringara*. In *Kalivesham* I tried out my experience with an actor. But I related it to *Kali* and then related it to the whole of *Nalacharitam*.

Udayan: If I am not wrong, it is *veera rasa* in a very deep sense and all other *rasas* are actually supportive of the *veer rasa*.

Pannikar: My *Kalivesham* was selected by a committee in a major festival of which Habib Tanvir was the President. It was communicated to me that my *Kalivesham* was selected by them. I asked them, whether they were attracted by it because the cast of the play numbers only twelve or thirteen. Then the organiser said, 'No, no! Everyone who was part of the selection committee was present, including Habib Tanvir, and all the plays were being read. They took notes on all the plays. Then we saw your production on CD and then we found immediately that this was something very new, something remarkably different from your other plays we wanted to project your Malayalam play with a deeper resonance.'

Udayan: You have done Bhasa, you have done *Ashcharyachudamani* and you have done Kalidasa …

Pannikar: And also Mahendra Vikram Verman and Bodhayan and Shakthi Bhadra.

Udayan: What are the differences that you found between Bhasa's plays and Kalidasa's, keeping in mind that we know the difference stated by Appu Kuttan Nair. What is your view on these two different writers? Let us say, Bhasa and Kalidasa.

Panikkar: That is enough, they are the basic ones. The others are also important. Mahendra Vikram Verman's *Mattavilasam* and Bodhayana's *Bhagvadajjukiyam* belong to a separate category of plays called *prahasan*. There the *rasa* is different. It is *hasya* and *vachika* is very predominant. But I have done them. Let us keep them separate. We could consider Saktibhadra's a magical genre. He has created two Ramas, two Laxmanas and two Sitas which no one has ever tried. You know, in Saktibhadra's *Maya Sita,* there are two Sitas. Ravana assumes the role of Rama. Sita thinks that it is Rama. and believing him, she goes in the aerial chariot, and from there Sita looks down to see another Rama! She is travelling with one Rama and the real Rama appears down there with Surpnakha as the Maya Sita. And there is a third Rama, who is Maricha dying in the guise of Rama. Laxmana sees Rama dying. When the real Rama comes in the final scene with Surpnakha as Sita and calls Laxmana, Laxmana looks and mistakes the real Rama as *rakshasa maya*, the Rama. According to him, his brother is dying and this is the person responsible his brother's death and now he is getting ready for war. This is a wonderful identity crisis in man! I made it a play of identity crisis. The production was very well appreciated. It is very different from other plays, this dramatic illusion by Shakthi Bhadra's magic. Coming to the comparison between Bhasa and Kalidas, they cannot be compared because Bhasa and Kalidasa represent two major trends in Indian theatre. Kalidasa represents the subtle poetic trend of storytelling which is different from the visual poetry which Bhasa portrays. Yes, Bhasa is said to be South Indian, it is accepted. Whatever, South Indian or North Indian, he is definitely different from Kalidasa. His storytelling is always strongly supported by *kriya* (action) and there is no theatre without *kriyamsha* running parallel to the poetry. As a matter of fact both are visual poetry. Kalidasa has also used the word, *Chakshush yajna* (visual *yajna* or sacrifice) and this is very much present but works at a different level. It is very difficult to predict Bhasa; very easy to predict Kalidasa. I reached Kalidasa through Bhasa. I was inspired by the images he used like the flowers, the bees, deer, creepers, of course according to the context of the text. That is possible. The difference between the two is very glaring. Both are very relevant because you don't have a third one to point out. You could talk of plays of the *prahasan* variety and *Lokdharmi* plays like *Mrichhakatikam* and *Mudrararakshasa* as the third and fourth. Apart from them this whole gamut of Sanskrit theatre whether it is a Sri Harsha or even Bhavabhuti, are all inspired by Kalidasa. Harsha is inspired very evidently by Kalidasa in his play *Priyadarshini* and *Ratnavati*. *Naganandam* of course is a slightly different play. *Naganandam* is done by the *Chakyar*s. We have yet to discover some local or some regional playwrights like Shakthi Bhadra to compare with Bhasa.

Udayan: Of all of Kalidasa's plays you first did *Malavikagnimitram* …

Panikkar: No. I did Kalidasa in reverse order. I first did *Shakuntala*. Then *Vikramorvashiyam* and then *Malavikagnimitram*. *Malavikagnimitram* did not initially excite me. I was not for it and then when I was with Kamlesh Dutta Tripathi I took up *Malavikagnimitram*. *Tripathiji* was narrating some new shades of the *Malavikagnimitram*—Agnimitra's father and son fighting at the border and Agnimitra always remaining worried about the country's well being. Although he seemed very much engaged with love making. Only that part was taken up by Karanth in his production. But there was another side to Agnimitra. During his time there was turmoil in the country which reflected in the court intrigues etc. These things came to my mind after long discussions with Tripathi ji.

Udayan: And therefore the *veera* dimensions …

Panikkar: Yes, I saw the *veera* dimensions. And then for me, the Ashoka tree becoming a character was very interesting.

Udayan: Yes, it was brilliantly done. It almost occupies the central stage.

Panikkar: It becomes a character.

Udayan: How did this idea come to you that all the three heroines of these plays were actually representatives of *prakriti* (nature)?

Panikkar: This idea occurred to me for the first time when I did *Shakuntala*. It came to me, at first unknowingly, but I was more concerned with the duty of the king: *prakriti-hitaya parthiva*. The *prakriti* came even at that time. *Prakriti hitaya parthiva* was not clear to me so I added *praja hitayah parthivah*. What is *prakriti*? *Prakriti* is nothing but *praja*. *Prakriti* includes *manushya prakriti* (human nature) and the *vishwa prakriti* (universal nature). It can be interpreted in many ways. In *Shakuntala* which I did earlier, I could not dive deep into the character of Shakuntala in this context of Nature. But only when I did *Vikramorvashiyam* was it evident that its central character, Pururava, has got a very rare gift from heaven which is Urvashi. He had the gift but he could not use it properly. Urvashi was nothing but Nature. How did that idea come? Because when he misbehaved, when he went after Udayavati, a *vidhyadhara balika*, a young, beautiful girl, Urvashi got offended. Urvashi felt very bad and she showed him her true self; she was nothing but Nature and he was misbehaving with Nature, not caring for her, and then she transformed into a creeper. Getting into Kumarvana she becomes a *lata*, a creeper. Kumarvana is a name but names are always baffling. Kumarvana is Kumara's Vana (forest of the brahmachari, Shanmugha), and a lady is not supposed to enter there. *Kumarvanum praveshya praveshanandram* she transformed into a creeper as she enters there implying that she is nothing but Nature. From then on I started rethinking *Shakuntala* as well. In the subsequent production of *Shakuntala*, I could easily get into the character's contextual relevance to Nature. She becomes a flower and bees come to her and try to molest her.

Udayan: In Srikanthan Nair's *Kanchan Sita*, Sita is Nature.

Panikkar: That Sita is Nature is told by Srikanthan Nair himself and we have discussed this earlier.

Udayan: It was beautifully done by Aravindan.

Panikkar: What we are doing with Bhavabhuti is precisely what Arvindan did with Srikanthan Nair. We too are inspired by Bhavbhuti. But we are not including everything from *Uttararamacharitam* in our performance text.

Udayan: And after doing Shakuntala as Nature you also interpreted Malavika in the same light.

Panikkar: Yes, in the same light but slightly different. You can see the difference but we have yet to underline it fully. I am working on it. You can also help me in this. In *Vikramorvashiyam* you have Urvashi. Urvashi is different from Shakuntala, she is celestial. She has got wonderful powers. She can also be terrible. There is a reference to her in the *Rig Veda*. The Pururava-Urvashi theme is there, where she is compared to the *Aadi* bird which can hide within its wings. She is also a horse and a wolf. There are three such images related to Urvashi. I have used all of them. These show that she is so powerful sexually that she cannot be easily satisfied. The king's feeling was probably that he had enough power to satisfy her but he got fed up with her. That is why he leaves her. She also throws him out at one point. I did it using the curtain. She pushes him out after using him and he falls, and in that fallen state he feels sad and thinks he would rather be with another girl, in peace. Uravshi's celestial power was too much for him. Nature is so powerful. Here Urvashi represents the Kali element in Nature, the strong element, the cruel element; something like a tsunami you could say. Malavika and Shakuntala are different from Urvashi. Urvashi is very strong.

Udayan: They are all three dimensions of Nature. They are three approaches to Nature actually. For example, Shakuntala will be Nature with whom you want to fall in love with. She becomes dear to you. She is attractive.

Panikkar: Yes, she is the innocent *ashrama mriga* (deer). I had shown a deer in the beginning. King Dushyant is going after the deer and the deer assumes the role of Shakuntala or some girl. This was shown even in the earlier production. Now I have further shown a flower and he smells her and his desire go around her as bees approach flowers. That's the difference. Urvashi is so strong but Shakuntala is innocent in the beginning and becomes furious in the fifth act.

Udayan: Malavika?

Panikkar: Yes. She is working in the palace incognito as a maid and she is watering the Ashoka tree when the king approaches her to make her his third wife.

Udayan: In fact in your production *Shakuntala,* when Shakuntala behaves in a slightly meek way, I didn't much like it. I felt that she is much braver. I told you this.

Panikkar: But she belongs to the hermitage. That is one probable reason. One should see how she comes out in the fifth act. She is very strong in the fifth act. That is the moment where she has to be strong. Where did you perceive her as meek?

Udayan: When she goes to Dushyanta's court. Initially it is alright, because when she is rejected, she is crestfallen. But when she continues like that, there I felt that …

Panikkar: Which act do you mean?

Udayan: In the scene where she goes to the court.

Panikkar: In the court, she comes wearing the veil and the veil is removed. Step by step, she is awakening to reality. The dialogues have all of these, her doubting, her questioning and the whole of it till she finally says, 'You are a *vanchaka* (cheat)'; this is the culmination. I think I have tried to follow the dialogues which the author had already written, whereas there is nothing to that effect in the beginning. It builds up step by step till she is totally dejected. She is even then trying to remind him of the old experiences where also the textual material limited me. It was difficult to find out a non-textual text if at all required. I accept that the acting could probably be made stronger. We can see this character in the context of comparison of the three heroines of Kalidasa.

Udayan: Because these are three ways in which Nature can be approached.

Panikkar: And as far as the lovers are concerned, their approach to them is also like man's approach to Nature.

Udayan: Yes, the three different approaches to Nature.

Panikkar: Three behaviours of Nature, three characteristics of Nature and how each one is approached.

Udayan: Uravashi is very raw, voluptuous, and all that, and by the time you come to Malvika, she is unattainable for a long time. In her case the togetherness is so difficult to find.

Panikkar: It is not there very much.

Udayan: Yes, it's not there. And the difficulty of being together with Nature is also the case with Urvashi.

Panikkar: In Malvika's case, Agnimitra's approach to Nature is very distant. He does not indulge her and is fearful, although she is not to be feared. He is only fearful about his wives, about circumstances.

Udayan: She is not fearful at all.

Panikkar: Not at all. But she cannot be approach. The approach is very difficult, he can establish contact with Nature only stealthily. Urvashi, on the other hand, is very cruel and strong and sexually overpowering. And the third one, Shakuntala, is very sensible, with equanimity and maturity because of her life in the hermitage. She, of course, was enamoured of Dushyanta, and had fallen in love. That is true but she has more maturity because of her association with Kashyapa.

Udayan: They may also be three forms of Devi. I mean Kalidasa was a *Devi bhakta* as they say, so it is quite possible that they may be two or three forms of Devi. Three forms of Parvati, the possibility is there. These may be the three ways of worshipping Devi.

Panikkar: Now that these plays are going to be done again and again, and I am also planning all three plays in one, these aspects which we discussed will really help me when the nuances are worked out.

***

Udayan: Whenever you start writing a play, you normally start by writing a poem. Is a poem already written on which you base the play? Or sometimes perhaps, ends up as a poem. How does it help in writing the play?

Panikkar: A particular situation or a state of being or *avastha* is thought of. *Avastha* works in you in different ways, creating creative roots. For example, I can say precisely about *Theyyatheyyam* that an *avastha* was at work for a long time in my mind. Writing *Theyyatheyyam* itself was a very long experience. Two stories were in my mind, they were told to me and then they were there in my mind for a long time. The first story was *Andalur Kavu* a Ramayana tale, Lakshamana Devataar Theyyam at a place in Malabar. The other story was the story of the experience of a Theyyam artiste who commits murder. He becomes a wanted fellow. I wanted to combine these two stories. The Ramayana story is the one where the Ramayana is retold in the rural tradition, where Devataar is Rama, Ankakkara is Lakshamana, Bepooran is Hanuman and Paranki is

Ravana. 'Feranki' means an outsider. I wanted to suggest the quality of outsiderness also.

Udayan: 'Feranki' is a very commonly used name for the Portugese.

Panikker: I am told that in Portuguese or some other language, the meaning of this word is 'outsider'.

Udayan: In all Indian languages this word was used for outsiders like the Portuguese and the British.

Panikker: I had these two stories in mind. The second story came to me when I was travelling through the villages of Malabar.

Udayan: Was that in the 1960s?

Panikker: Yes. This was the time when Arvindan was planning to take his third or fourth film *Kummatti*. He took me with him. I had to write the script for him. He wanted to cast someone for the main role of Kummatti, he had somebody in mind … ultimately he was the one who was cast. Before that we thought we would try somebody else. And so for that purpose we went to Kannur district. We stopped our car in front of a house. There was some confusion there. People thought we were the police! It was the house of a Theyyam dancer. His mother came out and said, 'He is not here. What do you want?' And we said, 'We want to meet him!'

Udayan: You had gone to meet him actually.

Panikkar: We had gone there to see if Aravindan could take him for that role. The person who took us there inquired and found that he was wanted by the police in a murder case. So that is how the story of the actor, an impersonator himself commiting a murder came to me.

Udayan: Then you wrote a poem?

Panikkar: Yes. I wrote the poem *Theyyatheyyam*. The storyline for the play came slowly. It is a different play among my other plays.

Udayan: Even with *Daivathar* and *Sakshi* did you write the poem first?

Panikkar: No. They were written earlier. My other play *Karimkutty* was told to me by my mother.

On the twenty-eighth day of a particular month in the year the paraiahs who worked in the fields were given a free day. They could do anything on that day. They could even take away your ladies from home if they were seen outside, without any questions asked…

Panikkar: They were free for only a day in the year.

Udayan: And what are they the rest of the time?

Panikkar: They are slaves. Karimkutty is one such dark-skinned slave. He is one among 400 slaves. I have equated these working class people to spirits with power. There are stories about spirits which are called *chaattan*s, or *shaitan*. *Chaatan*s are spirits who can be tamed, who can be made your own and then they will bring you anything.

Udayan: We were talking about Karimkutty.

Panikkar: *Chaatan* is a concept, it is a spirit and there is a sorcerer in the play who controls 400 minus ten *chaattan*s (we don't say the exact number directly as it is considered inauspicious). He is the owner or custodian of 390 *chaatan*s. We used only eight or ten people in the play. The leader of all these *chaatan*s is Karimkutty. Like the *chaatan*s they can do wonders, they can produce paddy which itself is a wonder. They are like spirits, black spirits. They are not bad spirits, they can help. Karimkutty, the senior *chaattan* can bring anything, even the rarest sweets.. Either he will help or the other *chaattan*s will do this. Even in the British period these *chaattan*s were believed to exist. There were houses where there were '*chaattan* troubles'. I have seen one such house which was supposedly haunted by *chaattan*s. During the times of British rule after the treasury was locked, a string was tied with a double knot because there was a belief that otherwise *chaattan*s would open it. It was believed that *chaatan*s did not have thumb and so could not open the knot! This is not in the play however. I am telling you this as a belief and because even the British rulers thought that *chaattan*s were there! The main point in my play is that the *chattan*s are equated with the working class.

Udayan: But you said they were slaves. As far as I know there was hardly any slave trade in India.

Panikkar: There was slave trade. It existed in Kerala. The pariah was owned by his master. He could not give his services to anybody else. There was a temple in a tribal area where there was a festival during which the slave exchange used to take place.

Udayan: Do you think this practice was very old?

Panikkar: It is a universal phenomenon and comes from man's desire that somebody should work for him. There were workers, who were called

Adimaa and they were owned by feudal lords. In Kuttanaad in Kerala, there was a very bad practice among certain families. They engaged pariahs in big canoes to attack people who went through the outer lake and confiscate their ornaments and give them to their masters. There is also a story that a well known family of this area was engaged in this activity. The family members owned an array of such canoes which were used to rob hapless travellers in the night. Gold ornaments would be brought to the gate of the family house in the morning. According to legend, the owner of the house once came to the gate and asked, 'Is anybody alive or have you killed them all?' The pariahs replied, 'We have killed everyone.' After seeing the ornaments at the gate, the owner asked this question because he knew that the ornaments belonged to his own womenfolk who were on their way to the Vaikom temple.

My play *Karimkutty* has these *chaattan*s and also a disciple who learns sorcery under him. The guru never teaches everything to the student. There is a belief in every discipline the gurus never teaches everything that he knows. He may not even impart all his knowledge to his own son. This disciple managed to learn some very small things from his teacher and that has made him wealthy. He is a nouveau riche man. He asks his guru for one *chaatan*. He starts advancing money to his guru and his guru is scared to accept it. At one point the disciple asked his guru, 'Give back my money or leave one *chaattan* for me.' Now the guru never expected this. There were four hundred minus 10 *chaattan*s with him but he did not want to part with any of them. The disciple finally left, but would come back every once in a while on an elephant to the accompaniment of musical instruments so that other people would know that he had come for his money. The guru would reply, 'Why are you asking for the money? You gave it to me as *dakshinaa*. You should not ask me to return it.'

To which the student replied, 'There is no question of *dakshinaa*, you have not taught me anything. You have not given me the *chaatan* I have been asking for, for so long. Now I cannot wait. I must get my money back.' Thus the guru was put to much difficulty. If he didn't return the money his name would be tarnished. Now the guru was but a poor man and had lost everything. But he asked his disciple to return on Friday. And the disciple agreed. The guru gave his word of honour under the belief that the chief of the *chaattan*s would not turn down his request. He then told the chief of *chaatan*s, 'Karimkutty, I am in dire need. I am in trouble, I need you to bring me money!'

And Karimkutty said 'Money I can give, provided you give me a promise about when you can return it. We *chaattan*s believe in truth and expect you to keep your word. If you can tell me the exact time when you will return the money, I will bring you any amount of money.'

Hearing this, the guru says, 'How dare you speak to me like this? I am your master, and you have no confidence in me!' And they quarrelled. Among 400 minus 10 *chaattan*s there is one called Sunderan *chaattan*. He falls in love with the guru's daughter, Poomala.

There is a belief that if you engage spirits, you are doomed to fall if you don't do it with care. Sunderan *chaattan* loves the girl and the girl would die if she didn't go with the *chaattan*. In the second act the guru comes to know that his daughter has run away with Sundaran *chaattan*. When Sunderan was out on the twenty-eighth day, which was the free day for slaves when they could do anything, he decides to take away the master's daughter. Sunderan *chaatan* with the help of other *chaattan*s take her away. From then on the guru's downfall begins.

In the third act the disciple comes on the appointed date that is, on Friday to his guru. He comes on the elephant, demanding his money. The guru asks him, 'What will you do if I am not able to give it back?'

'You give me a *chaatan*.'

Thus Karimkutty is sold to the disciple. The guru puts a rope around his neck and gives him away cruelly. The disciple takes the rope and happily goes away. From there on the guru's downfall is complete and all the four hundred minus ten *chaattan* throw stones at him. He is finished.

Udayan: It is a beautiful play.

Panikkar: There was a filmmaker, Priya Krishnaswami working in Pune. She came and prepared a script for the film. She asked for my permission. I discussed it with her. The script is still with me. She never made the film. But she had written the script very well.

Udayan: You directed it yourself?

Panikkar: The play? Yes. From that time onwards I directed all the plays.

Udayan: And so was the case with *Kalivesham.*

Panikkar: I directed *Kalivesham* also.

Udayan: What was the other play that you were referring to?

Panikkar: It is called *Kallurutty.* That production was done with folk elements and folk visuals. Once, I did *Karimkutty* differently where Karimkutty *chaattan* lies on the stage as a big effigy and when excorcised the character came out of the effigy. There was Kundunni who was the manager of the sorcerer. He couldn't see Karimkutty. 'Can't you see?' asks the sorcerer. 'Don't show me, I will fall down,'says Kundunni. 'No, no you can see. He is my servant like you,' says the sorcerer. 'You touch me so that you will be able to see him. But if you touch me, I will have to take a bath. But that's alright I will take another bath. You may touch me.' And then he touches him and sees Karimkutty.

Udayan: The other play that you were referring to was *Kallurutty.*

Panikkar: I had a long association with a tribal community of actors from Kannur. The tribe is called Mayilone.

Udayan: How come you had such a long association, I mean were you living there?

Panikkar: No, I conducted workshops there. I have a friend Jayraj who is the Chairman of Folkland, Kasargodu. He wanted me to conduct a few workshops, so I used to go there and then I got the opportunity to work with the Mayilone community. I came to know about them and their stories. I also interviewed a Mayilone artist. He passed away very recently. My play was dedicated to him. His name was Bolen. I also wrote a poem on him of the same name. *Bolen* is about a character who is indomitable, courageous and who never cares about the so called elites. He hates them. Bolem is not a common name. I got the story from him and also from Jayraj who was also with me helping to contact him.

Udayan: What was the story you got from them?

Panikkar: It was a story of two brothers. They were also Theyyams, gods. Pancharuli was the name of both of them. They had the same names, looked the same and behaved in the same way. They had a sister called Kallurutty. She had this wonderful power that when she rolled a stone, suddenly the whole of Nature would act in her favour. She was a powerful person, a child of Nature. She was also ultimately made into a goddess. There is a folk tale about her. She too becomes a Theyyam, later. Brothers and sister were very close, they loved each other.

Udayan: All three?

Panikkar: Yes, all three. They lived a peaceful life. There was a river which separated the rest of the country and the tribal area. There was sophisticated society living on one side of it and there was the tribal village on the other.

Udayan: I am asking you to tell me the story because I want to know how you handle a story and turn it into a play?

Panikkar: I know. So they were divided by this river. There was a ferry in the river. The ferry man was called Anthony. *Thony* means canoe, hence his name. He took people from one side to the other. He belonged to the Christian community. His work was to connect the two sides. There is another character in the play called Ugrani who is the representative, an officer of the British rulers. He belongs to a higher cadre, he is actually like an agent.

Udayan: A British agent in that area.

Panikkar: Yes, he is a powerful person. He crosses the river to go to the other side where he has acres of land growing *ganja* and he utilises the services of these brothers, Panacharulis. They are made to work and when the time comes for the *ganja* to be carried to this side of the river for sale, it was done by the Pancharuli brothers. He comes to supervise the harvesting of *ganja*.

Panikkar: Yes, when he comes here, he meets this girl Kallurutty and on seeing her, he wants her, by hook or by crook. He approaches her. The brothers come to the *ganja* fields, carrying their goods with them. Sometimes they go into the forest to drink their famous country liquor. Their sister Kallurutty interferes and says, 'Don't go, this is a very important festival which is going on and you should attend it.' But even then they stealthily manage to sneak off. They take their drinks and come back and join the rest. Ugrani happens to meet Kallurutty. He gives money to the Panachruli brothers and tells them to go and enjoy drinks. Ugrani wants the sack of *ganja* to be carried to the other side of the river to sell it. He gives money to the brothers, sends them away and tries to approach their sister.

She gets offended and she rolls her magic stone and Nature reacts very strongly against this offender, Ugrani. He cannot stand the rage of Nature that comes to her safety. He says to her, 'If you are not coming my way, I will teach you a lesson!' Then he goes away. The brothers with the sack of *ganja* are crossing the river. Anthony is curious. 'What is in the sack? It has a very strong smell. What are you going to do with it?' The drunken brothers say that under Ugrani's instructions that they were to take the sack to the other side of the river and go to the *chungam*, the excise checkpost.

They were supposed to go there with the sack and tell him that the sack was Ugrani's and they are authorised to take it with them. But since their sister refused Ugrani, Ugrani comes to the riverside and tells Anthony to take him to the other side. Anthony does so. The two brothers finally reach the excise post with the sack of *ganja*. 'This sack is Ugrani's. How can we take it as our own?' They wait for Ugrani's arrival.

When Ugrani arrives, he says, 'I don't know these men. What is this? Hai! This is wrong, they are breaking the law, and they should be punished!' Ugrani cruelly disowns them and they are caught and are put in jail in the fort. Kallurutty comes to know of this. Then in the folk tale she takes her *paatheya,* food for the journey, and comes to cross the river. 'Kallurutty, I will come with you.' Then she meets a villager who asks Anthony, the ferryman, to take them to the other shore. And Anthony replies, 'You may board the ferry but as for her, I will have to think.' He says so because he is one of Ugrani's men. She is not taken and the villager goes alone. She rolls her magic stone and the river makes way for her. She walks across and the ferry capsizes. Anthony struggles and she walks away. She finds her brothers with her magical powers. The brothers are set free and they all come back. While they come back Ugrani is ready with a plan. There is another sorcerer who is more powerful than this tribal girl, he seems to be a more sophisticated sorcerer. He is brought so that she could be subjugated.

And then the final fight between Kallurutti and Umrashan, the other sorcerer, takes place. Umrashan belonged to the community living on the other side of the river, opposite to the tribal side. Ugrani is given a promise by this Umrashan that he will see to it that she is tamed and given to him. 'She will come to your way,' he says and puts vermillion mark on Ugrani's forehead. 'We will see that she is brought down.' And there is a terrible fight between the two. Ultimately both of them are destroyed. These two,

Umrashan and Kallurutty, are also killed. The last song in the play describes that Kallurutty has become Theyyam. Umrashan is also deified. There is a place at Thrikannapuram where there is a temple where. Kallurutty's place is at the top of the temple and down there at some place is Umrashan's place.

Udayan: What changes did you bring about to the folk tale when you wrote this play?

Panikkar: I changed the meaning of the river, the river motif and the river divide and many other things. Anthony is very important. Anthony is not there in the folk tale, but in my version, he is the one who tries to connect the two worlds. It's a simple story. More than an interpretative script, it's just a flowing stream of a village folk tale with its ecological specialities.

The River becomes a strong symbol of the divide between the tribal and the British ruled world.

Udayan: We have seen in the earlier part of the conversation the way you use space …

Panikkar: That is very important in my Malyalam play *Kallurutty*. The way the river gives way to Kallurutty and the way the brothers are put in jail at the fort, the way the inside of the fort is seen on stage—all that is there. It was equally interesting to show the whole *kotta* (fort) breaking when Kallurutty rolls the stone.

Udayan: How does time move in your theatre? I say this because my teacher, the great filmmaker Mani Kaul, always said that one great function of art is to make you experience time and you can experience time only when you either slow it down or speed it up. I mean if you don't do that then time remains the same as the real time and you don't experience it. So how do you do it?

Panikkar: That is the very question that led Habib Sahab to make an observative that the pace of my plays is very slow. 'Is it not slow?' He asked. You can't say things that fast. Each event has its own time concept when you depict it. You cannot simply speed up things.

Udayan: In your plays, I would say there are different temporalities. They have different paces, different *laya*s, like sometimes time gets extended and becomes slower. At other times it is made to move faster and then you connect the two. At one time you are in fast *laya* then from there you enter into slower *laya*, then very slow *laya* and then once again you go into the fast *laya*. This is what one experiences in most of your plays. One experiences the movement of time in them. I am trying to say that the experience of time is multiple in your plays. *Tala*, rhythm, plays a great role in your plays in actually underlining whether time is becoming slower or faster. But sometimes you make time flow slower or faster through the movements of the actors, through the movement of the flow of the story. Time never flows in your plays just the way it flows in real life, or actual time.

Panikkar: Never, that cannot be so This is a very important difference of traditional Indian theatre from realistic theatre that you are pointing out. I don't have to explain it now, it is self explanatory. You have explained it. It is all a question of converting real time into virtual time.

Udayan: Even when the dialogue is delivered, you either extend it by a lot or very less. Stop it or make it move fast. This is as if a kaleidoscope of time is created and we relish multiple times there. Through that we relish *rasa*s. I mean forms of time become the vehicles to carry *rasa*s to us.

Panikkar: This is to be examined by you. Your observation seems interesting. But this is not something which I have done consciously. I cannot comment on how this happens in my creative process. I am still wondering how to find a tangible way of putting it and finding proof for it.

Udayan: I will give you proof. I will give you an example from your *Vikramorvashiyam*. At the beginning of that play a fight ensues between Pururuva and the Asura. This is when he is taking away Urvashi. The fight is very brief in your production but the way it is choreographed, one experiences the space. One realises that the fight is taking place, which I believe is most wonderfully done and at the same time one realises that it is taking place nowhere else but in the sky.

Panikkar: They are going through the sky and there are a lot of things happening which are very romantic where you have to definitely resort to a time concept which cannot be the real time concept of escaping and then trying to take her in the turmoil when he fought with the *asura* (sinful, power-seeking deities). Pururava fought with the *asura* who was carrying away Urvashi.

Udayan: He fought for the sake of Indra, on behalf of Indra.

Panikkar: Yes, because he was Indra's friend. Indra used to invite him for all performances and important events in *swarga* (heaven). So upon hearing Urvashi's cry, he goes and fights in the air and takes Urvashi into his aerial chariot. All this happens very quickly. The concept of time here in the fight scene and in scenes where Urvashi is saved and regained suddenly changes into a slower, romantic mode where many small things are enacted giving them a romantic touch. When the chariot suddenly stops he touches her shoulder and says, 'Oh after all this is *premankur*, the seedling of love,' so all this happens in slowed down time. This is natural. When *shringara* (the erotic) is expressed in Kathakali, the pace of the dance slows down. Here also after the war in the air, time slows down, gets suppressed.

Udayan: As if you are examining at ease the interaction between the two lovers in great detail. If you were not doing that it would not be clear. And so you really lengthened the scene and the time was slowed down. If one related it to the time taken for the fight scene it would seem disproportionate.

Panikkar: For your recollection I say that in that scene where Pururava comes with Urvashi you also forget at times that they are in that aerial chariot. When he describes he goes out of the chariot, into the air, and there you know that such rationale doesn't work but the feeling that they are there in the aerial chariot is sustained because it is moving. There is the charioteer who makes the movement but at the same time *pada* (poem) of the hero, the heroine and her friend Chitralekha are all enacted in rounds. Similarly the Brahmin family in *Madhyamavyayogam* passes through the dense forest. It is only through their movement that we are be able to feel the ups and downs and uneveness of the terrain and that on the way they have to cross the river and climb the hill. We gauge the height of the hill from the expression in their eyes.

Udayan: Also the depth of the mountain from the top is gauged through the movement of the group. The ease with which Bhima goes there speaks of how easy it is for him and how difficult for the Brahmin family and thus the comparison is made possible. Through two different timings, two different gaits are created.

Panikkar: What you are saying is perfectly correct about the timing.

Udayan: There are many times. Suddenly time becomes faster then it becomes very slow. It is never like one experiences it in reality and that is where comparison with realistic theatre will come in because in realistic theatre there is only one tempo similar to so called actual time. It will never be slowed down or turned faster.

Panikkar: This is a very important difference of traditional Indian theatre from realistic theatre that you are pointing out. I don't have to explain it now, it is self explanatory. It is all a question of converting real time into virtual time.

Udayan: This is the quality of poetry. I think you do it naturally in your theatre because you are a poet. I mean had you not been a poet it would have been very difficult for you because in poetry that is exactly what one sees. You slow down time, then you hasten it and all that comes together and constitutes what is called the experience of a poem. That precisely is the condition that was agreed upon by Ganesha and Veda Vyas before writing the *Mahabharata* where Ganesha said to Veda Vyas that he should not slow down while dictating the *Mahabharata* to him or else he would not write it. And in response to this Veda Vyas tells Ganesha that he agrees on this condition but there is one condition from his side as well and that was that Ganesha would not write anything dictated to him without understanding it. And therefore Veda Vyas sometimes slows down the things by creating difficult *shloka*s which Ganesha takes times to understand.

Panikkar: In the play there is no question of going slow or fast as such, there are variations of pace.

Udayan: These variations create the experience of time in your plays.

Panikkar: You have got me thinking now! I had not given a thought to this before. It is only when you say this now that it occurs to me that I might have done this. I understand what you said. What you said is true, poetry demands this, in writing poems this happens. Anyone who composes poems in the right way will understand what you have said.

Udayan: What is your experience of, let's say, the theatre of Habib Tanvir? What is it that you remember of his theatre?

Panikkar: His plays, whatever plays I have seen, all are Habib's style. It is the same in my case also. The style is almost the same. You cannot simply stop practising a style and suddenly resort to a different style. It is not possible for any writer. You take Dostoevsky's works. He has written several novels, all of which assert a quality which is Dostoevskyan. Similarly, Habib Sahab's style of work is the same. What I found in his storytelling was that it definitely banks on the Indian way of story telling which is prevalent in most of the folk forms including tribal forms of the heartland of India, which is different from the storytelling in many forms like Mudiyettu, Padayani, etc native to Kerala. It definitely marks a difference from mine. I am trying to compare and to understand through the comparison. There the *vachika* is very important; *rasa sankalpa* is not much and is definitely less. It is there to some extent. There is *bhava*, music and all these things but the *vachika* has a very dominant place in Habib's plays if my observations are correct. Here in my case, I use *vachika* only wherever it is very essential in most of my plays. Not in all plays. Even in our *Uttararamacharitam* you are more stingy than I, because you express maximum *bhava* through very few words. That is good but then I ask you, why don't we have two more lines? Too much *vachika* on one side and too less on the other. I always tried to strike a balance between *vachika, angika* and *sattvika*. Such levels of careful treatment, I am sure is not the norm in Habib Sahab's work and I say this without any disrespect for his work.

With complete appreciation I can say that his plays are a form of story telling which he got from our tradition as maintained in forms like of *Mach, Nacha* and such others. We too have this tradition of storytelling here in Kerala. *Poratunatakam* of Palakkad district and *Kakkarissinatakam* of the Travancore area are such traditions. We too have the same style of story telling where there is music and then dialogues then suddenly switching back to music. Habib Sahab has used it wonderfully well and combined it with visuals but they are not the visuals which create a stream parallel to that of *vachika* and visual relating to them, which create a relationship between the two. There is no such relationship. One stream goes one way and the other stream goes another way and they qualify each other to some extent but do not evoke each other. We don't always want to do *padartha abhinaya*. That is not expected. But in a play like that of Bhavabhuti's what is written is there; then what is my contribution? I have to contribute by making this written thing rendered. In rendering, too, there is poetry but in Habib's theatre these two lines run parallel, one does not exactly relate to the other. So a person who doesn't understand the language might find it difficult. All the same, this is not the acid test of the success of the play. When I say this I mean that it is also one of our Indian traditions of the regions of Madhya Pradesh, Uttar Pradesh, Chhattisgarh, etc. We too have this tradition and this is the tradition which is maintained and enlarged, restructured, recreated by Habib Sahab. This is what I felt about his *Charandas Chor*. I have seen his *Charandas Chor, Mrichhakatikam*, and other works.

Udayan: What about the theatre of Ratan Thiyam? I will give you the reason why I ask this question. One is of course that these two are also very good theatre directors. In Ratan Thiyam's work, the *vachika* and associated *abhinaya* is minimised and the static visual takes over. The *vachika* becomes very, very thin and it is through the composition of colours and movement that he primarily creates his theatrical experience.

Panikkar: His music is significant but he has very strong and convincing visuals. Sometime he celebrates the visuals. There is so much celebration in visuals! That definitely makes a class by itself and his storytelling is very much bound to the regional ethos of the North East.

Udayan: So is it possible that in the North East probably this visual dimension is very important?

Panikkar: It might be. You know that terrain is also refelected in the songs and the experience of the heights are reflected in the climbing movements in the Manipuri dance etc. That flow is there. The Manipuri dance Ponku Chola and many other local dances and expressions of the Manipuri tradition like the Thangtha are very dominant in Ratan Thiyam's productions, in his interpretations, in his celebrative process of a theatre situation.

Udayan: Is is same for Kanhai Lal also?

Panikkar: No, Kanhai Lal is different. I have seen Kanhai Lal's two or three productions. One is his *Tetu* and that was wonderful, it was symbolic. What should I say about him? His main strength was his wife, Savitri ji ... She is a very good actress. I saw her in Tagore's *Post Office* acting as a boy. She has a wonderful stage presence and her rendering was very powerful. His success cannot be thought of without her and of course his designs are very special. I have seen one of his productions here in Kerala. He incorporates certain western elements also to make the production powerful.

Udayan: Ratan Thiyam also does that. He takes a lot from western paintings.

Panikkar: There is no harm in it.

Udayan: Yes, there is no harm in it if it can be turned into a magnificient theatrical experience, which he does.

Panikkar: You don't have to follow a rule that you won't take anything from outside. It is fine to take from that tradition too. Why not!

Udayan: That is alright but you should be rooted and then everything should be fine.

Panikkar: Once you are rooted you can imbibe any other culture.

Udayan: People say that you should keep your windows open but I feel a lot of people only have open windows …

Panikkar: Without houses!

Udayan: How do you start your rehearsals? After you have chosen your play how do you go about doing the rehearsals?

Panikkar: My first concern is the *vachika* because the text is immediately related with the *vachika*. The storytelling which has its mundane moorings is the starting point or the springboard. We are related to the life which is told in the play. The text is the medium so it must be respected. For this I am mostly concerned with the music. The whole thing in a musical format can give me sufficient material, sufficient encouragement to think about visuals. The main point is music. So immediately when I take the play, I will be concerned with the language, the way you are concerned with your language …. I give ideas in simple language. This is what is required. If I communicate my ideas, then you, the writer of my play will bring out your poetic expression through images which will not be the normal way of expressing in everyday life. Do you know how to express otherwise?

Udayan: No.

Panikkar: You can express only like this. If I told you that I want a galloping horse you will certainly think about it and ideas about the galloping horse would come to you in poetic language. In the same way when that is to be translated to action the main thing is to decide the rhythm, to decide the total rhythm of the play and in connection with the total rhythm, the rhythm for any special occasion. There is a total outward rhythm structure and an inner musical structure. How to untie, how to tie situations? These are the main concerns for me, especially when I take on Sanskrit plays. And then of course, there are the visuals. Visuals will come to you only through music. By music I do not mean the sound pattern alone. It is also not the music in the sense of popular film music, or the music in the so called popular commercial theatre. I am not referring to that kind of music where you talk and after that the song comes. It is not just the song but the total thing, it is like the re-recording in film, a total music, that is form, content and all other inflections. Even the dialogues have musical effect. It should have the air thrust, *vayustobha*, depending on the *bhava*, so that is the total music. And we take only one unit at a time and think of how to elaborate this unit; elaboration not for the sake of elaboration, but to make it interesting to the audience without reference to any particular audience. The audience could be just myself. It should be satisfying to me. When you present it, it should finally be satisfying to me. Before you read it to me it should satisfy you first and only then are you in a position where you have the confidence that the rest can read it. That way, as *swayam prekshaka*, am a representative of the audiences that will be watching the play. And sitting there I have to report to me about the timing, the timing concept, speed or the *laya*.

Udayan: How did the actors come into that picture when you start rehearsing? Recently Sangeeta Gundecha wrote a nice piece on your doing *mangalacharan* of *Avimarakam* and the way you do things it seemed almost like a dream, the way you enter into a *manglacharan* and then open into images…

Panikkar: You are talking about *mangalacharan* of *Avimarakam*.

Udayan: Yes.

Panikkar: In the beginning of that play there is a *shloka* in which the earth is being lifted by the *Varaha* (the boar incarnation of Vishnu). This is related to the story of the play also. We find a very distant link and it is almost like you have to argue as to how to make a connection. I ask them to start with music. When the music is ready, then the actors will start, then the musicians will bring something new to it and I will make some corrections. In this way, I will get engaged with it. This is the one favourable thing about working with a group continuously. They often know what they are doing is nonsense. But even then that is made relevant by me and then I work on it. Sometimes I give them exercises to do and keep away and then they work out something.

All of them work jointly. Somebody may suggest something which may seen stupid, somebody else might correct it and at that point I leave. Now the music is already there and the *vachika* too is there. The rhythm is decided by me and given to them and then they work on it on their own. I come back after half an hour or so in certain cases and then ask them to show it to me. And while taking a look at what they have done I get the link to correct it. This is how we do it nowadays because I have confidence in my actors.

Sangeeta has written about the opening scene of *Avimarakam*, the one where the elephant enters. It was very interesting. The elephant is created by a group. The heroine is Kurangi. Kurangi, on her way to the temple, passes through the palace garden and Anjangiri, the elephant, approaches her. In the text, she is being attacked by the elephant and then Avimaraka, the hero comes to the scene and rescues her. When the music was set I asked them to create Anjangiri in different parts like the tusk by one actor and leg by another etc. I told them to create an elephant in this way. The scale and 'elephantness' of the elephant was to be created by six persons. So they did it and Kurangi enters the garden from behind. One could do it in different ways but I said, 'don't create a sense of horror or anything like that but take her very soothingly by the tusks and give her a swing and allow her to enjoy it because this is nobody other than Avimaraka himself in the guise of the elephant. The elephant comes again in the play. We leave it to the audience to decide what the elephant is—whether it symbolises public opinion or the love of Avimaraka for Kurangi. The elephantness is created and it is only to take her into a lullaby. Then he comes and plays with the elephant. The elephant in different parts then all fall apart.

Udayan: What about the element of time?

Panikkar: How should an elephant charge against a person? The usual concept was given up and here I wanted to make this elephant a symbol of love. Love for this girl. And Avimaraka was the saviour from the elephant— that is, a saviour from her love-sickness. This is more difficult from my other Bhasa productions. Earlier I had not tried out an interpretation like this but it was very effective.

Udayan: How did the idea of Kundalini, etc. come in the production of *Vikramorvashiyam*? I mean it starts with the *mangalacharan* and there is a very distinct indication for the ascendence of Kundalini. How do you relate to that tradition?

Panikkar: On the one hand, there is the image of the banyan tree. Pururava represents the banyan tree with its roots in the soil and its branches reaching up in search of heaven. But it again sends its roots back to the soil from the top. This is Pururava. He goes to heaven but always comes back. He has a constant relationship with Indra. Beneath this tree, Pururava does his *suryanamaskar*. After *suryanamaskar,* he stands in a particular position and then the Kundalini works. A girl goes around his body, she goes up his body. It is a foreshadowing of Pururava's *yatra* (journey). There is more than one symbol which is slightly confusing but I wanted this permanent symbol of the banyan tree there. And then Pururava is introduced with the Kundalini which is what helps him to go to heaven. He goes to heaven only by his Kundalini power. Kundalini too is in search of its counterpart, I mean *Ishwara*. So his going to heaven gives him an opportunity to come across Urvashi and save her from the hands of a demon who abducts her from heaven.

Udayan: In a sense you are interpreting this play through Kundalini and suggesting that whatever one is going to see is an imagination of Pururava through the means of Kundalini.

Panikkar: Right. So it takes on different meanings to different observers. This is your observation, what you felt. That too is correct. One may not use the word Kundalini because it is nowhere in my interpretation, production or text.

Udayan: How did that idea come to you?

Panikkar: From the beginning of its *mangalacharan* which is *vedanteshu yamahureka ek purusham. Purush* is going in search of *prakriti*. He is *ek purush*. Who is called *ek purush*? He can only be God. This man is godly. He has that spirit in him and that is why Kundalini works. *Vedanteshu yamahureka purusham vyapya sthitam rodasi.* Pururava means 'great sound'.

Udayan: Yes.

Panikkar: Great sound could be 'Om', the first sound.

Udayan: Yes, *Adinad.*

Panikkar: Or it could be the sound of the thunder after the lightning.

Udayan: Yes.

Panikkar: And Urvashi is the lightning.

Udayan: Yes.

Panikkar: Urvashi is always compared to lightning and Pururava is compared to the sound after the lightning, the *rava*, the thunder. They see each other in the sky.

Udayan: Thunder and lightning are together only for a few transient moments and then they separate. They have to separate and that is how the whole image works. But there is another very powerful image in your play: the image of wolves.

Panikkar: The image of wolves comes later.

Udayan: That represents the voluptuousness of Urvashi.

Panikkar: That is there in the *Rig Veda* because you know in the play the group has wolves at their back. *Adippakshi* (primordial bird) too is there. Urvashi hides herself and acts as *Adippakshi,* the bird which can hide in its wings.

Udayan: It can actually disappear in its wings and this is what happens with Urvashi, she too disappears within herself in Kumarvanam.

Panikkar: She disappears. That is a fact which is not stated at all in the text. It is not there in the text. It is a non textual reference from the *Rig Veda* which is a source of inspiration for Kalidasa also.

Udayan: It is not there in the text. Do you feel that the various *natya* (theatre) practices of India and its spiritual traditions like the Kundalini are somehow related? Do you feel they are two separate traditions or do they flow into each other?

Panikkar: Definitely the philosophical element is very much there in our arts. But such an interpretation of the *Natyashastra* came only much later, around the ninth century. Until then of course there were arguments going about the ultimate purpose and functions of abhinaya. Then came Abhinava Guptapadacharya. The philosophical element was present already but it was not pronounced or discovered or practised consciously. Probably this was discovered by him. *Pratyabhijna* is identifying that which we already know. The *rasasankalpa* reaches its philosophical level when you realise *ananda*. Mind has all the five layers and where does this fifth layer lie? The five layers of mind are the *annamaya kosha, pranmaya kosha, manomaya kosha, buddhimaya kosha* and *anandmaya kosha*. Art should appeal to all these *kosha*s. When it appeals to all these *kosha*s then the result is *bramhanand sahodara*, it is beyond the intellectual mind. Mental mind is the mind of feelings. Intellectual mind is *buddhimaya kosha, pranmaya kosha* is very peripheral and the other *manomaya kosha* is the mental imagination. All these *kosha*s are there but the ultimate experience is only in *anandmaya kosha*. It can easily be obtained through music, more than through any other art. This is why this practice is not considered at all by people involved in theatre. This cannot be attained as long as reason prevails. It is not possible to avoid reason. But here it is possible because we are presenting the *avastha* were you can enjoy the ascendence of the Kundalini in Pururava. If you are only following the text and not paying attention to the unsaid portions in the text, then you will not touch that question.

Udayan: Of *anandmaya kosha*.

Panikkar: Yes, that is true.

Udayan: Because through reason you cannot reach there.

Panikkar: Reason cannot take you to that *kosha*. I am frightened now at this point in our discussion! I am really afraid whether we are falling down or climbing up!

Udayan: By embracing reason can you enjoy the essence of music?

Panikkar: Not at all. Take for example the sense of feeling in a mother. There is no reason to it. You could say that there is because she has given birth. All these could be stated but the feeling is much more than that.

Udayan: Let us talk about your other play *Kalivesham*. You have told me a little bit about it and I found that it is quite a complex play.

Panikkar: The idea for this play was from the *Nalacharitam* Kathakali. But it is not merely a reproduction of it. *Nalacharitam* passes through the play as a link. I was inspired to do this play when I wrote a poem called *Kalisantaranam*. The issue in the poem is about how to escape from Kali. I have a friend, Vasudevan Namboodiripad, who is a very famous Kathakali guru. He is a Namboodiri Brahmin, a very pious man, who meticulously observed the dictates of the Namboodiri clan. He used to do all rituals like *sandhya vandana*, various mantras, etc. He and his son, who is also a Kathakali actor, are very close to us. We travelled together to Japan in a small group where he acted as a woodsman in my play *Ottayan*. We went to Japan by invitation of Tadashi Suzuki to participate in the Togamora Festival, a very famous festival organised by Suzuki. Wherever Vasudevan travelled he always kept his brahminical dictates in his personal routine with whatever facilities were available. He would even do puja in the available space and with available water. If water was not available from a natural source, he would take it from the tap. He never drank alcohol, and did not eat meat, and would not touch any one during his puja. Thus he was very pure and orthodox. In Kathakali he was famous for playing Kali. Kali Yug is the present age with all its negativities. In the *Nalacharitam* story in Kathakali, Kali possesses the hero, Nala. Nala was present at Damayanti's marriage, but so were all the gods incognito, like Vayu, Varuna, etc. They were all desirous of marrying Damayanti, but it is Nala who gets her. In my play, the point is Kalivesham, which implies the conflict between the character of Kali and the actor who is destined to take up such a negative role. The conflict takes place in the mind of the actor who is an orthodox individual. Kali instigates the actor to indulge in wine, women, playing dice and finally murder. Kali stands behind the actor. The Kathakali performance starts at night so Kali stands behind the actor. 'Get ready', he says, 'I am going to enter into you'. This way the character enters into the psyche of the actor. And this is the problem. Kali is looking for an opportunity to enter into Nala. Thus two entries are there. This is after the marriage of Nala and Damayanti. They are together and then Kali appears and Nala (the actor) also appears. Kali says to Nala (the actor) 'Take the role of a snake and threaten her.' And the actor says, 'But that is not part of the story.' Then Kali says, 'That is not the story! Who told you that was the story! You must act according to the order of the character!' Normally in theatre it is the actor who decides how the character should be designed but here it is the character that dictates to the actor what he should do! 'You take the role of the snake', he says and the actor makes the movement of the snake and comes to the notice of Damayanti. She looks at him and says 'Oh, what is this! Save me!' And Nala replies, 'I don't see anything here!' She again says, 'There is a snake coming to bite me, please ward it off, take it away from here!' And Nala replies 'Don't worry! So many people have come to attend our marriage … gods like Indra have come … this serpent too might have come to attend. Don't worry I will throw it away.' And he throws the snake away and Damayanti is happy.

Then the story goes on. Kali's design is how to enter Nala's body. In the story too he finds it difficult to enter because Nala is a very upright man and unless he commits some wrong deed it will not be possible for Kali to enter him. Therefore, he is always watching him closely. Nala loses his kingdom after marriage. There was a game of dice between Nala and Pushkara and Nala fails because Kali had entered the dice in favour of Pushkara. This is shown in the play too. Nala then wanders in the forest with Damayanti and Kali looks for an opportunity to get into him. Nala and Damayanti feel hungry and look for something to eat. They see some birds in the forest. Kali takes the role of a bird. Nala does not have any net to catch the bird and so he takes off the cloth he is wearing and throws it to trap the birds, but instead, they fly off with the cloth and Nala is left without any clothes. A tired Damayanti wishes to sleep and Nala takes her onto his lap. That was the time when Kali could try to enter his body. Kali is seen sitting under the Tanni tree which offers shade. This is a good opportunity for Kali to work on Nala's mind. Nala suddenly starts feeling that he should desert Damayanti. He slowly takes her from his lap, puts her on the ground and then turns and walks away. She gets up and asks, 'Where are you going? And Nala tells her, 'Your home Kundinapuri is very near so you go ahead, forget about me.' 'But why?' she asks. Damayanti is perplexed, but Nala behaves rudely and pushes her away at the instigation of Kali. Nala and Damayanti are separated. In the third act too he is wandering through the forest. The serpent Karkotaka gets trapped in a forest fire. The fire blazes from all sides and Karkotaka requests Nala to save him. And Nala asks, 'Are you going to cheat me like Kali?' to which Karkotaka replies, 'I won't.' Seeing that the snake Karkotaka is caught in the fire and if he did not save him, he would be killed, Nala says, 'You take ten steps along with me.' And he takes ten steps (that is in the original tale) and he is saved from the fire. The moment he is saved, Karkotaka bites him and Nala turns completely blue. It has nothing to do with Kali. He turns blue due to the bite of the serpent. Nala asks, 'What is this?' He wants to kill Karkotaka and Karkotaka says, 'This is for your good. This is very essential for you to pass through your bad days. This bite is not a curse but will help you in the future and you will pass through your bad days with my blessings.'

And he goes away. Now comes the ultimate fight between Kali and Nala (here Karkotaka also helps Nala). How does he find Kali? Kali is driven out of Nala's body by Karkotaka's bite. Nala fights Kali, takes out his sword and is about to kill him, when Kali pleads, 'Please spare me, I will go away.' Nala says, 'You should never disturb good people, you should have no place in the mind of good people.' After that Kali addresses the audience, 'Who is good and who is bad? Let me know so that I may find an abode.'

Udayan: This is also a play like most of the plays that you have done, and some of the plays that you have written that I know of where *veera* rasa is central.

Panikkar: There is another aspect of the play in the second act which I forgot to mention. The second act shows that the actor, after completing the entire play throughout the night, comes back home but even after this, Kali still remains in him. He looks around and finds Kali everywhere. His wife says, 'You do your *sandhya vandana*, you do whatever you want. You are free, this is your home!' She brings water and pours it into his hands. He holds the water in his hand to utter the mantra. But Kali interferes from behind.

Udayan: I feel this is important. It suggests that the Kali Yuga, a kind of an age of turmoil which we are living in, enters the mind and makes a person act in a certain way.

What you are saying is that if you give space to the *yuga* in your own being for have its way, then it will not leave you.

Panikkar: That is why I say about *yuga* dharmas against what you call *sthira* dharmas. In the case of evolving a subtext, we have to work on human behaviour during the rehearsals; even after the production, we work further during the rehearsals to improve the subtext. The changes are made in the nuances without hindering the basic interpretation so the changes effected are regarding the variables.

Udayan: You treat your own script in the same way as you treat other scripts; I mean, you go on creating subtexts, in your own scripts also.

Panikkar: I am very careful to wriggle out of my own prison! In this context we can come to the next point of *Uttararamacharitam*. For *Uttararamacharitam* two creative minds have come together and are working in unison with the same goal. Though both our goals are different, we are working on a subtext.

It's not a play written without reference to its possibilities of production. But just writing as it comes is also one way the mind works. And in your mind you create a stage and performance score. Working in another way you can write without any reference to theatrical possibilities at all. That is also possible. But here now both of us are applying ourselves in a context. Your primary concern is the literary aspect. Literary aspect means how to express it through the medium of imagery, poetry or figures of speech, etc., which are required for writing poems. When we discuss the play, I may be on a very plain level and we may start thinking about what happens next. This is the storyline. Now the storyline is definitely the text which is connected with what actually happened. From there, what is being worked out later from the text will also be another creative work. Even this script cannot be called the subtext which will remain unchanged till the very end but it is of help when I start rehearsals because through it we think, argue, discuss and figure out the whys and hows of the action in the play. Whereas if I take the original *Uttararamacharitam* and directly do it in Sanskrit, I will have to do a lot of editing as we have done.

In some other cases I have also found that sometimes some passages as they are in the original may not be very useful. In this case, too, I am sure there are many such. A subtext has different levels. One level is what we have worked on. Now, the question is how it could be carried out and in this process what additional visual inputs could be incorporated to make it effective. These things will come. We have worked out some of those as well. For example, in the *Chitrapata darshana* take the case of the three pictures moving across the stage. It is all there in the text but we have selected only those pictures which would be applicable to our treatment. We could add other pictures, like that of Ganga, but they were planned keeping visuals in our mind. This is our working process. I think nowadays nobody writes with this attitude, with this approach unless it is specifically planned as we did. Suppose you had written a play like this without reference to me at all but keeping in mind that you should make this play actable then the whole thing would have been different. In that case the director has to treat it again.

Udayan: In fact I was noticing that whenever I would write something, immediately in your mind a certain imagery would open up, certain theatrical movements would open up. You would immediately place this line or dialogue in that context and would test it and you would listen to the dialogue being spoken by a character in your mind and then you would listen to the resonance of that dialogue in the imagery and only then you would accept it.

Panikkar: You can work out the whole process which we have done and use that in your book. It will be useful for a workshop for playwrights. Its material could comprise of what we have created through our experience. In fact, we were thinking about a playwright's workshop when I was there as Vice Chairman of the Sangeetha Nataka Akademi. I failed to conduct one because I could not convince the Akademi about my vision and its efficacy. It demands certain things. A poet like you and a director like me who have some understanding should come together and work in a workshop situation. If you hold your autonomy and I hold mine then a playwright's workshop will not work. It has to be a joint effort.

Udayan: Yes, it would move only if the two wheels act together.

Panikkar: The selection of the personnel and their equations cannot be looked into by the Akademi. It should evolve out of personal relationships like this and readiness to interact out of love for culture; love for the work. How can any Akademi organise all this?

Udayan: No public institution can ever do that of its own. When a director and a poet or a playwright come together and work it out, only then will they be able to create a new script. Or they may take an old script like we did in the *Uttararamacharitam* and develop it into a new one.

Panikkar: You have developed a script for *Uttararamacharitam* with me. But let's try an experiment. You try to develop another script for *Uttararamacharitam* on your own forgetting what you did with me. You write it the way you write your poems. I will also do the same. Then we can meet and compare our work. I am sure both such scripts of the same play would be quite different from each other.

Udayan: They will be very different.

Panikkar: They could be put together.

Udayan: We could do such experiments, they are worth trying out!

Panikkar: You know why I say this? Because I have to work on it in my own way anyway, now that we are going to part.

Udayan: Yes, that's true

Panikkar: I will take this script that we have created in workshop, to my theatre where I am going to interact with the actors who are ready to present this and you will also go to your own chamber. You go and rethink the characters, about the whole play freely and bring out something as I will also do.

Udayan: That would be very interesting, if you could do that.

Panikkar: Purely for literary purposes.

Udayan: I do agree.

Panikkar: That will definitely give us an insight into two autonomies. Of the writer and the director and of their coming together.

Udayan: You have spoken about the significance of Kalari in the training of the actors; I'd like to request you to say more about the total training of the actors, because you know, in many other theatre groups, actors remain quite untrained. I mean they get trained only while they are doing a play but that is not training. What do you suggest?

Pannikar: Indian theatre demands at least three aspects of acting *vachika*, *angika* and *sattavika*. In their respective perspectives, *sattvika* comes later in training. In training actors, my approach was to give training in *angika* which is the basic, because only through the *anga* the actor communicates, only through the body. Within the body there are so many elements that come out like *shabda* (sound, word). *Shabda* also is part of the body, it comes out of the body and expression too; mind also is part of the body and expresses through the body, through the organs specially through the eyes, face and expressions. So *angika* is the basic and the most essential and fundamental acting from where we should start.

In organising the actor's *angika*, I have taken Kalari as a neutral art, neutral in the sense that it is not an art form to tell a story nor does it have a grammar like Kathakali. I think I have explained this in detail earlier. Kathakali has a grammar, Kudiyattam has a grammar. In Kudiyattam, they have evolved a technique. Kathakali too has a technique, where, for example, when two persons or two characters fight, they do it according to an established technique. They may have one or two ways of doing it, or they may have one or two rhythm patterns for a particular expression. This is precisely what makes it an art form because here, form is very important to distinguish that. Kalari too is a form but I look at it not as grammar but basically as a group of alphabets. We can create alphabets of communication through body language by taking elements from Kalari. Kalari is an offense and defense methodology. In Kalari, they also teach how to use weapons— that is also relevant, because in warfare, using your weapon is also important, but more than that, for teaching purposes, for preparing an actor, we use Kalari to learn body balance. He learns to be conscious about the whole, all the parts of the body.

Udayan: Make each part of the body, your eyes.

Pannikar: Wherever you want, you should be able to apply your concentration on the body. That is the basic thing which makes an actor. The actor is the *prajapati* of the theatre, *nataeva prajapati* can be made a desirable dictum. *Kavireva prajapati* is a known saying in *sahityam*, in literature the *kavi* or poet is the *prajapati*. Here in theatre the *kavi* is the *prajapati,* but he abdicates his position to *nata*, to actor because he has to communicate with the audience, and this he can do only through the actor. A poet or director for that matter can communicate with the audience only indirectly, they cannot directly do it unless the poet reads his own poems. But when he reads it out like that, he is not an actor but is really only reading out the text. But by reading his poem, he tries to, of course, communicate his ideas, etc … the way you were reading your poem to me earlier, you wanted to communicate to me your ideas. To that extent you have to articulate your meanings through air thrust, but the articulation is very important in the case of the actor for communication with the audience. So there lies the relevance of *vachika*. What I have been doing is trying to learn the rudimentary practice of Kalari and then I have also added things which I have explained to you earlier. I was working with Gopi, who is trained in Kalari, as an actor and then we worked on a methodology for how an actor should be trained in Kalari. We have introduced *vachika* by incorporating rhythms where the actor himself vocalises the rhythms and thus comes the *vachika*. We have combined Kalari with *vachika* and extended the possibilities of the alphabets prepared by Kalari, by adapting from the *charis* of the *Natyashastra* and to some extent certain other chapters like *gatiprachara* too and incorporating them into Kalari. That is how we extended Kalari to theatre and then naturally in preparing the methodology of an actor's training. Kalari movements are supported by *shushkaksharas* (meaningless syllables) and we attributed *bhava* to it and thereby *rasa*. Training in *sattvika abhinaya* was added like this: when there are two persons, two actors, then one will attack the other by articulating *bol*s and through movements or expressions and the other actor's expressions will be of defense. We have included in practice and in different ways, offence and defense methodologies which all are directed towards evolving theatre alphabet.

Udayan: I would just want to clarify a bit. The *bol*s or the words that the actors speak to attack to each other, do they have meanings or not?

Panikkar: There is no meaning in them at all but meaning is attributed to them by adding mental acting. You see if you were attacking, you would pronounce the *bol*s in a certain way, so the *bhava* is being brought out through the use of the air thrust with which we spell out the *bol*s.

Udayan: And then the other actor would himself defend with another set of *bol*s?

Panikkar: No, The *bol*s sould not be different, they would clash if they are different. Here the vocalisation is adjusted according to the *bhava*. The *bhava* should be according to the voice and the movements, so the *angika, vachika* and *sattvika* are brought together. Once this is attained, the training will go in the proper direction. This is very simple but at the same time in practice it will have a wonderful effect. Such was my experience in preparing the actors in this direction. In the case of music *sapta swara*s and all the *jandavarisas* and all the regular music lessons are practiced separately also. How *bhava* for the purpose of acting is introduced in the music also is being taught. The *moorchchna* of a raga is sung and then how it takes a curve by withdrawing the raga and thursting the *bhava* with necessary air thurst is practised with great care, from music to dialogue a *bhava* curvature is created

Udayan: And while they are being trained the *sattvika* will also come into being, because they'll have to act?

Panikkar: Naturally.

Udayan: *Sattvika* also gets a place in training through *shushkaksharas*.

Panikkar: It was not there in Kalari, we introduced it.

Udayan: It was not there.

Panikkar: We took it from the Kalari situation and added more to the whole thing so as to make it a comprehensive acting methodology.

Udayan: Yes. At one level this attack and defense is a kind of *sattvika abhinaya*, here one kind of *sattvika abhinaya* comes into being, but there are so many shades of *sattvika abhinaya*. Are they also being done in the same way?

Panikkar: Yes. Soft method of *vatsalya* with movements, that is also there and it can be even further extended.

Udayan: Yes, all *sancharis* (fleeting emotions) can also be done in this way.

Panikkar: There is a chapter in the *Natyashastra* where it deals with gait. When you go for a marriage, how should your face be? How would you exaggerate a happy walk? Of course your walk will justify the purpose. Suppose you go to a place where someone close to you has died, how would you behave? *Chakyar*s show you a lot of such things. See how you behave even in your daily life when you face a particular situation. That too could made into a *natyadharmi* way of presentation

Udayan: Yes, then it would start signifying.

Panikkar: And then there are so many exercises in the *natyadharmi* way: how you drive out a person, how you chase a person, how a predator chases a deer. There are techniques for both the deer and the predator … it all comes out in our productions. That is why I said these are alphabets.

Udayan: Yes, that's true and then you keep them neutral, independent of the narrative.

Panikkar: Exactly.

Udayan: So they are not already incorporated into any narrative. Then the narrative can be freely created. And then you can go on adding these many *sancharis*.

Panikkar: Go on adding as many *sancharis* as the text demands. Like in *Uttararamacharitam,* we have created some very interesting situations which demand a certain behaviour of the body. And when two persons are on the stage and one does an *ekaharya*, is he freer than when he has to share it with another person. See when two persons come on the stage *kakshya* (orbit, it could either be an active orbit, *abhyantarkakshya* or passive, *(bahyakakshya)* also comes in. When an actor who remains in the *bahyakakshya* and a man who remains in *ekaharya* in the *abhyaantar kakshya*, how would they interact and how would the attention of the audience tilt from one person to the other? When it tilts to the other, then the other would be in the *abhyantarkakshya*, even in the presence of the audience.

I will give you an example of the right way of doing it. Suppose I am on the stage. I am in the *abhyantarkakshya*. Now I see someone there: he's coming and I look beyond the audience, He is continuing to come. Until his voice is heard from outside, he is in the *bahyakakshya*. When he comes and occupies the stage and attracts the audience, he is in the *abhyantarkakshya*, he takes up that place. Sometimes both are in the *abhyantarkakshya*, not in the visual range of the audience, but within the range of attention of the audience, then they are in the *abhyantarkakshya*.

Udayan: So the *abhyantarkakshya,* in the sense, is the area of attention of the audience. And the *bahyakakshya* may be there on the stage itself, but it is outside the area of the attention.

Panikkar: Yes. Even while the character is present on the stage, he could be in the *bahyakakshya.*

Udayan: And continuously you play between the two while you are doing the play. You bring the actor or the situation into the *abhyantarkakshya*—that means in the area of the attention of audience or taking it away from the area of attention.

Panikkar: And in Indian theatre it is possible to enact what you have heard or what you have seen. What is not there could also be enacted as seen. If the thing is present and you want to show that you have not seen it, that too can be done. In *Kalivesham* we discussed earlier, it is shown that Kali is there, Kali can be seen by the actor, but his wife cannot see him and that's why she asks, 'To whom are you talking? Who is there?' It is established that she has not seen Kali.

Udayan: The same would happen with *Chhaya* (shadow) Sita in *Uttararamacharitam.* Sita is very much there but because of a certain boon from Ganga she remains invisible to Ram. Ram is not able to see her. In the play this event becomes so emotional that it becomes difficult to act it out.

Panikkar: Yes, that is done by *kakshya vibhajan* (division of orbits).

Udayan: Then the *kakshya* becomes much more complex. In that particular scene in *Uttararamacharitam* Ram will behave in a way that he has not seen Sita but Sita will have to be on the stage. She will be in the *prekshaka* (audience)'s area of the attention but not of Rama's.

Panikkar: Yes, the *prekshaka* can see Sita there but Rama cannot. There Rama has to enact that he has not seen Sita and Sita has to enact that she is not being seen by Rama.

Udayan: And thereby in the minds of the *prekshaka*, Sita will be there but will disappear. Appear and disappear.

Panikkar: Appear and disappear. That is the *kakshya*. Practical lessons of *kakshya* were thought of by a playwright like Rabindranath Tagore in his play *Raja*. That's why I did it. Not only because of that alone but because of several other reasons. The king makes his visit which can be felt by Surangama but the Rani cannot see. The maid also, whether she can see or whether she can feel is kept in the dark. That's a very interesting confusion which I worked out. The beam of light comes and falls at a point where she, the maiden arranges the materials for the prayer and she does the puja as if he is there. We are not sure whether he is seen by this maid or not. But from *bahyakakshya*, a beam of light comes into the *abhyantarkakshya*. All these possibilities are there in such a small space. In Kathakali, in such small spaces, they wage battles.

Udayan: The *Mahabharata*?

Panikkar: Yes, they do *Mahabharata* on the small stage. There is this concept of the imaginary, virtual space and time. That is the wonder of Indian theatre. Westerners also speak about space time continuum and all that but here you know we do such wonderful experiments with space and time.

Udayan: That's true.

Panikkar: The *kakshya vibhajan* creates such a unique possibility in the Sanskrit theatre.

Udayan: How is the actor during training made conscious of this issue of the *kakshya*? Is he/she trained in this too?

Panikkar: Yes, it is there.

Udayan: How?

Panikkar: It is in the training itself. During *ekaharya* that is, only one person attacking something that is imagined, could be done with two persons, the attacker and the attacked. But if the attacked is not there, and the attacker is assuming the role of attacked as well, that is *ekaharya*. He moves like the attacker. And then he turns and becomes the attacked. So there you know such an interaction is practised.

Udayan: I feel in such a situation when the attacker is attacking, the attacked is in the *bahyakakshya*. When he is acting as the attacked, the attacker comes in the *bahyakakshya*.

Panikkar: Yes.

Udayan: So he becomes conscious of both here.

Panikkar: *Chakyars* have done wonderful work in all these aspects. They have created it in their theatre manuals and practice also. There is a famous passage, 'Shikhinishalabho' in *Subhadra Dhananjayam* Kudiyattam in which Arjuna has gone to the Prabhasatirtha, where he finds wonders like the snake keeping company with the mongoose and the deer drinking the milk of the leopard and flies falling into the fire coming out unburnt. He finds all these anomalies there. I remember, in particular, the scene of the mother leopard giving milk to the young deer. They enact the whole situation using space in a creative manner. The space is used by the actor as the leopard which gives the milk, and immediately as the deer creating a very tight configuration like in a photograph. For one moment the actor is the leopard giving milk and the next moment he turns around and becomes the deer drinking milk.

Udayan: This means that the *bahyakakshya* and the *abhyantarkakshya* are not physical spaces?

Panikkar: No, there the space itself invades the imagination of the viewer, thereby making audience also imagine it. They do not merely remain a moribund audience but start participating. They are given a function to imagine.

Udayan: Which would mean that *abhyantarkakshya* at one time can spread on the whole stage and then may shrink to the extent of that udder being put into the mouth of, let us say, a deer and then it may once again get spread out.

Pannikar: It could be focused as well as spread out.

Udayan: ... which means that the *rhythm* is also created out of this spreading and shrinking of the *abhyantarkakshya* or both of these *kakshyas* that is. *abhyantarkakshya* and *bahyakakshya*.

Panikkar: This *kakshya* is further qualified by the use of the curtain. The curtain becomes a very creative medium for dividing the *kakshya*s. I have used the curtain in that way. In the established traditions of Kathakali and Kudiyattam we get only precise situations where a character comes to the projection; during entry and exit. We have used it in different ways. In Kathakali one curtain is used as a canopy and another as a half curtain and the figure of the character gets projected in the carved out space.

Udayan: In Kathakali and Kudiyattam because there is no curtain as such. I mean in the front.

Panikkar: Only moving curtain.

Udayan: So the curtain is also used as a neutral prop.

Panikkar: In Kathakali and Kudiyattam and in Indian theatre generally, even in traditional folk theatre and in our Mudiyettu type of ritual theatre too, the curtain is used not to cover but to uncover.

Udayan: To uncover?

Panikkar: Yes. It's only to bring it to the notice of the audience with a double effect. It's a method, a device to project, so it's not to cover as a curtain in proscenium theatre halls does where the front is completely covered with a curtain, which opens sideways or up. That sort of curtain came to us only from Parsi theatre.

Udayan: What uses do you put the curtain to?

Panikkar: I have put it to many uses like showing fire, for creating a path, taking a person through a way which is very labyrinthine and then two peoples meeting, as in the case of Hidimba and Bhima meeting in *Madhyamavyayogam*. They come on both sides of a curtain and with the curtain they go round. The curtain moves and so do they. There are many ways in which I used curtains. In *Shakuntala*, the curtain was used as a means to remember the old experiences by Dushyanta which led to his ultinate realisation.

Udayan: You have brought the curtain into the area of the *kakshya vibhajan* in a much bigger way.

Panikkar: There are many instances in which the curtain works as an effective medium to present the change of attitude, the *antardwandua* or inner conflict and the like. Raja Rama in *Uttararamacharitam* makes his entry behind the curtain in all pomp and splendour. The items of caparison held behind him like the fan made of peacock feather (*alavttam*), etc. representing *veera* or the heroic or kingly quality. He takes a round in the curtain and when reaching the old position, the stage hands holding the signs of pomp slowly bring them down to the musical accompaniment and accordingly, the facial expression of Ram takes to *karuna rasa*.

Udayan: So this is done with the curtain held in front of the character and the character moving around it while the *bhava* gets transformed. Tell me one thing. A very simple question that I have in my mind is that in all your training process done even with absolutely neutral alphabets, as you so wonderfully say, does the culture of the actor, from where he comes, have any role to play? I mean is it possible to teach the *sancharis* lets say, to a person from an absolutely a different tradition, or culture?

Panikkar: It is possible. I asked two actors from Madhya Pradesh to come and join the production. They came to Thiruvananthapuram and worked with us.

Udayan: They came all the way here, to Kerala?

Panikkar: Yes, to Kerala, to my theatre. I arranged for their stay. They wanted very sincerely to work with me. There are others too. There were quite a number of participants in the camp, in the workshop held at Calcutta and later in Delhi by the Sangeet Natak Akademi in which I was also a member of the teaching faculty. Some of the participants requested the Akademi that they may be allowed to work with either Ratan Thiyam or myself. So two of them came here.

Udayan: My question was about teaching a person from an absolutely different tradition

Panikkar: When I worked with NSD students, they could easily learn their roles. I sometimes asked them to create roles freely, if there was some Chhau or Kathak dancer. Kathak is not strange to me. So such creativity can be easily accommodated, the 'other' for me.

Udayan: That's true. But what I was asking is something different, because when I say from 'other culture', I mean somebody from foreign countries, from the West for example.

Panikkar: Now a few Estonian actors have come here. They did a wonderful job. I think we have recorded it, you can see it, how they proceeded. One of my plays *Aaramban* was written to teach direction. Teaching direction is not easy. Not at all possible but I wanted one of the actresses to do a play, which I wrote for her based on a western myth and which was done by her. It was a short piece where I used *bols*, I used music, our music, it may have sounded differently but that was understandable because they were using a new language. They didn't know anything about the language in which the play was written—the language, its syntax, everything else was new to them. When it is not easy even for Indians, what can you expect from foreigners?

Udayan: Was it difficult for you to train them in *sattvika abhinaya*? I mean did you find it difficult? I am talking only about the training and not about the performance.

Panikkar: In the training process, the actor is led to encounter a unit of acting by dissecting it into a three sections. Pre-acting, acting and post-acting. The text which forms the material for vocal acting occupies mostly the middle part. This should be enlivened and supported by a thrust in the beginning, which constitutes a period of preparation. Then it ripens into the *abhinaya* proper, the *vachika*. It further proceeds to post acting. The time factor in creating these three areas of acting, especially the first and the last is so short and suggestive that it helps the actor to gain momentum and preserve his energy without it being wasted away. Take the example of a person encountering a dog. When he faces the dog he enacts taking a stone which forms the pre acting and then he throws it uttering a to frighten off the dog, which is the *abhinaya* proper with some sort of *vachika* attached to it. What happens after throwing the stone, if the dog runs away, he has to establish that through his look and reactions.

Udayan: You teach the students such lessons in detail? Do you find it easy to communicate with all?

Panikkar: With some people I have found it difficult, but that difficulty was crossed by constant practice. The Estonians, I must say, were so demanding, they went on demanding things from us! I had to teach them the whole *rasa* theory and then I had to also invite a specialist on *rasa* because I too wanted to learn more, it's such a tricky area! Especially when it is combined with practice. So I told them what I knew from practice. I said, 'I will teach you but I will get you another professor, Shri Pooapur Krishnan Nair who is a better theory person.'

I then asked my actors and the Kathakali actors to demonstrate. They did not leave us till they got what they wanted! They were very inquisitive. They were here for one month and on the concluding days of their stay they put up a show. One girl among them was a ballet dancer, she was taught three items in Mohiniyattam by Sarita. She picked it up and danced very well. Famous musician and violin maestro Shashi Kumar taught them a wonderful curvature lessons from *swara* to *swara* and they were made to sing. Shashi Kumar also composed their song in the raga *Balehari* and selected that song for study in his master class and he tuned their song exactly as they sang. They were using a *raga* very similar to the Indian *raga*, *Balehari*, *Sa Re Ga Pa Dha Sa is arohana* (ascending scale) and *Sa Ni Dha Pa Ma Ga Re Sa*, in the *avarohan* (in the descending scale), while in the *arohan*, *Sa Re Ga Pa Dha Sa* that is, *Ma* and *Ni* are not there. Then they started singing the same thing in *swara*s, in notations. He asked one to sing the notation, the other to sing the song.

Udayan: And they learnt it through?

Panikkar: They learnt it through. Then they knew that the music is just one music, it can't be different. So the curvature from *Re* you have to go to *Ga. Re Ga Ma.* This curvature type of music is not there in the linear musical traditions. They specially learned this curvature in music as well as in *bhava*s.

Udayan: In fact the great veena player Ustad Zia Moiuddin Dagar of the Dhrupad *gharana* used to say that the mystery of music lies in how you go from one *swara* to the other, and nothing else.

Panikkar: Exactly.

Panikkar: At least, as far as Indian music is concerned.

Udayan: If you want to understand music, this is the crux of the matter.

Panikkar: You must meet with Shashi. He gives much input to our theatre music. Even now, my son Srikumar continues taking lessons from him.

Udayan: When my teacher and the great filmmaker Mani Kaul teaches me Dhrupad, he tells me that all mystery of music lies in this and nothing else- the journey from one *swara* to the other.

Panikkar: The general feeling is that classical music has attained proficiency from folk music, this is only the truism. But folk music is also difficult. I have composed a song for my singer son Sri, a love song of Kuttanad. You can find in it the nuances of that area. A girl has come from the countryside for harvest, a duckman falls in love with her, this is theme.

This peculiar tune is there in the region of Kuttanad, so I was inspired from that. But then it is still difficult, more difficult than classical music. There is a system already established in the so called classical. But here there is only feeling.

Udayan: We have not discussed much about the patronage of the arts. I think that the growth and development of the arts, particularly of performing arts is very critically dependent on the nature of the patronage.

Panikkar: Sometimes patronage can do harm also. That is what we were discussing … about the patronage in Kerala's music. You know there is a trinity of composers: Tyagarajswami, Dikshitar and Shyamashastri. The king Swathi Thirunaal was also a *vaggeyakara*. He lived only up to the age 32. He was a great composer. I always say that whenever he composed his *padam*s in Kerala's own style, he was very genuine and when he composed other *kriti*s, like *kirtana*s, he was just imitating the trinity; any one of the three. He had, of course, a great liking and respect for the trinity, so it was not his fault. During his time the only musical system officially available in Kerala was Carnatic music. The indigenous system of Kerala music was totally neglected. Its performers were not considered artists. So in this case, wrong patronage affected the local music because the king did not patronise it and he was trying to propagate what was available from outside our region. This happened at a time when royal support was very much needed for the indigeous music. So patronage can go wrong.

At the same time, the king patronised all artists. Patronising and not patronising, both happened side by side. All local *Bhagvatar*s were patronised by the same king, Swathi Thirunaal. But what did he patronise? His patronage was not for giving status to the existing system of music available in the land. *Adhinivesh* that is, something coming from outside was trying to put us down, trying to supercede our legacy. *Adhinivesh* from any quarter, whether it's from your own people or the next door neighbour … is equally bad.

Udayan: How did the patronage system work for the *Chakyar*s?

Panikkar: What I have said about Swathi Thirunaal is just one aspect of his. I have great respect for all his contributions, he was a great man but he and his predecessors as well as other kings in Cochin and other small principalities were all patronising different art forms including Kathakali. Velakali was patronised by the king of a small country, Ambalapuzha, who was a landlord king.

Sometimes, the patron is also an artist with sensibility like Deva Narayana of Ambalapuzha. He had an artistic and sensitive mind, because of which the martial art of Velakali had developed. So Kathakali had the rare privilege of getting patronage not only from kings but also from landlords. They used to have their own artistes. The Brahmin community, the Namboodiris, like Olapamanna, Illam, patronised Kathakali. The *Chakyar*s were solely patronised by the temples. Temples, of course, were given land by the ruling kings. They had large acres of land so patronage was very much available for the *Chakyar*s. That is why when that situation changed and when all the landed property of such temples were given away and the lands went to the hands of those who had their possession, the situations had completely changed.

Udayan: What happened to the patronage?

Panikkar: The patronage was no more there from individual landlords. The feudal system was no more in existence. Temples too suffered due to this change.

Udayan: But when the temples were patronising the *Chakyar*s, it was the whole society which was actually patronising them and not only the ruling elite; the society in general was patronising them.

Panikkar: The temple was also in the direct control of the king. The king was the ultimate authority. As far as Hindus were concerned, all that we have as temple belongings and everything else ultimately belonged to the state and the government was nothing other than the king. It was the king who ran the government.

Udayan: So the temple patronising *Chakyar*s actually meant that the temples gave land to the *Chakyar*s that they got from the kings.

Panikkar: Yes, of course. They were to do some work in the temple. In certain temples even now, the *Chakyar*s have to perform.

Udayan: What is the possibility of a patronage system now in our times?

Panikkar: That is what I say, when the situation changed and landlordism disappeared, then the support system also changed.

Udayan: By changed, you mean democracy came?

Panikkar: Yes. And the democratic government started establishing institutions like academies. Various sorts of schemes came. You know, a new support system came into being.

Udayan: But even now it's very weak.

Panikkar: It is very weak but we can't say it is completely weak in the case of Kudiyattam. Kudiyattam had the rare good fortune to be accepted by the National Sangeet Natak Akademi. They have come to support Kudiyattam. I remember when Keshshav Kothari was the Secretary, he came to Kerala. It was in the year 1990. From that time onwards they identified the groups here, the gurus here, but of course their number was on the decrease. But three, four *gurukulams* were very active, Mani, Irinjalakuda and Paimkulam. So they were identified. And then Kalamandalam came by that time. Kalamandalam started the Kudiyattam and Kathakali wing. So that way, Kalamandalam was already getting support from Government. Even from the very beginning of Kalamandalam, Vallathol struggled a lot. That was the transition period when Cochin, Travancore and Malabar were three separate units. Vallathol managed to get support from the Cochin Government.

Udayan: In the modern democratic system what kind of patronage can now be made to theatre, I mean to contemporary theatre. In fact I mean all kinds of theatre, not only to Kudiyattam, which, I consider, is contemporary even today …

Panikkar: They should all be properly supported.

Udayan: Otherwise theatre like Kudiyattam will finally end up as nothing but a relic.

Panikkar: Even after getting financial support from the Akademi and even after getting the approval from UNESCO that it is the great intangible heritage of humanity, I have my own apprehensions about its future; the main reason being that all the great masters of Kudiyattam have gone. In their absence no competent artist with the caliber of traditional brilliance is available. The community of *Chakyars* is almost extinct. In the new generation, there are very few artists who believe that art can live only by strengthening the training if the art has to do justice to its great tradition. There is a tendency in some of the exponents to indulge in off-beat experiments. Their view may be appreciated beccause it is one way to keep abreast with the changes in the outside art world. But this should not be done at the expense of the most inevitable aspect of training. Experiments are definitely welcome, but for the development and sustenance of a great art of international importance like Kudiyattam, it is most essential to maintain the system in all its strength, vibrance and purity. We have now a Kudiyattam Centre here in Thiruvananthapuram formed by Sangeet Natak Akademi, New Delhi. In its formative period I was the Chairperson of this centre by virtue of the fact that I was Vice Chairman of the Akademi in New Delhi of which this centre forms a constituent unit. When I was working in this centre I tried my best to attract contemporary theatre people, theatre critics and university students. Many of them came for the workshops and seminars. The result was very encouraging. There used to be lively discussions about acting. Most of the participants realised that theatre artistes in our time require awareness of our traditions and also imbibe the worthy elements in theatre. I was always arguing while I was in the Akademi that the purpose for which the Centre for Kudiyattam was established in Kerala was to make it a great centre of research on Indian theatre attracting the whole attention of the theatre world and to provide opportunity to organise research schemes on the legacy of Kudiyattam and all the connected aspects of theatre preserved in many of the vibrant Indian performing arts. In none of our institution do we have a systematic curriculum to learn *Natyashastra*.

Udayan: This is essential for the study of Indian theatre. If it is not possible in India where else will this text be learnt?

Panikkar: Such a study will not be complete without taking into consideration what is being done in practical theatre where the principles of *Natyashastra* are put to practice. There are many tribal forms where you come across the tenets of *Natyashastra* put to practice. Without taking these into our theatre studies how can we claim that we have a theatre of our own?

Udayan: Which means that one form of patronage to those art forms can a way of making them a live and vital and can also mean that they are included in the education system.

Panikkar: Exactly.

Udayan: And then they become part of the everyday education in schools and colleges, so that people have a live contact with them.

Panikkar: Yes. They should not become a relic of the past.

Udayan: The way things are getting lost is really tragic.

Panikkar: It will always be present with us. We will be able to renew them and reinterpret them.

Udayan: Yes, that's true

Panikkar: But many theatre scholars in our country insist that there should be one *Caucasian Chalk Circle* or some such absurd play every year in our curriculum. This is what is being done in the National School of Drama.

Udayan: This is ridiculous.

Panikkar: They don't even take a Tagore play! Even though Tagore is not the final word on *Natyashastric* tradition, but whatever tradition is there, should be learned. They should do a Tagore play, they should do a Dharamveer Bharati play or they should do a Girish Karnad play every year! They should also do a Kalidasa or Bhavabhuti play. They should try all these. But it is not being done except for some sporadic attempts here and there.

Udayan: But they are not part of the curriculum. The curriculum basically comprises of western theatre.

Panikkar: And all imagination works around western theatre. And they are calling it Realistic theatre.

Udayan: This is wrong.

Panikkar: The present question is whether Naturalism-Realism is the only thing or whether non-Realism is all rubbish. In such productions they use music, they use body language, but in a very poor way ... because they have not learnt it properly from our tradition or from *Natyashastra*.

Udayan: Yes.

Panikkar: So unless and until we insist on the text of *Natyashastra* and we don't need to learn it fully, one doesn't have to learn all the 36 chapters, we will not be able to make our theatre grow.

Udayan: Yes.

Panikkar: They only need teach the basic chapters that deal with *angika*, *sattvika, vachika,* and *aharya abhinaya.* That is enough. *Aharya* is not really required but then since it goes with the others, we could learn it as well …

Udayan: So they become conscious of these four components of acting separately.

Panikkar: And then you know the *chari*s, the *karana*s etc. Now they think that *karana*s are not our subject, Padma Subramanyam, the dancer will deal with it, it is a separate issue. This separation tendency, without seeing things in a holistic way, has defeated our theatre.

Udayan: Yes. And secondly in the NSD all the regional theatres should be given representation.

Panikkar: No, it was not given.

Udayan: Because from the very beginning the NSD evolved a very strange notion on our regional theatre in different languages, it grew with a wrong notion of the country. Now because of that, Western theatre seems to be relevent for us, it is proposed as the universal theatre and the multiplicity of our regional cultures is totally ignored.

Panikkar: Exactly. Underline this. If you want to retain the principle of Indian theatre you'll have to accept that regions can only create 'national'. So we should have regional theatres. We should have regional-national theatres, regional-national schools of drama, making one apex body in Delhi or wherever you want. There can be an exchange between two regions, let's say between North East and South and such likes. Suppose you take 20 students (20 is the maximum number we take from the whole nation now), give 20 students to each region and make them interact on what regional theatre studies they have undergone.

Udayan: There may be five such centres: north, south, east, west and central.

Panikkar: Let the Government of India give them proper support. We should break this NSD into five.

Udayan: Then the NSD can function differently and more efficiently.

Panikkar: As an apex body.

Udayan: It can function to find the links between the regional cultures …

Panikkar: That should be the sixth!

Panikkar: And the present funds need not even be increased to a great extent, in any case present funds are very large. Or they can double the funds or increase them by threefold.

Udayan: And give them to these regions …

Panikkar: Exactly. Now they have a regional centre in Bengaluru. But the whole concept is different. It is their office, their regional office controlled by the NSD. It should not be like that. It should be more active in imbibing and renewing the regional tradition and also the *margi* system as envisaged in the *Natyashastra*.

Udayan: The centres should be given autonomy.

Panikkar: Autonomy should be there and then finally they should be made responsible only to reach the apex body for final results, etc. All the students may go to the apex body for the final degree or whatever.

Udayan: Matanga's *Brihaddeshi* gives the notion of many *deshi* that is, regional forms which are related to each other. How can they be unrelated to each other?

Panikkar: No, then there is no point.

That is why I said, suppose they give 10 or 20 students to Kerala; they should undergo training for say, three years. If it is three years, they should learn here for one and a half years or two years and then exchange them with Manipur or Assam or the Central region, Madhya Pradesh. When we give admission to this centre, 40 per cent local people, the people who are, let's say, coming from Kerala, should be given admission and then there can be 60 per cent coming from different regions. These things should be maintained in this way—only them, as you said will, it not exclude the other regions, only then will it have links with other regions too.

Udayan: I too think that it should be something like this.

Panikkar: Of all students day scholars or local students should be 40 per cent and remaining 60 per cent students essentially should be from the other regions.

Udayan: The fallacy has been on two levels in Indian performing art training and policy: one that we have thought of 'the national' as something neutral and thereby the western became the universal. That is in the National School of Drama. On the other hand, we have also not worked enough to find the links between the various regional traditions.

Panikkar: Yes, that's very true.

Udayan: We should have done that, so that an institute like, the National

School of Drama s'ould be given this responsibility of finding the links between various regional theatres.

Panikkar: Links may not be possible at one stretch, but slowly it can be introduced in the syllabus. That is why I said 60 per cent of the students should come from other regions and then you can do an exchange.

Udayan: You know, till the British came to India, all these regions were interconnected. The links were there. If at all we are interested in making India an Indian nation and if we are interested in creating a national drama, we should have these links. We should have this notion of interlinks between these regions.

Panikkar: It is a very good suggestion. That can be achieved only by proper support schemes. And these regional schools of national drama should take care of forms like Kudiyattam and Kathakali and other such regional theatres. They should not be treated as museum pieces. They should be in a position to generate theatre, theatre theories and practice. Without that how do we connect ourselves to our traditions? And how do we go forward and create our future?

Udayan: Yes, otherwise our traditional arts will die voicelessly.

Panikkar: But let us hope for the best as we conclude.

APPENDIX 1
Timeline: Kavalam Narayana Panikkar's Theatre Activities in India and Abroad

1966: Directed *Thiranottam* for Kerala Kalamandalam

1980: Directed and presented Bhasa's *Dootavakyam* (in Sanskrit) at the Kalidasa Samaroh, Ujjain

1982: Directed and presented 4th Act of *Vikramorvasiyam* at the seminar in the Kalidas Samaroh, Ujjain with Sopanam.

Directed *Ottayan* for Nrithalaya Aesthetic Society, Singapore

Participated at the International Theatre Festival at Toga-Mura, Tokyo, Japan and conducted theatre workshops

1983: Directed Bhasa's *Urubhangam* in Hindi for the National School of Drama, New Delhi final year students

Conducted theatre workshops at Common Wealth Institute, London and Theatre Laboratory at Wales, UK

Conducted Kathakali and theatre workshop at the International Theatre Festival in Kolkata

1984: Directed *Sooryasthan* (Hindi translation of Malayalam) for the National School of Drama, New Delhi

1985: Presented Sanskrit plays *Karnabharam* and *Bhagavadajjukkam* in the Festival of India

Directed and presented *Urubhangam* and *Bhagavadajjukkam* at the University of Wisconsin, USA

Directed *Mattavilasa* (in Hindi) for the National School of Drama, New Delhi Repertory Company

Directed *Mattavilasam* (Malayalam) for the School of Drama, Trichur

Participated in the International Theatre Festival at Delphi, Greece

1986: Participated in the seminar on India Theatre at the University of Warsaw, Poland

1987: Presented Bhasa's *Karnabharam* and *Madhyamavyayoga* at the Festival of India, USSR

Directed Tagore's *Raja* for the National School of Drama, New Delhi

1987: Organised the International Theatre Festival on Bhasa (again in 1989, 1994 and 2000)

1988: Presented Sanskrit plays *Karnabharam* and *Bhagavadajjukkam* at the Tokyo International Festival

1989-90: Visited Greece with the Sopanam Group for a Indo-Greek project on the two epics *Illiad* and *Ramayana*

1991: Participated in Carnantum Festival in Austria with the Sopanam Group

1995: Visited China as a member of the Indian Delegation

Directed Kalidas's *Vikramorvasiyam* (in Sanskrit) in the Kalidas Samaroh, Ujjain with local artists.

1996: Presented Bhasa's *Madhyamavyayoga* at the Festival of India in Bangladesh

1997: Participated in the ITI Festival in South Korea with the Sopanam Group

2000: Participated in the International Theatre Festival Lamama, Italy

2001: Directed and presented Jean Paul Sartre's play *Trojan Women* in Malayalam with the sponsorship of Alliance Francaise in Thiruvananthapuram

Directed and presented Sanskrit play *Karnabharam* and Malayalam adaptation of Shakespeare's *The Tempest* in the National Theatre Festival organised by the National School of Drama, New Delhi

Presented *Kallurutty* (Malayalam) in the Akka Festival, Mysore

Presented Sanskrit play *Karnabharam* with Nandikar for the National Theatre Festival in Kolkata

2002: Directed and presented Bhasa's Sanskrit play *Pratima* and the Malayalam play *Kallurutty* at the National Theatre Festival organised by the National School of Drama, New Delhi

Directed and presented the Sanskrit play *Vikramorvysiyam* with the members of Nrithyalaya Aesthetic Society, Singapore

Wrote, directed and presented Malayalam play *Kalivesham* in many theatre festivals in India

Wrote, directed and presented *Kalanetheeni* in English

Produced and directed Bhasa's *Charudattam* in Sanskrit and presented it in many theatre festivals in India

2004-05: Directed *Theyyatheyyam* in Hindi. Presented by second year students at the National School of Drama, New Delhi

Translated and directed *Maya* by Mahakavi Sakthibhadra

2006: Produced and directed Kalidasa's *Malavikagnimitram*

2007-08: Produced and directed Kalidasa's *Abhigyan Shakuntalam*

2009-10: Produced and directed Bhavbhooti's *Uttarramcharitam* in Hindi

2011: Wrote, directed and presented *Nizhalayanam* in Malayalam

APPENDIX 2
Publications by K.N. Panikkar

Malayalam poems	**Publisher**
1. Cheena Paravakal (1955)	Keralaputra, Alleppey
2. Kannermanka (1958)	Keralaputra, Alleppey
3. Kompum Kulampum (1959)	Keralaputra, Alleppey
4. Premarasmy (1960)	National Book Stall, Kottayam
5. Kavalam Kavithakal (1993, 2008)	Thirusadassu, Vaikom
6. Kali Sandharanam (2000)	D.C.Books, Kottayam

Malayalam plays	**Publisher**
1. *Sakshi* (1968)	National Book Stall, Kottayam
2. *Thiruvazithan* (1969)	National Book Stall, Kottayam
3. *Jabala Sathyakaman* (1970)	National Book Stall, Kottayam
4. *Daivathar* (1976, 1990)	Poorna Publications, Calicut
5. *Karimkutty* (1985)	National Book Stall, Kottayam
6. *Natakachakram* (Five Plays) (1990)	
a. *Agnivarnante Kalukal*	
b. *Marattam*	Poorna Publications, Calicut
c. *Pazhaya Vritham*	
d. *Bhagavadajjukiyam*	
e. *Bhootham*	
7. *Kaikuttappadu* (1993)	Poorna Publications, Calicut
8. *Avanavan Kadamba* (1978)	Poorna Publications, Calicut
9. *Kavalathinte Randu Natakangal* (1987)	
a. *Sooryathanam*	National Book Stall, Kottayam
b. *Pashugayatri*	
10. *Puranadi* (Five Plays)	
a. *Arani*	
b. *Faust*	D.C. Books, Kottayam
c. *Puranadi*	

d.   *Thuppan*

e.   *Apprakkan*

11. *Kavalam Natakangal* (Twenty-three Plays) (2008) Haritham Books,

Kozhikode

a.   *Sakshi*

b.   *Thiruvazhithan*

c.   *Jabalasathyakaman*

d.   *Daivathar*

e.   *Sooryathanam*

f.   *Avanavan Kadamba*

g.   *Ottayan*

h.   *Karimkutty*

i.   *Kaikuttappadu*

j.   *Kalanetheeni*

k.   *Omanathinkal*

l.   *Koima*

m.   *Pasugayathri*

n.   *Agnivarnate Kalukal*

o.   *Marattam*

p.   *Bhootham*

q.   *Aaramban*

r.   *Ambhambhada Rabhana*

s.   *Apprakkan*

t.   *Puranadi*

u.   *Theyyatheyyam*

v.   *Kallurutty*

w.   *Kalivesh*

Malayalam translations

1.   BHASABHARATHAM, 1987—Bhasa's Five Plays:

i.   *Urubhangam*

ii.   *Dootha Ghatolkhajam Sopanam*

iii.   *Madhyamavyayogam*

iv.   *Dhoothavakyam*

v.   *Karnabharam*

2. *Bhagavadajjukam* 1980 (3 Plays)
    i.   *Ottayan* (Kavalam)   Poorna Publications, Calicut
    ii.   *Bhagavadajjukiyam* (Bodhayana)
    iii. *Mattavilasam* (Mahendra Vikrama Varman)
3. *Trojan Sthreekal,* 2001   Alliance Franchaise
    (*The Trojan Women* by Jean Paul Sartre)
4. *Oru Madhyavenal Rakinavu*
    (*A Midsummer Night's Dream*) &   D.C. Books, Kottayam
    Kodumakattu (*The Tempest*) by Shakespeare
    (Shakesperinte Sampoorna Krithikal)

Children's publications

1. *Kunjhichirakukal* (Two Plays)   State Institute of Children's
    (*Kunjhichirakukal* and *Vishnu Maya*)   Literature, Trivandrum
2. *Kummatti*   National Book Trust, New Delhi

Plays translated to English

1. *The Lone Tusker*
    (*Ottayan* Translated by   Seagull Publications, Calcutta
    Prof. K.S.Narayana Pillai &
    Karimkutty by Paul Zacharia)
2. *The Right to Rule* (*Koyma*)   Seagull Publications, Calcutta
    (Translated by Paul Mathew)
3. *The Domain of the Sun* (*Suryasthan*)   Seagull Publications, Calcutta
    (Translated by Gopala Krishnan)
4. *Theyyatheyyam*   Sahithya Akademi, Indian
    (Translated by Vasanthi Sankara Narayanan)   Literature 2002
5. *Arambachekkan*   PAS Books-Contemporary
    (Translated by Erin B.Mee)   India
6. *Marattam School of Letters*
    (Translation by V C Harris)   M.G. University

Other publications

1. *Folklore of Kerala* (1991)   National Book Trust, New Delhi

APPENDIX 3
Plays Written/Directed by Kavalam Narayana Panikkar

No.	NAME OF THE PLAY	WRITTEN BY	DIRECTED BY
1.	*Sakshi* (Malayalam 1964)	Kavalam	Kumara Varma & Dr K.K.Panikkar
2.	*Jabala Satyakaman* (Malayalam 1972)	Kavalam	
3.	*Daivathar* (Malayalam 1973)	Kavalam	Kumara Varma
4.	*Tiruvazithan* (Malayalam 1974)	Kavalam	Mani Alanchery
5.	*Avanavan Kadamba* (Malayalam 1975) (Hindi 1986)	Kavalam	G. Aravindan Kavalam
6.	*Bhagavadajjukam* (Sanskrit) (Malayalam 1976)	Bodhayana Translation: Kavalam	Kavalam
7.	*Ottayan* (Malayalam 1977)	Kavalam	Kumara Varma
8.	*Madhyamavyayoga* (Sanskrit 1978)	Mahakavi Bhasa	Kavalam
9.	Dootavakyam (Sanskrit 1980)	Mahakavi Bhasa	Kavalam
10.	*Sooryasthanam* (Malayalam 1979) (Hindi 1984)	Kavalam Translation: J Sharma	Kavalam Kavalam
11.	*Thirumudi* (Malayalam 1980)	Kavalam	Bharath Gopi
12.	*Shakuntala* (Sanskrit 1982)	Mahakavi Kalidasa	Kavalam
13.	*Vikramorvasiyam* (Sanskrit 1982)	Mahakavi Kalidasa	Kavalam
14.	*Karimkutty* (Malayalam 1983)	Kavalam	Kavalam
15.	*Mattavilasam* (Sanskrit) (Hindi 1984)	M.V. Varman Translation: N.C. Jain & Urmi B. Gupta	Kavalam
16.	*Pashu Gayatri* (Malayalam 1979) (Mevadi 1979)	Kavalam Translation: Deepak Joshi	M.S. Satheesh Bhanu Bharti

No.	NAME OF THE PLAY	WRITTEN BY	DIRECTED BY
17.	*Karnabharam* (Sanskrit 1984)	Mahakavi Bhasa	Kavalam
18.	*Koyma* (Malayalam 1986)	Kavalam	Kavalam
19.	*Urubhangam* (Hindi 1983) (Sanskrit 1987)	Mahakavi Bhasa Translation: B.B. Aggrawal	Kavalam Kavalam
20.	*Marrattam* (Malayalam 1987)	Kavalam	M.S. Satheesh
21.	*Kalanetheeni* (Malayalam 1988)	Kavalam	K. Kaladharan
22.	*Kinarvattom* (Malayalam 1988)	W.B. Yeats Translation: Kavalam	Siva Mohan Thampi
23.	*Raja* (Bangla) (Hindi 1989) (Malayalam 2006)	Rabindranath Thakur Translation: Ageya Translation: P. N. Kurup	 Kavalam Kavalam
24.	*Arani* (Malayalam 1990)	Kavalam	Kavalam
25.	*Kakkuttappadu* (Malayalam 1990)	Kavalam	K. Kaladharan
26.	*Agnivarnante Kaluka*l (Malayalam) *Maharaj Agnivarna ke Pair* (Hindi)	Kavalam Translation: M.S. Bishambaran	 Bansi Kaul
27.	*Theyya Theyyam* (Malayalam 1991) (Hindi 2004-05)	Kavalam Translation: B. R. Bhargava	Kavalam Kavalam
28.	*Marukidathy* (A Tribal Party) (Malayalam 1991)	Kavalam	Kavalam
29.	*Faust* (Malayalam 1992)	Kavalam	Erin B. Mee
30.	*Cavalry* (Malayalam 1993)	W.B. Yeats Translation: Kavalam	K.T. Abraham
31.	*Swapna Vasavadattam* (Sanskrit 1993)	Mahakavi Bhasa	Kavalam
32.	*Bhishmar* (Malayalam 1994)	Sardar K.M.Panikkar	Kavalam
33.	Swapna Katha (Hindi 1994)	Bharat Ratna Bhargava Adaptation of three Bhasa's plays	Kavalam
34.	*Kunjichirakukal* (Children's Play) (Malayalam 1995)	Kavalam	Malini P.V

No.	NAME OF THE PLAY	WRITTEN BY	DIRECTED BY
35.	*Poranadi* (Malayalam 1995)	Kavalam	Kavalam
36.	*Dootavakyam* (Sanskrit 1996)	Mahakavi Bhasa	Kavalam
37.	*Vikramorvashiyam* (Sanskrit 1996)	Mahakavi Kalidasa	Kavalam
38.	*Apprakan* (Malayalam 1998)	Kavalam	Bharath Gopi
39.	*Prathima* (Sanskrit 1999)	Mahakavi Bhasa	Kavalam
40.	*The Tempest* (English) (Malayalam 2000)	William Shakespeare Translation: Kavalam	Kavalam
41.	*Trojan Women* (Malayalam 2001)	Jean Paul Sartre Translation: Kavalam	Kavalam
42.	*Kallurutty* (Malayalam 2001)	Kavalam	Kavalam
43.	*Kalivesham* (Malayalam 2003)	Kavalam	Kavalam
44.	*Kalanetheeni* (English 2002)	Kavalam	Kavalam
45.	*Charudattam* (Sanskrit 2002)	Mahakavi Bhasa	Kavalam
46.	*Maya* (Sanskrit) (Malayalam 2005)	Mahakavi Sakthibhadra Translation: Kavalam	Kavalam
47.	*Vikramorvashiyam* (Sanskrit 2005)	Mahakavi Kalidasa	Kavalam
48.	*Malavikagnimitram* (Sanskrit 2006) (Vidooshaka's passages in Hindi)	Mahakavi Kalidasa Bharat Ratan Bhargava	Kavalam
49.	*Shakuntalam* (Sanskrit 2007-08)	Mahakavi Kalidasa	Kavalam
50.	*Aramban* (Malayalam/English 2009)	Kavalam	Kavalam
51.	*Uttararamacharitam* (Sanskrit) (Recreated in Hindi 2010)	Bhavbhooti Udayan Vajpeyi	Kavalam Kavalam
52.	*Nizhalayanam* (Malayalam 2011)	Kavalam	Kavalam
53.	*Chandalika* (Bangla) (Malayalam 2011)	Rabindranath Thakur Translation: P. N. Kurup	Kavalam

APPENDIX 4
Film Songs by K.N. Panikkar

SL NO.	FILM	PRODUCER	MUSIC DIRECTOR	NO. OF SONGS	YEAR
1.	*Rathinirvedam*		Devarajan	4	1982
2.	*Alolam*	St. Josephs Cine Arts	Ilayaraja	4	1982
3.	*Ilakkangal*	Satru Films	M.B. Sreenivasan	3	1982
4.	*Marmaram*	Satru Films	M.S. Viswanathan	4	1982
5.	*Ittillam*	'A' One (Productions)	A. T. Ummer	4	1982
6.	*Sooryan*	Anjaneya Films	Arjunam	3	1982
7.	*Itavela*	Satru Films	M.B. Sreenivasan	3	1982
8.	*Alkottathil Thaniye*	Century Films	Shyam	3	1982
9.	*Ithiripoove Chuvanna Poove*	Grihalakshmi Films	Ravindran	3	1982
10.	*Aroodham*	Angle Films	Shyam	8	1982
11.	*Aaravam*	Creative Arts	M. G. Radhakrishnan	4	1982
12.	*Atirathram*	Century Films	M. S. Viswanathan	5	1983
13.	*Padayottam*	Navodaya Productions	Gunasingh	4	1983
14.	*Daivathe Orthu*	Navodaya Productions	M.G. Radhakrishnan	4	1983
15.	*Arunayude Prabhatham*	Navodaya Productions	Arjunam	3	1983
16.	*Arorumariyathe*	Angel Films	Shyam	3	1984
17.	*Sandyakkenthinu Sindooram*	Angel Films	Shyam	4	1984
18.	*Adhyayam Onnu Muthal*	Ranjith Arts	M. S. Viswanathan	4	1984
19.	*Kattathe Kilikkoodu*	Grihalakshmi Films	Jhonson	2	1984
20.	*Kaveri*	Dakshineswari Films	V. Dakshinamurthy & Ilayaraja	3	1985

SL NO.	FILM	PRODUCER	MUSIC DIRECTOR	NO. OF SONGS	YEAR
21.	*Kummatti*	General Pictures	M. G. Radhakrishnan	6	1985
22.	*Thampu*	General Pictures	M. G. Radhakrishnan	3	1985
23.	*Thampuratti*	General Pictures	G. Devarajan	4	1985
24.	*Udayam Padinjaru*	Saptasagara Movies	Jerry Amaldev A. T. Ummer	3	1986
25.	*Sarvakalasala*	Gandhimathil Films	M. G. Radhakrishan	3	1987
26.	*Nilakkuriji Poothappol*	Kalamandir Productions	Ousceppachen	3	1987
27.	*Pooram*	Good Knight Films	M. G. Radhakrishnan	2	1988
28.	*Ulsavappittennu*	Thomsun Films	G. Devarajan	4	1989
29.	*Puravrutham*	Karthika Films	Mohan Sithara	2	1989
30.	*Marattam*	Suryakanthi	Kavalam		1989
31.	*Anmaniranjavan Sreenivasan*	Kalamandir Productions	Johnson	3	1990
32.	*Aham*	Sri Sankara Arts	Ravindran	4	1991
33.	*Pidakozhi Koovunna Noothandu*	Urvara Arts	S. P. Venkitesh	3	1994
34.	*Janani*		Ousceppachen	2	2000
35.	*Kannezhuthi Pottumthottu*		M. G. Radhakrishnan	3	1998
36.	*Sesham*		Sarath	2	2002
37.	*Kadannal Koodu*		Mohan Sithara	2	2002
38.	*Nerkuner*		Kavalam	1	2004
39.	*Bharathan*		M.Jayachandran & Kavalam	2	2007
39.	*Manchadikuru*		Kavalam	4	2008

APPENDIX 5
Awards and Fellowships Receieved
by K.N. Panikkar

Kerala Sahitya Akademi Award	Best Playwright	1974
State Film Award	Best Lyricist	1978 & 1982
Critic Circle of India Award	Best Sanskrit Play Productions	1982 & 1984
National Award, Central Sangeet Natak Akademi	Direction	1983
Nandikar (Kolkata) National Award		1988
Ford Foundation Fellowship		1985 to 1989
Emiritus Award—Ministry of HRD		1995
Kalidasa Samman, Madhya Pradesh Government	For Play Direction	1995
Kerala Bala Sahitya Institute Award	Best Malayalam Children's Playwright	1998
Kerala Sangeetha Nataka Akademi	Senior Fellowship for Drama	2000
Sangeet Natak Akademi, New Delhi	Fellow	2002
Padmabhushan		2007
Tanvir Samman	Direction	2007
One India One People		2009
Vallalthol Sammanam	Total contribution on literature	2009
Sangeethavikas	Award for the book *Samakalika Sangeetham*	2009